Magali Arriola//J.G. Ballard//Georges Bataille//Jean Baudrillard//Mark Beasley//Walter Benjamin//Walead Beshty//Svetlana Boym//Giuliana Bruno//Italo Calvino//J.J. Charlesworth//Barbara Clausen//Le Corbusier//Jonathan Crary//Tacita Dean//Jacques Derrida//Denis Diderot//Geoff Dyer//Richard Grayson//Jörg Heiser//Martin Herbert//Andreas Huyssen//Patri… …r//Darian Leader//Mark … …ose Macaulay//Tom McD… …lla Léith//Jeremy Millar//… …wer//Ralph Rugoff//Eric Sch… …mel//Iain Sinclair//Robert S… …san Stewart//Adrian Stokes… …//Paul Virilio//Gilda Williams

Ruins

Whitechapel Gallery
London
The MIT Press
Cambridge, Massachusetts

Edited by Brian Dillon

RUINS

Documents of Contemporary Art

Co-published by Whitechapel Gallery
and The MIT Press

First published 2011

Whitechapel Gallery is the imprint of Whitechapel Gallery Ventures Limited

ISBN 978-0-85488-193-2 (Whitechapel Gallery)
ISBN 978-0-262-51637-2 (The MIT Press)

A catalogue record for this book is available from the British Library

Library of Congress Cataloging-in-Publication Data

Ruins / edited by Brian Dillon.
p. cm. – (Whitechapel : Documents of contemporary art)
Includes bibliographical references and index.
ISBN 978-0-262-51637-2 (pbk. : alk. paper)
1. Ruins in art. 2. Arts, Modern–20th century. 3. Arts, Modern–21st century. I. Dillon, Brian, 1969–
NX650.R84R85 2011
709–dc22
2011011787

10 9 8 7 6 5 4 3 2

Series Editor: Iwona Blazwick
Commissioning Editor: Ian Farr
Project Editor: Sarah Auld
Design by SMITH
Justine Schuster
Printed and bound in China

Cover, Rachel Whiteread, *House* (25 October 1993–11 January 1994), concrete cast of nineteenth-century terraced house, Grove Road, London E3. © Rachel Whiteread. Photograph: Edward Woodman. Commissioned and produced by Artangel.

Whitechapel Gallery Ventures Limited
77-82 Whitechapel High Street
London E1 7QX
whitechapelgallery.org
To order (UK and Europe) call +44 (0)207 522 7888
or email MailOrder@whitechapelgallery.org
Distributed to the book trade (UK and Europe only) by Central Books
www.centralbooks.com

The MIT Press
55 Hayward Street
Cambridge, MA 02142
MIT Press books may be purchased at special quantity discounts for business or sales promotional use. For information, please email special_sales@mitpress.mit.edu or write to Special Sales Department, The MIT Press, 55 Hayward Street, Cambridge, MA 02142

Whitechapel Gallery

Documents of Contemporary Art

In recent decades artists have progressively expanded the boundaries of art as they have sought to engage with an increasingly pluralistic environment. Teaching, curating and understanding of art and visual culture are likewise no longer grounded in traditional aesthetics but centred on significant ideas, topics and themes ranging from the everyday to the uncanny, the psychoanalytical to the political.

The Documents of Contemporary Art series emerges from this context. Each volume focuses on a specific subject or body of writing that has been of key influence in contemporary art internationally. Edited and introduced by a scholar, artist, critic or curator, each of these source books provides access to a plurality of voices and perspectives defining a significant theme or tendency.

For over a century the Whitechapel Gallery has offered a public platform for art and ideas. In the same spirit, each guest editor represents a distinct yet diverse approach – rather than one institutional position or school of thought – and has conceived each volume to address not only a professional audience but all interested readers.

IT
IS
AN
EMPTY
DESOLATE
PLACE,
AND
I'M
SURE
IT
IS
THIS
DESOLATION
THAT
MAKES
DUNGENESS
SO
UTTERLY
ATTRACTIVE:
THAT
IN
ITS
EMPTINESS
IT
CAN
BECOME
SO
FULL

Tacita Dean, *Sound Mirrors*, 1999

MODERNITY IN RUINS

THE MILITARY-INDUSTRIAL SUBLIME

Brian Dillon
Introduction//A Short History of Decay

We live now, though we might say that we have always lived, in a time of ruination. The first decade or so of the twenty-first century has seen what appears to be a distinct flourishing – in the realms of global events, popular culture and the work of visual artists – of images of catastrophe and decay. In the wake of the destruction of the World Trade Center in 2001, and in the midst of the wars that followed in Afghanistan and Iraq (with their images of exploded Buddhas in Bamiyan and toppled statues of Saddam Hussein, respectively) we have been faced once more with the assault on urban and architectural materiality as a symbol of geopolitical strife. At the close of the last decade, economic ruin led to a rash of images of architectural and urban-planning disaster – housing developments that would never be inhabited, office blocks that could not be completed – and a renewed awareness of the long decline of major industrial sites and cities of the last century: the plight of Detroit became the prime example. In general, a sense of the waning of the modernity and modernism of the twentieth century was in the air, alongside an awareness of the decaying machinery of colonialism and a vexed nostalgia for the aesthetic forms and iconography of the former Soviet Bloc. At the same time, the prospect of planetary ruination through climate change – a lingering disaster to replace the swift nuclear one imagined half a century ago – did not fail to nourish further ruinous fantasies and apprehensions.

Much of the art, thought and literature described in this book is a response to this contemporary state of ruinous affairs. In recent years many artists have turned to themes and imagery of decay and destruction – more especially, the remains of buildings and landscapes that now seem like relics of the last century. There has been a proliferation – particularly in photography, film and video – of work that explores (often in melancholic mode, but frequently too with a sense of still raw materiality) the ruins of modernist architecture, the defunct infrastructure of the cold war, territories decimated by industrial or environmental disaster, the relics of the economic hubris of the last decades of the twentieth century. We may think, for example, of the anachronistic dramas and reconstructions mounted by Gerard Byrne among the remains of mid-century modernism; Cyprien Gaillard's investigations of the terminal motif of the postwar housing block; Ângela Ferreira's treatment of modernist fragments in colonial and post-colonial Africa; the sculptural and monumental remnants of defunct Soviet-era regimes and deposed leaders that have been filmed by Carey Young and alluded to or elaborated upon by David Maljkovic. But such works are part of a more venerable continuum of ruin aesthetics, with its immediate precursors in artists and thinkers of the 1960s and 1970s, beyond that period in the paradoxes of modernism itself, and its more distant ancestors in the long history of ruin appreciation that is evident in (especially) Western art from the late renaissance onwards. This book provides a survey of the contemporary state of, and justifications for, ruin aesthetics – but it looks back too to the wastelands, fragments and scenes of destruction from earlier epochs that artists have drawn on in recent years.

The anthology begins with several key texts of the early enthusiasm for ruins: a craze that culminated with the elaboration in the late eighteenth century of a Romantic aesthetics of fragmentation, failure and picturesque decline. But the main focus of the selection of extracts (from artists' writings, philosophy, urban theory and fiction, among other genres) is more recent, and the topic divides broadly into four sections. The first considers the modern ruin, and the ruin's relation to modernity. The second explores the specific role of military and industrial ruins in contemporary art, focusing in detail on the relics of the cold war. The third section is concerned with landscape and environment in the wake of the work of Robert Smithson and other artists of the 1960s and 1970s. The final section addresses the relation of the ruin to a future or futures: its capacity to invent or imagine a time to come, even as it seems to fall back into time past. Throughout the essays and passages from more extensive works excerpted here, the ruin appears in its material specificity, as an allegory for global or regional political forces, as an aesthetic trope that condenses images and ideas from different genres, as an invitation to thought and as the site of a sublime (though also sometimes comical or even kitsch) haunting.

Ruins embody a set of temporal and historical paradoxes. The ruined building is a remnant of, and portal into, the past; its decay is a concrete reminder of the passage of time. And yet by definition it survives, after a fashion: there must be a certain (perhaps indeterminate) amount of a built structure still standing for us to refer to it as a ruin and not merely as a heap of rubble. At the same time, the ruin casts us forward in time; it predicts a future in which our present will slump into similar disrepair or fall victim to some unforeseeable calamity. The ruin, despite its state of decay, somehow outlives us. And the cultural gaze that we turn on ruins is a way of loosening ourselves from the grip of punctual chronologies, setting ourselves adrift in time. Ruins are part of the long history of the fragment, but the ruin is a fragment with a future; it will live on after us despite the fact that it reminds us too of a lost wholeness or perfection.

According to the scholar and novelist Rose Macaulay, whose 1953 book *Pleasure of Ruins* is one of the classic studies of the subject, the ancient Greeks and Romans had little real aesthetic feeling for the ruin as such – but there are hints of such a taste in wall paintings at Pompeii and Herculaneum, and of course the ultimate destiny of those cities (as of Rome) was to become themselves the inspirations for much later ruin enthusiasts.[1] Though ruins feature here and there in the mediaeval imagination, it is not really until the renaissance – that is, until the advent of a modernity that conceives itself in relation to the remains of the past – that the ruin becomes an essential aesthetic concept and recurrent image in Western art. At first ruins function merely as an allegorical backdrop, but by the time of Piranesi – whose *Prisons* and complex vistas of classical architecture invent the atmosphere of much of the ruinous art that followed – they are central to the scene: material reminders of a dead past but pointing also to the inevitable desuetude of present architectural (and more broadly cultural or political) schemes.

By the eighteenth century, a recognizable 'ruin lust' was well established in European culture. It ghosts some of the key aesthetic debates of the century – concerning the categories, for example, of the sublime, the picturesque and the gothic – and is present both in painting and in the craze for artificial ruins that is so much a part of garden and landscape design of the era. In 1770, in his *Observations on Modern Gardening*, Thomas Whately wrote: 'At the sight of a ruin, reflections on the change, the decay and the desolation before us, naturally occur; and they introduce a long succession of others, all tinctured with that melancholy which these have inspired.'[2] And in 1792, in *Les Ruines, ou Méditation sur les révolutions des empires*, the Comte de Volney hymned the sight of ruins as a sublime reminder of the passing of all human dreams and devices: 'Hail, solitary ruins! holy sepulchres and silent walls! you I invoke; to you I address my prayer. While your aspect averts, with secret terror, the vulgar regard, it excites in my heart the charm of delicious sentiments – sublime contemplations.'[3]

In aesthetics and art criticism, the essential formulation of this new sensibility directed at decay and fragmentation comes in Denis Diderot's *Salon of 1767* – before the ruin, he writes, 'we contemplate the ravages of time, and in our imagination we scatter the rubble of the very buildings in which we live over the ground; in that moment solitude and silence prevail around us, we are the sole survivors of an entire nation that is no more. Such is the first tenet of the poetics of ruins.'[4] This sense of having lived on too late, of having survived the collapse of past dreams of the future, is key to the ruinous optic that still animates certain artists today. It finds a particularly resonant expression in an essay of 1840 by Thomas Babington Macaulay, who predicted that in the distant future Catholicism (this in the context of an essay on the history of the papacy) 'may still exist in undiminished vigour when some traveller from New Zealand shall, in the midst of a vast solitude, take his stand on a broken arch of London Bridge to sketch the ruins of St Paul's'.[5] Macaulay's New Zealander, gazing upon the wreckage of the metropolis, became a recurrent motif for many decades – the most notable example is Gustave Doré's engraving *The New Zealander* of 1870. It is this dual valence of the ruin as image or reality, exemplified by Diderot and Macaulay – its capacity to place us at the end of a historical continuum or cast us forward into the future ruin of our own present – that traditional ruin aesthetics bequeaths to later artists and thinkers.

In 1911, in his essay 'The Ruin', the German sociologist Georg Simmel described a late iteration of the ruin aesthetic of the previous two centuries – a vision of the ruin as essentially an accommodation between nature and culture, the artificial object sliding imperceptibly towards an organic state, until in the end nature has its way and we can no longer legitimately speak of a 'ruin' at all. 'Architecture', he writes, 'is the only art in which the great struggle between the will of the spirit and the necessity of nature issues into real peace, in which the soul in its upward striving and nature in its gravity are held in balance.'[6] In the ruin, however, nature eventually begins to have the upper hand: the 'brute, downward-dragging, corroding, crumbling power' produces a new form, 'entirely meaningful, comprehensible, differentiated.'[7]

Simmel's is in some ways still a Romantic conception of the ruin – it tends towards an organicism that the new century would undermine both aesthetically and historically. In particular, the ruin of the recent past becomes a telling object for many artists and writers. We may think of Walter Benjamin's *Arcades Project*, the great encyclopaedic portrait of Paris ('the capital of the nineteenth century') on which he worked until his death in 1940: a fragmentary work organized around the image of the Parisian shopping arcades that were already, in the first decades of the new century, falling into disrepair and pointing to the decay of nineteenth-century modernity and optimism. (In the late 1920s, when Benjamin was broaching the topic of the afterlife of the nineteenth century, Georges Bataille had already celebrated, in the pages of his journal *Documents*, the real and metaphoric dust that it had left behind.) Or we can consider, a decade or so later, Rose Macaulay's reflection on the ruins of the recent past. Writing in the final pages of *Pleasure of Ruins* just a few years after the Second World War (during which she lost her home and library), Macaulay asks her reader to imagine a bombed out building where 'the stairway climbs up and up, undaunted, to the roofless summit where it meets the sky.'[8] Can such a structure properly be considered a ruin, with all of the Romantic and even nostalgic feelings the word implies? Macaulay is ambiguous on the subject.

Modernism itself, in this period, contracts an ambiguous relationship with the ruin. In part, the urban renovations imagined by such architects as Le Corbusier depend upon a vision of the city laid waste by demolition – in a thorough fulfilment of the process begun, for example, by Baron Haussmann in

Paris in the 1860s – or even by aerial bombardment. As Anthony Vidler avers of the projected Corbusian *ville radieuse*: 'the past was either eradicated or transformed, in an eighteenth-century manner, into ruin fragments in the park. ... The city [had] become no more nor less than a cemetery of its own past.'[9] In the immediate postwar period, Vidler argues, these vistas of rubble were achieved realities, and the prospect of a vastly more destructive nuclear future consequently haunts the bunker-like Brutalist architecture of, among others, Peter and Alison Smithson. And the kitsch version of this thinking had been perfected already, before the war, in Albert Speer's concept of 'ruin value', according to which the monumental architecture of Hitler's projected Germania was conceived with an eye to its future picturesque decay.

The artists whose work is discussed or excerpted in this book draw inevitably on this complex and often confused history of ruin aesthetics. But the art of recent years takes its impetus most obviously from a conjunction of artistic, literary and theoretical work produced in the late 1960s and early 1970s. The writings of Robert Smithson – especially as they pertain to and explore the industrial and infrastructural landscape of New Jersey – are exemplary in this regard. Entropy, the key concept in Smithson's work, reminds us that the ruin is always dynamic and in process, giving rise to what Smithson calls 'dialectical landscapes' that hover between the deep geological past and a catastrophic future. In September 1967, Smithson took a bus from the Port Authority terminal in Manhattan to the outskirts of the city of Passaic, where he was born, and wrote about the excursion in an essay, 'A Tour of the Monuments of Passaic, New Jersey', which he published in *Artforum* the following month.[10] Among riverside detritus and the half-formed structures of a new highway, Smithson affects to have found a new 'eternal city': a terrain strewn with decayed 'monuments' to rival those of Rome. His tone is mock-erudite and ironic, but Smithson also coins a crucial term for later artists: the artefacts that he describes and photographs are not Romantic relics but 'ruins in reverse'. They are caught in a dialectical state between being built and falling into disuse and decay – Smithson's ruins make the future look old-fashioned and the past seem as if it has arrived from some unknowable time to come.

This sense of confused chronologies also marks the key literary and theoretical statements regarding the modern ruin in this period. In 1975 the French urban theorist Paul Virilio published *Bunker Archaeology*: a study of the relics of the defensive Atlantic Wall erected by the Nazis on the French coast during the Second World War. The massive concrete structures seemed to Virilio, who had discovered them as a young man at the end of the war and started photographing them a decade later, to emerge from a distant (perhaps prehistoric) past and to point to a science-fiction future.[11] At the same time, they somewhat resembled the raw

THAT MONUMENTAL
PARKING LOT DIVIDED
THE CITY IN HALF, TURNING
IT INTO A MIRROR AND
A REFLECTION – BUT THE
MIRROR KEPT CHANGING
PLACES WITH THE
REFLECTION. ONE NEVER
KNEW WHAT SIDE OF
THE MIRROR ONE WAS
ON. THERE WAS NOTHING
INTERESTING OR EVEN
STRANGE ABOUT THAT
FLAT MONUMENT, YET
IT ECHOED A KIND OF
CLICHÉ IDEA OF INFINITY;
PERHAPS THE SECRETS
OF THE UNIVERSE ARE
JUST AS PEDESTRIAN –
NOT TO SAY DREARY.
EVERYTHING ABOUT
THE SITE REMAINED
WRAPPED IN BLANDNESS
AND LITTERED WITH
SHINY CARS – ONE AFTER
ANOTHER THEY EXTENDED
INTO A SUNNY NEBULOSITY.
THE INDIFFERENT BACKS
OF THE CARS FLASHED
AND REFLECTED THE
STALE AFTERNOON SUN.
I TOOK A FEW LISTLESS,

**ENTROPIC SNAPSHOTS
OF THAT LUSTROUS
MONUMENT.**

Robert Smithson, *A Tour of the Monuments of Passaic, New Jersey*, 1967 concrete masses of Le Corbusier's late style and the productions of later Brutalist architects in Britain and the United States. In time, the Atlantic Wall would also be explored by the English novelist J.G. Ballard, whose fictions of the 1960s and 1970s – *The Atrocity Exhibition, Concrete Island, High Rise* – already mined the same aesthetic of ruinous mingling of past, present and future. For Virilio and Ballard, the monumental edifices of the twentieth century – tower blocks, car parks, modernist pleasure palaces, military bunkers and silos – were already looking like dilapidated reminders of past dreams, whether utopian or totalitarian.

In the 1990s the collapse of certain aspects of the modernist dream – as perhaps best embodied in the image of the residential tower block – became explicitly a subject for visual artists. In a work such as Martha Rosler's 1993 video *How Do We Know What Home Looks Like*, the decayed and contested architecture of modernism appeared both outdated and up-for-grabs: a fading utopian inheritance that barely hung on to its (then routinely disparaged) potential for collective aspiration. Rosler's intimate exploration of Le Corbusier's Unité d'Habitation at Firminy-Vert, in south-central France, showed a dilapidated building that had been in part redecorated by its tenants with aspirantly bourgeois wallpapers and private souvenirs, but still retained a sense of embattled technological community, typified by the radio station installed on its roof. It was, however, among artists who referred, directly or obliquely, to the end of the cold war and the collapse of the Soviet Bloc that the theme of ruin flourished in the 1990s and beyond. Tacita Dean's film *Sound Mirrors* (1999) brooded over the remains of British pre-war acoustic early-warning technology that seemed to presage the silos and satellite dishes of the cold war, while later Berlin-based films such as *Fernsehturm* (2001) and *Palast* (2004) more readily reflected on the ageing or half-demolished architecture of the East. That strand of explicitly Ballardian ruin lust has continued too in certain works by Jane and Louise Wilson – notably, their treatment of Victor Pasmore's Apollo Pavilion in the postwar new town of Peterlee, in *A Free and Anonymous Monument* (2003), and their own return to the Atlantic Wall in *Sealander* (2006) – and in the vastly ambitious project of the Center for Land Use Interpretation to document (among many other types of landscape) the defunct sites and artefacts left behind by the US nuclear-weapons and space programmes in the second half of the twentieth century.

These artists and other like them drew also on cinematic precursors, both in their thematics and style. Chris Marker's *La Jetée* (1962) projects its protagonist back into the past following a nuclear war that has left Paris in ruins – the film is punctuated by images of wreckage and statuary fragments, and even the supposedly pristine past of his too-perfect memory is a museum of sorts, well stocked with aged mementoes. In terms of ruinous landscape or environment, cinema also provides crucial exemplars. The ruined 'Zone' of Andrei Tarkovsky's

Stalker (1979) is a model for the metaphorically productive non-places explored by such artists as Darren Almond and Adam Chodzko; the poisoned industrial hinterland that haunts the central characters of Michelangelo Antonioni's *Red Desert* (1964) is a precursor to the sites of environmental degradation studied, for example, by the Center for Land Use Interpretation. And the documentary fictions of Patrick Keiller – a tireless chronicler of the decay of English landscape and cities – have much in common with, and have been for a decade an abiding influence on, gallery-based artists. All this quite aside from such instances of futuristic ruin as Hollywood has long projected: the post-apocalyptic stock in trade of films such as *Planet of the Apes* (1968), with its vision of New York reduced to a skewed Statue of Liberty protruding from the sand.

The scope of significance of the ruin, or the idea of ruination, in contemporary art is broached first, then, by the problem of modernism – or more accurately the afterlife of modernism – outlined above. This remains a fertile area of enquiry and of making for younger artists. A project such as Roger Hiorns' *Seizure* (2008), which involved filling a flat at a modest late-modernist housing complex with bright blue copper-sulphate crystals, is a case in point. But here we see the complex timescales that such work often invokes today. Instead of merely highlighting the present moment's distance (in political and social as well as chronological terms) from the structure and its history, *Seizure* projected visitors back into a deep geological past and into a fantasized future: a modernism remade as a bizarre science-fiction interior. In a different medium and register, the paintings of Julie Mehretu mine the architectural history of the modern metropolis to produce impossible cityscapes with ramifying geometries and dizzying perspectives: something like Piranesi's *Prisons* for the age of globalization and (in recent years) its discontents. And a film such as Runa Islam's *Empty the pond to get the fish* (2008) further complicates the common turn among contemporary artists towards an archaeology of modernism by depicting a building originally constructed for the 1958 World's Fair in Brussels and subsequently transported to Vienna to serve as the Museum of the Twentieth Century.

The political meanings that attach to the ruin are not exhausted today by the context of the aftermath of the cold war that so interested artists of the 1990s and the first years of the new century. Among the works surveyed in this book are those that address the most charged spaces and artefacts of twentieth-century European history. The sculptures and installations of Miroslaw Balka frequently make reference to the Nazi death camps – the artist grew up in a village from which almost the entire Jewish population had been deported in 1942 – in their presentation of monolithic volumes and anonymous spaces. In her film and photographic series *The J. Street Project* (2002–5) Susan Hiller recorded the 303 thoroughfares (streets, alleyways, modest paths) in Germany that are still named after the Jewish communities that once resided, worked or traded there – the 'ruin' in question is often no more than the name itself and the memories that adhere to it or have been erased there. Ruins are often, as here, the objects of more or less ironized archives: Walid Raad, under the working name of the Atlas Group, has essayed similar studies (though in this case veiled in fiction and myth) of events and sites from the wars in Lebanon from the mid 1970s to the 1990s.

This archival impulse has also been brought to bear on diverse forms of land use and misuse, and the ruins that they have left behind. Most ambitiously, the Center for Land Use Interpretation has sought to map the ghost places of the United States: defunct missile facilities and former test sites, dead mining towns, industrial wastelands, empty housing complexes, the technological remains of the space programme. The research undertaken by CLUI is also part of a growing interest among artists and writers in derelict or degraded landscapes, and in the intrusions of nature into decayed urban settings. (Geographers have coined the term 'drosscape' for the points on the map where nature and culture meet in ruinous disarray.) In the works of writers as diverse as W.G. Sebald, Geoff Dyer and Rebecca Solnit, the places that have in recent years animated many contemporary artists are mapped and theorized.

Perhaps the most enigmatic aspect of the time of ruination is the manner in which it points towards the future rather than the past, or rather uses the ruined resources of the past to imagine, or reimagine, the future. This is the logic already of Walter Benjamin's 'Theses on the Philosophy of History' – he speaks of blasting aspects of the past 'out of the continuum of history' in order to forge a new revolutionary future.[12] We can see this process at work, for example, in the art of The Otolith Group, whose redeployment of the aesthetics and politics of the past is invariably oriented towards an idea of future liberation, be it imagined in the wake of the work of Chris Marker, among the ageing buildings of Le Corbusier's Chandigarh in India or the electronic music of the 1990s. According to this way of thinking and working, the ruin is a site not of melancholy or mourning but of radical potential – its fragmentary, unfinished nature is an invitation to fulfil the as yet unexplored temporality that it contains. Ruins, as many of the artists surveyed and writers and critics excerpted here suggest, are freighted with possibility, even with utopian promise.

1 Rose Macaulay, *Pleasure of Ruins* (1953) (London: Thames & Hudson, 1984).

2 Thomas Whately, *Observations on Modern Gardening* (1770), quoted in Rose Macaulay, *Pleasure of Ruins*, op. cit., 29.

3 Comte de Volney, *The Ruins* (1792), English translation (London: Edwards Brown, n.d.) 10.

4 Denis Diderot, 'Le Salon de 1767' (Paris, 1767); trans. John Goodman, in *Diderot on Art. II: The Salon of 1767* (New Haven and London: Yale University Press, 1995) 196–7.

5 Thomas Babington Macaulay, 'Review of Leopold von Ranke's *The Ecclesiastical and Political History of the Popes during the Sixteenth and Seventeenth Centuries*, trans. Sarah Austin', Edinburgh Review, no. 72 (October 1840) 258.

6 Georg Simmel, 'The Ruin' (1911 text, based on an earlier essay), in *Essays on Sociology, Philosophy and Aesthetics*, ed. Kurt H. Wolff (New York: Harper & Row, 1965) 259.

7 Ibid., 261.

8 Rose Macaulay, *Pleasure of Ruins*, op. cit., 454.

9 Anthony Vidler, 'Air War and Architecture', in Julia Hell & Andreas Schönle, eds, *Ruins of Modernity* (Durham & London: Duke University Press, 2009) 34.

10 Robert Smithson, 'The Monuments of Passaic', *Artforum* (December 1967); reprinted under Smithson's full title in *Robert Smithson: The Collected Writings*, ed. Jack Flam (Berkeley and Los Angeles: University of California Press, 1996) 68–74.

11 Paul Virilio, *Bunker Archaeology*, trans. George Collins (New York: Princeton Architectural Press, 1994).

12 Walter Benjamin, 'Theses on the Philosophy of History' (1940), in *Walter Benjamin: Illuminations*, ed. Hannah Arendt and trans. Harry Zohn (London: Fontana, 1992) 245–55.

I see buildings falling in Glasgow. I see rubble. I ask myself where that rubble goes. I discover that it's crushed and then used to build new pedestrian streets – so people are walking on the ghosts of tower blocks

Cyprien Gaillard, 'New Romantic: In Conversation with Jonathan Griffin', 2010

MODERNITY IN RUINS

Denis Diderot
The Salon of 1767//1767

[...] Our glance lingers over the debris of a triumphal arch, a portico, a pyramid, a temple, a palace, and we retreat into ourselves; we contemplate the ravages of time, and in our imagination we scatter the rubble of the very buildings in which we live over the ground; in that moment solitude and silence prevail around us, we are the sole survivors of an entire nation that is no more. Such is the first tenet of the poetics of ruins. [...]

The ideas ruins evoke in me are grand. Everything comes to nothing, everything perishes, everything passes, only the world remains, only time endures. How old is this world! I walk between two eternities. Wherever I cast my glance, the objects surrounding me announce death and compel my resignation to what awaits me. What is my ephemeral existence in comparison with that of a rock being worn down, of a valley being formed, of a forest that's dying, of these deteriorating masses suspended above my head? I see the marble of tombs crumble into powder, and I don't want to die! And I begrudge the effect on weak tissue of fibres and flesh of a general law that even bronze can't contravene! A torrent drags each and every nation into the depths of a common abyss; myself, I resolve to make a solitary stand at the edge and resist the currents flowing past me.

If the site of a ruin seems perilous, I shudder. If I feel safe and secure there, I'm freer, more alone, more myself, closer to myself. It's there that I call out to my friend, it's there that I miss my friend; it's there that we'd enjoy ourselves without anxiety, without witnesses, without intruders, without those jealous of us. It's there that I probe my own heart; it's there that I interrogate his, that I take alarm and reassure myself. Between this place and the abodes of the city, the native ground of tumult, the seat of interest, passion, vice, crime, prejudice and error, the distance is great.

If my soul were predisposed to tender feelings, I'd surrender to them without restraint; if my heart were calm, I'd savour the full sweetness of its quietude.

In this vast, solitary, deserted sanctuary, I hear nothing, I'm isolated from all life's difficulties.

No one hurries me along and no one is within earshot; I can speak to myself out loud, give voice to my afflictions and shed tears without restraint. [...]

Denis Diderot, extract from 'Le Salon de 1767' (Paris, 1767); trans. John Goodman, in *Diderot on Art. II: The Salon of 1767* (New Haven and London: Yale University Press, 1995) 196–7; 198–9.

Georg Simmel
The Ruin//1911

[...] Wherever we perceive aesthetically, we demand that the contradictory forces of existence be somehow in equilibrium, that the struggle between above and below come to a standstill. But the form which yields only a perception is rejected by the ethical-psychic process, with its incessant moving up and down, its constant shifting of boundaries, and the playing of the inexhaustible forces in it, one against the other.

By contrast, the profound peace which, like a holy charmed circle, surrounds the ruin, conveys a sense of this constellation, of the obscure antagonism which determines the form of all existence, now acting among merely natural forces, now occurring only within psychic life, and now, as in the present case, taking place between nature and matter. This antagonism – although here too it is in disequilibrium in that it lets one side preponderate as the other sinks into annihilation – nevertheless offers us a quietly abiding image, secure in its form. The aesthetic value of the ruin combines the disharmony, the eternal becoming of the soul struggling against itself, with the satisfaction of form, the firm limitedness, of the work of art. For this reason, the metaphysical-aesthetic charm of the ruin disappears when not enough remains of it to let us feel the upward-leading tendency. The stumps of the pillars of the Forum Romanum are simply ugly and nothing else, while a pillar crumbled – say, halfway down – can generate a maximum of charm.

To be sure, we may well be inclined to ascribe this peacefulness to another motive: the character of the ruin as past. It is the site of life from which life has departed – but this is nothing merely negative, added to it only by thought, as it is for the countless things which, once immersed in life and accidentally cast on its bank, are by their very nature capable of being easily caught again by its current. In the case of the ruin, the fact that life, with its wealth and its changes, once dwelled here constitutes an immediately perceived presence. The ruin creates the present form of a past life, not according to the contents or remnants of that life, but according to its past as such.

This also is the charm of antiquities, of which only a narrow-minded logic can assert that an absolutely exact imitation equals them in aesthetic value. No matter if we are deceived in an individual case: with this piece which we are holding in our hand, we command in spirit the entire span of time since its inception; the past with its destinies and transformations has been gathered into this instant of an aesthetically perceptible present. Here, as in the case of the ruin, with its extreme intensification and fulfilment of the present form of the past, such profound and comprehensive energies of our soul are brought into play that there is no longer any sharp division between perception and thought. Here psychic wholeness is at work – seizing, in the same way that its object fuses the contrast of present and past into one united form, on the whole span of physical and spiritual vision in the unity of aesthetic enjoyment, which, after all, is always rooted in a deeper than merely aesthetic unity.

Thus purpose and accident, nature and spirit, past and present, here resolve the tension of their contrasts – or, rather, preserving this tension, they yet lead to a unity of external image and internal effect. It is as though a segment of existence must collapse before it can become unresistant to all currents and powers coming from all corners of reality. Perhaps this is the reason for our general fascination with decay and decadence, a fascination which goes beyond what is merely negative and degrading. The rich and many-sided culture, the unlimited impressionability, and the understanding open to everything, which are characteristic of decadent epochs, do signify this coming together of all contradictory strivings. An equalizing justice connects the uninhibited unity of all things that grow apart and against one another with the decay of those men and works of men which now can only yield, but can no longer create and maintain their own forms out of their own strength.

Georg Simmel, extract from 'Die Ruine: Ein ästhetischer Versuch', earlier version published in *Der Tag*, no. 96 (Berlin, 1907), the final text in *Philosophisches Kultur* (Leipzig: Kröner, 1911); trans. David Kettler, in *Essays on Sociology, Philosophy and Aesthetics* (New York: Harper & Row, 1965) 264–6.

Adrian Stokes
The Pleasures of Limestone//1934

[...] There is a contemporary consciousness of the decay of building stones, due to its great increase and to the expense it involves. For the modern increase of decay we have to thank the modern plasticity in the use of this and other materials. Such indifference is often aggravated in its effects by the curative procedures of a mercenary science. Again, machine dressing is sometimes stated to bruise the stone no less than a blunt chisel. But infinitely greater destructive powers are at work, such as the soot and acids contained in urban atmosphere, and cement mortar jointings so strong or so dense as to impregnate both stone and brick with soluble salts. Exfoliation, florescence, the dreaded crypto-florescence (an internal wall-white or wall-cancer) and other diseases, are the outcome.

In truth, all stone weathering is stone disease. No stone resists the action of atmospheric agencies indefinitely: otherwise we would have no sediments, no soil, no natural sculpture. Chemical change belongs to the beauty and liveliness of stone: it is the natural carving that records Time in immediate form with the pattern and colour of surface. Only a few of these effects, therefore, are repulsive, exfoliation in particular, especially when it appears to be the result of a bacterial infection. As for durability, fine building stones that have been well treated and that are washed by the rains last long enough, even in the sulphurous air of London.

Of all weathering, that of limestone, as a rule, is the most vivid. It is limestone that combines with gases in the air, that is carved by the very breath we breathe out. It is limestone that forms new skins and poetic efflorescence: above all, limestone is sensitive to the most apparent of sculptural agencies, the rain. None the less, the exposed limestone that is well watered may escape harmful sulphate crusts; and such calcium carbonate as is removed by water may well be deposited elsewhere on the building, not in sufficient quantities as to be grotesque or dangerous, but enough to intimate the sculptural communion between the masonry and the water piercing and renewing its stones. It is partly this weathering effect in particular that causes limestones to be the most attractive of building materials. Clayey stones are not good for building, and their light is often dull; while the weathering of sandstones is often an unrelieved crumbling away, if, as is usually the case, the cementing materials between the grains are more sensitive than the grains themselves. A slight crumbling of the cement entails the flaking of what might seem disproportionately large pieces from a rock otherwise so hard. Or else, sandstones of a hard, siliceous cement approximate in character to the abrupt and impervious granite which may become friable before the assaults of frost and other thermal changes, or, in the sea, before the activities of the rock-boring clam; but which seems to lack any communion with the elements that is continuous. It is not often that we see granite in the sensitive state of Cleopatra's needle, responsive after thousands of years in Egypt to the untoward atmosphere of London.

Even granite is heightened by human touch. Continual contact with hands and clothes causes nearly all stones to develop a smooth surface which is seldom observed to flake off. Examples of such surface are to be seen on those parts of ancient buildings that are accesible to the sculpture of touch. But, naturally, nowhere is this effect more palpable than in Venice, particularly on the banisters of the bridges. [...]

Rain, we have said, does not, as a rule, wash the weathered limestone appreciably away; yet it sculptures it more than other stone. One is aware of an intimacy in the *contact* between the marble fountain, for instance, and its water which here produces a gleaming surface veined with unsuspected colours, here magnifies fossil or granular structure. It is a matter of degree (for all stone is influenced by water), the degree of intimacy in their connection; and we have seen that the connections between limestone and water are diverse and poetic. One need know nothing about stones to distinguish a limestone fountain from one of granite. The sense of saturation they convey is different. The granite fountain seems impervious, the water glassy: the limestone or marble fountain, on the other hand, seems to become organic beneath the water, to be sluiced, refreshed. It is not impervious, though solid and gleaming. The water is the finery of a caressing mother. There is re-enacted the strong, resistant, coagulation of stone birth. A wet statue on a limestone basin truly bathes. For purer limestones and marbles have an inner glow that disarms petrifaction of deathliness, though there is retained all the outwardness and objectivity of death. We sense a double petrifaction of this kind, the one in the making of the stone, the other in the making of the statue. Such quality, in combination with the comparative facility with which limestone can be cut, lends itself to the particular naturalism which we identify with Europe. Its origin, of course, and the scenes of its triumph, have been along the Mediterranean basin where marble and pure limestone abound, and where the geography is the limestone geography *par excellence*.

The compactness of their grains causes the purer limestones to be not only robust, as we have seen, but also to possess in many cases this flesh-like glow. The radiance or glow of the purer limestones and marbles causes them, in combination with the impressive fact of their solidity, to be the symbols of life concreted into static objects, of Time concreted as Space. [...]

Adrian Stokes, extracts from 'The Pleasures of Limestone', *Stones of Rimini* (London: Faber & Faber, 1934); reprinted edition (New York: Schocken, 1969) 47–52.

Rose Macaulay
A Note on New Ruins//1953

[...] New ruins have not yet acquired the weathered patina of age, the true rust of the barons' wars, not yet put on their ivy, nor equipped themselves with the appropriate bestiary of lizards, bats, screech-owls, serpents, speckled toads and little foxes which, as has been so frequently observed by ruin-explorers, hold high revel in the precincts of old ruins (such revelling, though noted with pleasure, is seldom described in detail; possibly the jackal waltzes with the toad, the lizard with the fox, while the screech-owl supplies the music and they all glory and drink deep among the tumbled capitals). But new ruins are for a time stark and bare, vegetationless and creatureless; blackened and torn, they smell of fire and mortality.

It will not be for long. Very soon trees will be thrusting through the empty window sockets, the rose-bay and fennel blossoming within the broken walls, the brambles tangling outside them. Very soon the ruin will be enjungled, engulfed, and the appropriate creatures will revel. Even ruins in city streets will, if they are let alone, come, soon or late, to the same fate. Month by month it grows harder to trace the streets around them; here, we see, is the lane of tangled briars that was a street of warehouses; there, in those jungled caverns, stood the large tailor's shop; where those grassy paths cross, a board swings, bearing the name of a tavern. We stumble among stone foundations and fragments of cellar walls, among the ghosts of the exiled merchants and publicans who there carried on their gainful trades. Shells of churches gape emptily; over broken altars the small yellow dandelions make their pattern. All this will presently be; but at first there is only the ruin; a mass of torn, charred prayer books strew the stone floor; the statues, tumbled from their niches, have broken in pieces; rafters and rubble pile knee-deep. But often the ruin has put on, in its catastrophic tipsy chaos, a bizarre new charm. What was last week a drab little house has become a steep flight of stairs winding up in the open between gaily-coloured walls, tiled lavatories, interiors bright and intimate like a Dutch picture or a stage set; the stairway climbs up and up, undaunted, to the roofless summit where it meets the sky. The house has put on melodrama; people stop to stare; here is a domestic scene wide open for all to enjoy. Tomorrow or tonight, the gazers feel, their own dwelling may be even as this. Last night the house was scenic; flames leaping to the sky; today it is squalid and *morne*,[1] but out of its dereliction it flaunts the flags of what is left. [...]

Ruinenlust has come full circle: we have had our fill. Ruin pleasure must be at one remove, softened by art, by Piranesi, Salvator Rosa, Poussin, Claude,

Monsù Desiderio, Pannini, Guardi, Robert, James Pryde, John Piper, the ruin-poets, or centuries of time. Ruin must be a fantasy, veiled by the mind's dark imaginings: in the objects that we see before us, we get to agree with St Thomas Aquinas, that *quae enim diminutae sunt, hoc ipso turpia sunt*,[2] and to feel that, in beauty, wholeness is all.

But such wholesome hankerings are, it seems likely, merely a phase of our fearful and fragmented age.

1 [sad, mournful, dismal.]

2 [Things that are lacking in something are thereby unsightly.]

Rose Macaulay, extracts from *Pleasure of Ruins* (London: Thames & Hudson, 1953) 453–5.

Walter Benjamin
The Arcades Project//1927–40

[...] 'In speaking of the inner boulevards', says the *Illustrated Guide to Paris*, a complete picture of the city on the Seine and its environs from the year 1852, 'we have made mention again and again of the arcades which open onto them. These arcades, a recent invention of industrial luxury, are glass-roofed, marble-panelled corridors extending through whole blocks of buildings, whose owners have joined together for such enterprises. Lining both sides of these corridors, which get their light from above, are the most elegant shops, so that the arcade is a city, a world in miniature, in which customers will find everything they need. During sudden rain showers, the arcades are a place of refuge for the unprepared, to whom they offer a secure, if restricted, promenade – one from which the merchants also benefit.' The customers are gone, along with those taken by surprise. Rain brings in only the poorer clientèle without waterproof or mackintosh. These were spaces for a generation of people who knew little of the weather and who, on Sundays, when it snowed, would rather warm themselves in the winter gardens than go out skiing. Glass before its time, premature iron: it was one single line of descent – arcades, winter gardens with their lordly palms, and railroad stations, which cultivated the false orchid 'adieu', with its fluttering petals. They have long since given way to the hangar. And today it is the same with the human material on the inside of the arcades as with the materials of their construction. Pimps are the iron bearings of this street, and its glass breakables are the whores. Here was the last refuge of those infant prodigies that saw the light of day at the time of the world exhibitions: the briefcase with interior lighting, the metre-long pocket knife, or the patented umbrella handle with built-in watch and revolver. And near the degenerate giant creatures, aborted and broken-down matter. We followed the narrow dark corridor to where – between a discount bookshop, in which colourful tied-up bundles tell all sorts of failure, and a shop selling only buttons (mother-of-pearl and the kind that in Paris are called *de fantaisie*) – there stood a sort of salon. On a pale-coloured wallpaper full of figures and busts shone a gas lamp. By its light, an old woman sat reading. They say she has been there alone for years, and collects sets of teeth 'in gold, in wax and broken'. Since that day, moreover, we know where Doctor Miracle got the wax out of which he fashioned Olympia. They are the true fairies of these arcades (more salable and more worn than the life-sized ones): the formerly world-famous Parisian dolls, which revolved on their musical socle and bore in their arms a doll-sized basket out of which, at the salutation of the minor chord, a lambkin poked its curious muzzle. [...]

All this is the arcade in our eyes. And it was nothing of all this. They [the arcades] radiated through the Paris of the Empire like grottoes. For someone entering the Passage des Panoramas in 1817, the sirens of gaslight would be singing to him on one side, while oil-lamp odalisques offered enticements from the other. With the kindling of electric lights, the irreproachable glow was extinguished in these galleries, which suddenly became more difficult to find – which wrought a black magic at entranceways, and peered from blind windows into their own interior. It was not decline but transformation. All at once, they were the hollow mould from which the image of 'modernity' was cast. Here, the century mirrored with satisfaction its most recent past. Here was the retirement home for infant prodigies [...]

When, as children, we were given those great encyclopaedic works *World and Mankind*, *New Universe*, *The Earth*, wouldn't our gaze always fall, first of all, on the colour illustration of a 'Carboniferous Landscape' or on 'Lakes and Glaciers of the First Ice Age'? Such an ideal panorama of a barely elapsed primaeval age opens up when we look through the arcades that are found in all cities. Here resides the last dinosaur of Europe, the consumer. On the walls of these caverns, their immemorial flora, the commodity, luxuriates and enters, like cancerous tissue, into the most irregular combinations. A world of secret affinities: palm tree and feather duster, hair dryer and Venus de Milo, prosthesis and letter-writing manual come together here as after a long separation. The odalisque lies in wait next to the inkwell, priestesses raise aloft ashtrays like patens.[1] These items on display are a rebus: and [how] one ought to read here the birdseed kept in the fixative-pan from a darkroom, the flower seeds beside the binoculars, the broken screws atop the musical score, and the revolver above the goldfish bowl – is right on the tip of one's tongue. After all, nothing of the lot appears to be new. The goldfish come perhaps from a pond that dried up long ago, the revolver will have been a *corpus delicti*, and these scores could hardly have preserved their previous owner from starvation when her last pupils stayed away. [...]

One knew of places in ancient Greece where the way led down into the underworld. our waking existence likewise is a land which, at certain hidden points, leads down into the underworld – a land full of inconspicuous places from which dreams arise. All day long, suspecting nothing, we pass them by, but no sooner has sleep come than we are eagerly groping our way back to lose ourselves in the dark corridors. By day, the labyrinth of urban dwellings resembles consciousness: the arcades (which are galleries leading into the city's past) issue unremarked onto the streets. At night, however, under the tenebrous mass of the houses, their denser darkness bursts forth like a threat, and the nocturnal pedestrian hurries past – unless, that is, we have emboldened him to turn into the narrow lane. [...]

Plush as dust collector. Mystery of dustmotes playing in the sunlight. Dust and the 'best room'. 'Shortly after 1840, fully padded furniture appears in France, and with it the upholstered style becomes dominant.' Max von Boehn, *Die Mode im XIX. Jahrhundert*, vol. 2 (Munich, 1907) 131. Other arrangements to stir up dust: the trains of dresses. 'The true and proper train has recently come back into vogue, but in order to avoid the nuisance of having it sweep the streets, the wearer is now provided with a small hook and a string so that she can raise and carry the train whenever she goes anywhere.' Friedrich Theodor Vischer, *Mode und Zynismus* (Stuttgart, 1879) 12. Dust and Stifled Perspective. [...]

1 [Plates for the Eucharist.]

Walter Benjamin, extracts from *Das Passagen-Werk* (manuscript, 1927–40); trans. Howard Eiland and Kevin McLaughlin, *The Arcades Project* (Cambridge, Massachusetts: Harvard University Press, 1999) 103; 872–4.

Georges Bataille
Dust//1929

DUST – The storytellers have not realized that the Sleeping Beauty would have awoken covered in a thick layer of dust; nor have they envisaged the sinister spiders' webs that would have been torn apart at the first movement of her red tresses. Meanwhile dismal sheets of dust constantly invade earthly habitations and uniformly defile them: as if it were a matter of making ready attics and old rooms for the imminent occupation of the obsessions, phantoms, spectres that the decayed odour of old dust nourishes and intoxicates.

When plump young girls, 'maids of all work', arm themselves each morning with a large feather duster or even a vacuum cleaner, they are perhaps not completely unaware that they are contributing every bit as much as the most positivist of scientists to dispelling the injurious phantoms that cleanliness and logic abhor. One day or another, it is true, dust, supposing it persists, will probably begin to gain the upper hand over domestics, invading the immense ruins of abandoned buildings, deserted dockyards; and, at that distant epoch, nothing will remain to ward off night-terrors, for lack of which we have become such great book-keepers ...

Georges Bataille, 'Poussière' (Dust) entry in first instalment of 'Le Dictionnaire critique', *Documents*, no. 1 (Paris, 1929); trans. Iain White, in *Encyclopaedia Acephalica* (London: Atlas Press, 1995) 42–3.

Celeste Olalquiaga
Dust//1998

> The grey film of dust covering things has become their best part.
> – Walter Benjamin, 'Dreamkitsch', 1927

[...] In the one short piece where he discusses kitsch, Walter Benjamin employs the metaphor of dust to describe the rundown state of dreams in modernity. Attuned to the fate of the aura, he says, dreams are no longer removed from concrete experience, but tangible and near. They have lost their romantic dimension, their 'blue distance', fading into a sad greyness that figuratively represents the disintegration which befalls dreams when they cease being imaginary and enter the polluted atmosphere of everyday life.[1]

Benjamin associates this colourless state with the dust that accumulates on forgotten objects, establishing an analogy between what he calls the extinct world of things (things infused with aura, of course) and the worn-out condition of dreams: both are now in the realm of the banal, that is, of kitsch. What makes dreams and things kitsch, therefore, is their tangibility – the fact that they no longer stand 'two metres away from the body', but have become instead familiar and accessible. The connection of kitsch and decay is underscored by their mutual susceptibility to physical touch. And, as is always the case with the aura, the loss of distance is occasioned by technology, which Benjamin likens to bills of currency, in other words, to exchange value: bills and technology stand for the exterior of things, as opposed to their essence. In this way, Benjamin seems to perpetuate the classic opposition between essence and appearance that implicitly underlies the official status of kitsch as a superficial phenomenon and art outcast.

Benjamin's apparent dichotomy between outside and inside, body and soul, assumes that once things have been touched by the deadly hands of commodity fetishism, they wilt like flowers. And truly, only in the faraway dimension of conceptual distance (or of memory) can things remain beyond the mortal trials of time and space, the wear and tear of age and use. This auratic distance is better understood with the help of what Benjamin distinguishes as 'cult value', a traditional relationship to objects whereby these are infused with a sacred quality characteristic of cultures with a magic or theocentric view of the world. In turn, cult value is related to use value, where the worth of things is directly derived from their relationship to human activity, instead of subordinated to the laws of market exchange, or exchange value. [...]

Although Benjamin longs for cult value, he recognizes its modern disintegration as the breaking down of old hierarchies which places essence over appearance and, consequently, believes technology has a revolutionary potential. Similarly, although for him the novel promotes an individualistic experience that is radically different from the communal one of oral and epic literary traditions, it enables for this very reason a creative understanding of the world (rather than an acceptance of handed-down beliefs) which can open the way for its transformation.

What is most relevant about Benjamin's kitsch essay, therefore, is that it describes the consequence of the shift from a mode of experience based on a sacred distance to a mode based on perceptual proximity. For Benjamin, modernity replaces the cyclic flow of traditional time with a mirage of movement constituted by sheer repetition: the new as the 'ever-always-the-same'. This condition is exposed by dust, which can slowly accumulate on things given their ultimate immobility, since the proliferation in space does not grant things movement (that is, transformation) in time.

Ironically, or perhaps by some intuitive acknowledgment, stillness was feared by the pragmatic idealism of the nineteenth century, where everything had to have a reason, an explanation, or a function. Victorian interiors, apparently merely ornamental, had a practical purpose: to cover the emptiness left behind by the absence of tradition. Material proliferation was legitimized by the pretended usefulness of things that contained other things – albums, armoires, boxes, glass cases – often protecting them from this era's arch-enemy, dust. Interiors themselves, like the arcades of a few decades earlier, were created to protect objects from the outside, keeping them safe for contemplation.

The vast production of the late 1800s was geared to protecting, showing, holding – an obsession that accounts for this period's fastidious arrangements, where nothing is out of place and all the different elements participate in an obligatory meaningfulness. Dust is a cumbersome residue that taints what it touches and must be eradicated: dust is seen as dirt, a persistent contamination exuded by death onto the world of the living. Already the 1851 Crystal Palace featured two devices to combat dust: a structural feature whereby the wooden planks of the palace's floors were left slightly separate so that the dust could fall through them, and a bizarre 'vacuum coffin guaranteed to prevent decay'.

Eventually, nineteenth-century production surpassed the spaces that so generously embraced it, overflowing them to such a degree that they almost drowned under the weight of their own culture. Satiated, this society then turned around and lashed out against its own abundance amidst self-accusations of superfluity and waste. After all, its objects were no longer connected to anything vital, but were the emblems of a cultural death perpetrated by commodification, the remnants of an aura (however mythical) whose brutal disintegration marked the end of an era. So, while Benjamin's dust metaphor states that dust – kitsch, the banal – is a worthless, extrinsic detritus, at the same time it exposes the cultural condition that made this metaphorical dust possible: the loss of use value and the disintegration of the aura.

This assertion can be extended to suggest that dust grants things a peculiarity that reconstitutes them as a new experience, validating instead of disqualifying them. To this effect, I would like to propose that even though dust – or boredom – settles on things that do not move, dust itself may also be seen as the last breath of tradition, and therefore different from the deadly repetition of modernity. The dust that falls on modern things is the decay of the aura, the decomposition of a previous era that, like the tons of shells and detritus that continuously sink to the ocean bottom, creates a new layer of sediment. The dust of modernity, a mix of boredom and death, is the most tangible aspect of the new historical time, a thin patina of shattered moments remaining after the frenzy of multiplication has subsided or moved away.

It should come as no surprise, then, that Benjamin equates dust with kitsch, since both are constituted by what I am distinguishing here as the debris of the aura. What is at stake for kitsch and dust is the transformation of reality from unitary to fragmented, from continuous to chaotic, along with a shift in the way we perceive, which goes from ritualistic to a pragmatic apprehension. The layer of dust makes things into opaque phantoms of themselves in the same way that kitsch is the distorted copy, or brilliant shadow, of a unique original that it transforms while replicating. And in so far as kitsch is like dust – a fragmented reminder of something now gone, a mundane proliferation that infiltrates homes at will, a bizarre form of object appropriation – then kitsch is liable to the same accusations and cleansing operations that dust must endure.

Dust is what connects the dreams of yesteryear with the touch of nowadays. It is the aftermath of the collapse of illusions, a powdery cloud that rises abruptly and then begins falling on things, gently covering their bright, polished surfaces. Dust is like a soft carpet of snow that gradually coats the city, quieting its noise until we feel like we are inside a snow globe, the urban exterior transmuted into a magical interior where all time is suspended and space contained. Dust makes the outside inside by calling attention to the surface of things, a surface formerly deemed untouchable or simply ignored as a conduit to what was considered real: that essence which supposedly lies inside people and things, waiting to be discovered. Dust turns things inside out by exposing their bodies as more than mere shells or carriers, for only after dust settles on an object do we begin to long for its lost splendour, realizing how much of this forgotten object's beauty lay in the more external, concrete aspect of its existence, rather than in its hidden, attributed meaning.

Dust brings a little of the world into the enclosed quarters of objects. Belonging to the outside, the exterior, the street, dust constantly creeps into the sacred arena of private spaces as a reminder that there are no impermeable boundaries between life and death. It is a transparent veil that seduces with the promise of what lies behind it, which is never as good as the titillating offer. Dust makes palpable the elusive passing of time, the infinite pulverized particles that constitute its volatile matter, catching their prey in a surprise embrace whose clingy hands, like an invisible net, leave no other mark than a delicate sheen of faint glitter. As it sticks to our fingertips, dust propels a vague state of retrospection, carrying us on its supple wings. A messenger of death, dust is the signature of lost time.

Indeed, dust is where faded dreams and touch intersect, where the blue horizon fades to grey. Benjamin's distinction between dreams and touch reflects the aura's underlying hierarchy of value. In a time when the manufacturing of objects has given way to their mechanical and mass production, pre-industrial times are considered superior for representing a direct connection between producer/consumer and object; they are granted a transcendental dimension for seemingly bridging the gap between sensorial perception and symbolic apprehension. Within the parameters of use value the aura remains intact; the connotations of authenticity and uniqueness permeating process, object and subject.

Not so with mass production, which replaces use value with exchange value, where the emphasis is on accessibility and pragmatism. Having descended from the Mount Olympus of exclusivity, objects need no longer to surpass their immediate function on Earth, but can be relished instead for their corporeal existence. Like fallen angels, objects lose or rather ruin their auras upon descent, arriving with little more than a crumbling, dusty shadow of their once iridescent haloes. Deprived of supernatural immunity, the shaken-down aura falls prey to all the vicissitudes of earth-bound things: it can be touched, traded, copied and tampered with; it is but a fragment of its former existence. It is kitsch. [...]

1 Walter Benjamin, 'Traumkitsch' [Dreamkitsch] (1927), in *Ausgewahlte Schriften*, vol. 2 (Frankfurt am Main: Suhrkamp, 1966) 158–60.

Celeste Olalquiaga, extracts from *The Artificial Kingdom: A Treasury of the Kitsch Experience* (New York: Pantheon Books, 1998) 87–95; 140–46

Susan Stewart
Separation and Restoration//1996

The delicate and hermetic world of the souvenir is a world of nature idealized; nature is removed from the domain of struggle into the domestic sphere of the individual and the interior. The souvenir is used most often to evoke a voluntary memory of childhood, a motif we find either in souvenirs, such as scrapbooks, of the individual life history or in the larger antiquarian theme of the childhood of the nation/race. This childhood is not a childhood as lived; it is a childhood voluntarily remembered, a childhood manufactured from its material survivals. Thus it is a collage made of presents rather than a reawakening of a past. As in an album of photographs or a collection of antiquarian relics, the past is constructed from a set of presently existing pieces. There is no continuous identity between these objects and their referents. Only the act of memory constitutes their resemblance. And it is in this gap between resemblance and identity that nostalgic desire arises. The nostalgic is enamoured of distance, not of the referent itself. Nostalgia cannot be sustained without loss. For the nostalgic to reach his or her goal of closing the gap between resemblance and identity, *lived* experience would have to take place, an erasure of the gap between sign and signified, an experience which would cancel out the desire that is nostalgia's reason for existence.

In the cultivation of distance which we find in the uses of the souvenir – the distance of childhood and the antique – the third facet is distance in space – the souvenir of the exotic. Just as authenticity and interiority are placed in the remote past, the exotic offers an authenticity of experience tied up with notions of the primitive as child and the primitive as an earlier and purer stage of contemporary civilization. Jean Baudrillard writes in *Le Système des objets* that the exotic object, like the antique, functions to lend authenticity to the abstract system of modern objects, and he suggests that the indigenous object fascinates by means of its anteriority. This anteriority is characteristic both of the exotic object's form and its mode of fabrication and links it to the analogously anterior world of childhood and its toys. Thus the authenticity of the exotic object arises not in the conditions authored by the primitive culture itself but from the analogy between the primitive/exotic and the origin of the possessor, the authentic 'nature' of that radical otherness which is the possessor's own childhood. In Baudrillard's terms, modern is 'cold' and the antique and the exotic are 'warm' because contemporary mythology places the latter objects in a childhood remote from the abstractions of contemporary consumer society.

Such objects allow one to be a tourist of one's own life, or allow the tourist to appropriate, consume and thereby 'tame' the cultural other.

Just as in reverie, narrative is used to invent the symbolic, so by a similar process travel writing functions to miniaturize and interiorize those distanced experiences which remain outside contemporary lived relations. The tourist seeks out objects and scenes, and the relation between the object and its sight is continued, indeed articulated, in the operation of the souvenir. Robert Jennings and Company's tourist books from the 1830s are typical of this romantic genre. In *The Tourist in Biscay and the Castilles*, Thomas Roscoe writes of Bayonne: 'Being involuntarily detained, we employed the leisure thus created in seeking out the picturesque, which generally lurks, like unassuming characters, in quiet and out-of-the-way places. Nor were we by any means unsuccessful in our pilgrimage, though dire was the number of dirty lanes and alleys, both within and without the walls, which we threaded in search of it. In spite of the spirit of improvement, numbers of antique houses, not at all dilapidated, are still found here, and each of these would form an interesting study for the pencil.' While Roscoe emphasizes the picturesque, W.H. Harrison, in *The Tourist in Portugal*, has a more antiquarian focus, concluding that the reader has been presented with 'all the objects we deemed worthy of his attention ... and all we know about them'. The function of the tour is the estrangement of objects – to make what is visible, what is surface, reveal a profound interiority through narrative. This interiority is that of the perceiving subject; it is gained at the expense of risking contamination (hence the dire and dirty lanes) and the dissolution of the boundary of that subject. The process is later recapitulated more safely within the context of the familiar, the home, by means of the souvenir.

The exotic object represents distance appropriated; it is symptomatic of the more general cultural imperialism that is tourism's stock in trade. To have a souvenir of the exotic is to possess both a specimen and a trophy; on the one hand, the object must be marked as exterior and foreign, on the other it must be marked as arising directly out of an immediate experience of its possessor. It is thus placed within an intimate distance; space is transformed into interiority, into 'personal' space, just as time is transformed into interiority in the case of the antique object. Consider Gulliver's souvenirs of his adventures: from Lilliput the cattle, sheep, gold pieces and 'his Majesty's picture at full length'; from Brobdingnag 'the small collection of rarities' – 'the comb I had contrived out of the stumps of the King's beard; and another of the same materials, but fixed into a paring of her Majesty's thumbnail, which served for the back', the collection of needles and pins, some combings from the queen's hair and her rings, a corn cut from a maid of honour's toe, his breeches made of mouse's skin, and a footman's tooth. These souvenirs serve as evidence of Gulliver's experience and as measurements of his own scale, just as the giant's ring and booklet serve to authenticate the audience's experience. Like all curiosities, these souvenirs function to generate narrative. More than the souvenirs of Lilliput, which are most often whole and animal and serve as models and representative elements of sets, the souvenirs of Brobdingnag are partial and human; they are samples of the body which simultaneously estrange us from the body. But unlike the souvenirs of mortality discussed earlier, these souvenirs are taboo items collected from the body's refuse. These beard stumps, nail parings, hair combings and corns do not diminish the body by their absence or appropriation; rather, they speak to its dual capacities of excess and regeneration. They transform the human into the other and yet allow the possessor to know intimately that other in parts. Gulliver's souvenirs of Brobdingnag are not 'ordinary': they speak to his degree of involvement with the Brobdingnagians – his partial yet intimate vision. They are 'authentic' souvenirs in the same way that the objects of magical tasks in fairy tales ('you must bring me three hairs from the giant's head') are evidence of an experience that is not vicarious but lived within an estranged or dangerous intimacy. They acquire their value only within the context of Gulliver's narrative; without such a narrative, they are not only meaningless, they are also exaggerations of the disposable.

Unlike the ancient object, which, though it arises from the distant past, is endowed with a familiarity more 'warm' than the present, the exotic object is to some degree dangerous, even 'hot'. Removed from its context, the exotic souvenir is a sign of survival – not its own survival, but the survival of the possessor outside his or her own context of familiarity. Its otherness speaks to the possessor's capacity for otherness: it is the possessor, not the souvenir, which is ultimately the curiosity. The danger of the souvenir lies in its unfamiliarity, in our difficulty in subjecting it to interpretation. There is always the possibility that reverie's signification will go out of control here, that the object itself will take charge, awakening some dormant capacity for destruction. This appropriation of reverie by the object forms the basis for certain horror stories: 'The Monkey's Paw', or the ghost stories of M.R. James, for example. In such tales curiosity is replaced by understanding only at the expense of the possessor's wellbeing.

In most souvenirs of the exotic, however, the metaphor in operation is again one of taming; the souvenir retains its signifying capacity only in a generalized sense, losing its specific referent and eventually pointing to an abstracted otherness that describes the possessor. Nelson Graburn, writing on 'fourth world arts', has suggested:

> As 'civilized societies' come to depend more and more upon standardized mass-produced artefacts, the distinctiveness of classes, families and individuals disappears, and the importation of foreign exotic arts increases to meet the demand

for distinctiveness, especially for the snob or status market. One gains prestige by association with these objects, whether they are souvenirs or expensive imports; there is a cachet connected with international travel, exploration, multiculturalism, etc. that these arts symbolize; at the same time, there is the nostalgic input of the *handmade* in a 'plastic world'. (Introduction, *Ethnic and Tourist Arts: Cultural Expressions from the Fourth World*, ed. Nelson H, Graburn, 1976)

Thus such objects satisfy the nostalgic desire for use value at the same time that they provide an exoticism of the self. Ironically, the demand for such objects creates a souvenir market of goods distinct from authentic traditional crafts, that is, crafts designed in light of use value. And these souvenir goods are often characterized by new techniques of mass production. There is thus a directly proportional relationship between the availability of the exotic experience and the availability of 'exotic objects'. Once the exotic experience is readily purchasable by a large segment of the tourist population, either more and more exotic experiences are sought (consider travel posters advertising the last frontier or the last unspoiled island) or, in a type of reverse snobbery, there is a turning towards 'the classic' of the consumer's native culture. In those cities where one finds a wide range of 'ethnic' restaurants frequented by those not of the same ethnicity, one is also likely to find restaurants advertising 'classic American cuisine', a phrase which itself cannot work without a French deglazing.

For the invention of the exotic object to take place, there must first be separation. It must be clear that the object is estranged from the context in which it will be displayed as a souvenir; it must be clear that use value is separate from display value. There is perhaps no better example of this process than the radical generational separation in America which results in certain nostalgic forms of lawn art. While we see the exotic and the cultural other explored in forms such as pink flamingos and slumbering Mexicans, the most common forms are antiquarian ones such as wagon wheels, donkey carts, sleighs and oxen yokes. These metonymic forms are the articulation of abandoned use value. Prominently displayed, they speak to the industrialization of the occupants of the house, occupants who have become tourists of their parents' ways of life.

Yet to create 'tourist art' is to create display value from the outset and to bypass this gradual transformation. Separation is accomplished spatially rather than temporally here. Thus it is necessary to invent the pastoral and the primitive through an illusion of a holistic and integrated cultural other. As for tourist souvenirs themselves, they increasingly tend in both form and content to be shaped by the expectations of the tourist market that will consume them. Graburn points out that since makers of souvenirs must compete with imported, manufactured souvenirs, native arts tend toward smaller sizes – not simply small souvenirs, but miniatures of traditional artefacts. Among the advantages of miniaturized articles are 'applicability for decorative use, economy of materials and a doll-like, folkloristic quality not associated with the real article'. Those qualities of the object which link it most closely to its function in native context are emptied and. replaced by both display value and the symbolic system of the consumer. William Bascom has found that in African art this tourist influence has resulted in three stylistic trends, all arising out of Western aesthetic principles. First, there is a tendency toward Western ideas of naturalism and realism; traditional modes of stylization were replaced by nineteenth-century European conventions of the picturesque. Second, there is a tendency toward an opposite extreme: the grotesque. Bascom concludes that this work 'may reflect both European preconceptions about the savagery or strength of African sculpture as well as the influence of German Expressionism on European artistic taste'. The third tendency is toward gigantification. Yoruba carvers, for example, reproduce bells or clappers used in Ifa divination—bells that are normally 8 to 16 inches long and 1 inch in diameter – in versions that are 3 feet long and 3 inches in diameter. Gigantification allows the maker to charge more for the product, yet at the same time may involve less labour because it requires less attention to detail. Similarly, Graburn writes that 'Eskimo soapstone sculptors and Cordova *santeros* calculate that far less time and effort is spent making large, expensive carvings than the more typical small ones.' Thus the tourist aesthetic ensures that the object is continually exoticized and estranged. And, ironically, objects that are originally valued by tourists precisely because of their connections to a traditional, holistic and paradisal culture are transformed, exaggerated and modified by the fluctuating demands of that same tourist market.

In the uses of the souvenir, the other side of separation is restoration – here the false promise of restoration. The souvenir must be removed from its context in order to serve as a trace of it, but it must also be restored through narrative and/or reverie. What it is restored to is not an 'authentic', that is, a native, context of origin but an imaginary context of origin whose chief subject is a projection of the possessor's childhood. Restoration can be seen as a response to an unsatisfactory set of present conditions. Just as the restoration of buildings, often taking place within programmes of 'gentrification' in contemporary cities, has as its basis the restoration of class relationships that might otherwise be in flux, so the restoration of the souvenir is a conservative idealization of the past and the distanced for the purposes of a present ideology. We thus might say that all souvenirs are souvenirs of a nature which has been invented by ideology. This conclusion speaks not only to the display of Victorian sea shells under glass but also to the broader tendency to place all things natural at one degree of removal from the present flow of events and thereby to objectify them.

The only proper context for the souvenir is the displacement of reverie, the gap between origin/object/subject which fields desire. Whereas the collection is either truly hidden or prominently displayed, the souvenir, so long as it remains 'uncollected', is 'lost', removed from any context of origin and use value in such a way as to 'surprise' and capture its viewer into reverie. The actual locale of the souvenir is often commensurate with its material worthlessness: the attic and the cellar, contexts away from the business and engagement of everyday life. Other rooms of a house are tied to function (kitchen, bath) and presentation (parlour, hall) in such a way that they exist within the temporality of everyday life, but the attic and the cellar are tied to the temporality of the past, and they scramble the past into a simultaneous order which memory is invited to rearrange: heaven and hell, tool and ornament, ancestor and heir, decay and preservation. The souvenir is destined to be forgotten; its tragedy lies in the death of memory, the tragedy of all autobiography and the simultaneous erasure of the autograph. And thus we come again to the powerful metaphor of the unmarked grave, the reunion with the mother with no corresponding regeneration of the symbolic. [...]

Susan Stewart, 'Separation and Restoration' section of 'Objects of Desire', *On Longing* (Durham, North Carolina: Duke University Press, 1996) 145–51 [footnotes not included].

Walter Benjamin
Theses on the Philosophy of History//1940

VII

Consider the darkness and the great cold
In this vale which resounds with misery
– Bertholt Brecht, *The Threepenny Opera*

To historians who wish to relive an era, Fustel de Coulanges recommends that they blot out everything they know about the later course of history. There is no better way of characterizing the method with which historical materialism has broken. It is a process of empathy whose origin is the indolence of the heart, *acedia*, which despairs of grasping and holding the genuine historical image as it flares up briefly. Among mediaeval theologians it was regarded as the root cause of sadness. Flaubert, who was familiar with it, wrote: '*Peu de gens devineront combien il a fallu être triste pour ressusciter Carthage.*' [Few will be able to guess how sad one had to be in order to resuscitate Carthage.] The nature of this sadness stands out more clearly if one asks with whom the adherents of historicism actually empathize. The answer is inevitable: with the victor. And all the rulers are the heirs of those who conquered before them. Hence, empathy with the victor invariably benefits the rulers. Historical materialists know what this means. Whoever has emerged victorious participates to this day in the triumphal procession in which the present rulers step over those who are lying prostrate. According to traditional practice, the spoils are carried along in the procession. They are called cultural treasures, and a historical materialist views them with cautious detachment. For without exception the cultural treasures he surveys have an origin which he cannot contemplate without horror. They owe their existence not only to the great minds and talents who have created them, but also to the anonymous toil of their contemporaries. There is no document of civilization which is not at the same time a document of barbarism. And just as such a document is not free of barbarism, barbarism taints also the manner in which it was transmitted from one owner to another. A historical materialist therefore dissociates himself from it as far as possible. He regards it as his task to brush history against the grain.

Walter Benjamin, 'VII', from 'Über den Begriff der Geschichte', *Geschichtshistorische These* (1940); trans. Harry Zohn, 'Theses on the Philosophy of History', in *Walter Benjamin: Illuminations*, ed. Hannah Arendt (New York: Schocken Books, 1969) reprinted edition (London: Fontana, 1992) 254.

Jacques Derrida
Memoirs of the Blind//1990

[...] As soon as the draughtsman considers himself, fascinated, fixed on the image, yet disappearing before his own eyes into the abyss, the movement by which he tries desperately to recapture himself is already, in its very present, an act of memory. Baudelaire suggested in *Mnemonic Art* that the setting to work of memory is not *in the service of* drawing. But neither does it lead drawing as its master or its death. It is the very operation of drawing, and precisely its *setting to work*. The failure to recapture the presence of the gaze outside of the abyss into which it is sinking is not an accident or weakness; it illustrates or rather figures the very chance of the work, the spectre of the invisible that the work lets be seen without ever presenting. Just as memory does not here restore a past (once) present, so the ruin of the face – and of the face looked in the face in drawing – does not indicate ageing, wearing away, anticipated decomposition, or this being eaten away by time – something about which the portrait often betrays an apprehension. The ruin does not supervene like an accident upon a monument that was intact only yesterday. In the beginning there is ruin. Ruin is that which happens to the image from the moment of the first gaze. Ruin is the self-portrait, this face looked at in the face as the memory of itself, what *remains* or *returns* as a spectre from the moment one first looks at oneself and a figuration is eclipsed. The figure, the face, then sees its visibility being eaten away; it loses its integrity without disintegrating. For the incompleteness of the visible monument comes from the eclipsing structure of the trait, from a structure that is only remarked, pointed out, impotent or incapable of being reflected in the shadow of the self-portrait. So many reversible propositions. For one can just as well read the pictures of ruins as the figures of a portrait, indeed, of a self-portrait.

Whence the love of ruins. And the fact that the scopic pulsion, voyeurism itself, is always on the lookout for the originary ruin. A narcissistic melancholy, a memory – in mourning – of love itself. How to love anything other than the possibility of ruin? Than an impossible totality? Love is as old as this ageless ruin – at once originary, an infant even, and already old. Love doles out his *traits*; he sights, he comes on site, and sees without seeing – this blindfolded love 'this old child, blind archer, and naked', as Du Bellay says of Cupid.[1] The ruin is not in front of us; it is neither a spectacle nor a love object. It is experience itself: neither the abandoned yet still monumental fragment of a totality, nor, as Benjamin thought, simply a theme of baroque culture.[2] It is precisely not a theme, for it ruins the theme, the position, the presentation or representation of anything and everything. Ruin is, rather, this memory open like an eye, or like the hole in a bone socket that lets you see without showing you anything *at all*, anything *of the all*. This, *for* showing you *nothing at all, nothing of the all*. 'For' means here both *because* the ruin shows *nothing at all* and *with a view to* showing *nothing of the all*. There is nothing of the totality that is not immediately opened, pierced, or bored through: the mask of this impossible self-portrait whose signatory sees himself disappearing before his own eyes the more he tries desperately to recapture himself in it. Thoughtful memory and ruin of what is in advance past, mourning and melancholy, the spectre of the instant (*stigme*) and of the stylus, whose very point would like to touch the blind point of a gaze that looks itself in the eyes and is not far from sinking into those eyes, right up to the point of losing its sight through an excess of lucidity. An *Augenblick* without duration, 'during' which, however, the draughtsman feigns to stare at the centre of the blind spot. Even if nothing happens, if no event takes place, the signatory blinds himself to the rest of the world. But unable to see himself properly and directly – a blind spot or transcendental *trait* – he also blindly contemplates himself, attacks his sight right up to the exhaustion of narcissism. The truth of his own eyes as seer, in the double sense of this word, is the last thing that can be taken by surprise – *naked*, without attribute, without glasses, without a hat, without a blindfold on the head, in a mirror. The naked face cannot look itself in the face, *it cannot look at itself in a looking glass.*

1 [footnote 62 in source] Joachim Du Bellay, *L'Olive* (1549), sonnet 26 (Geneva: Droz, 1974).

2 [63] Benjamin speaks of 'the baroque cult of the ruin': 'that which lies here in ruins, the highly significant fragment, the remnant, is, in fact, the finest material in baroque creation.' (*The Origin of German Tragic Drama*, trans. John Osborne [London and New York: Verso, 1977] 178).

Jacques Derrida, extract from *Mémoires d'aveugle: l'autoportrait et autres ruines* (Paris: Éditions de la Réunion des musées nationaux, 1990); trans. Pascale-Anne Brault and Michael Naas, *Memoirs of the Blind: The Self-Portrait and Other Ruins* (Chicago, University of Chicago Press, 1993) 68–9.

Le Corbusier
Towards a New Architecture//1923

[...] There is a formidable industrial activity at present in progress, which is inevitably and constantly at the back of our minds; at every moment either directly, or through the medium of newspapers and reviews, we are presented with objects of an arresting novelty whose why and wherefore engrosses our minds, and fills us with delight and fear. All these objects of modern life create, in the long run, a modern state of mind. Bewilderment seizes us, then, if we bring our eyes to bear on the old and rotting buildings that form our snail-shell, our habitation, which crush us in our daily contact with them – putrid and useless and unproductive. Everywhere can be seen machines which serve to produce something and produce it admirably, in a clean sort of way. The machine that we live in is an old coach full of tuberculosis. There is no real link between our daily activities at the factory, the office or the bank, which are healthy and useful and productive, and our activities in the bosom of the family which are handicapped at every turn. The family is everywhere being killed and men's minds demoralized in servitude to anachronisms.

Every man's mind, being moulded by his participation in contemporary events, has consciously or unconsciously formed certain desires; these are inevitably connected with the family, an instinct which is the basis of society. Every man today realizes his need of sun, of warmth, of pure air and clean floors; he has been taught to wear a shiny white collar, and women love fine white linen. Man feels today that he must have intellectual diversion, relaxation for his body, and the physical culture needed to recuperate him after the tension of muscle or brain which his labour – 'hard labour' – brings. This mass of desires constitutes in fact a mass of *demands*. Now our social organization has nothing ready which can answer these needs.

Another point: what are the conclusions of the *intellectuals* face to face with the actualities of modern life?

The magnificent flowering of industry in our epoch has created a special class of intellectuals so numerous that it constitutes the really active stratum of society. In the workshop, in the technical departments, in the learned Societies, in the banks and in the great stores, on newspapers and reviews, there are the engineers, the heads of departments, legal representatives, secretaries, editors, accountants who work out minutely, in accordance with their duty, the formidable things which occupy our attention: there are the men who design our bridges, ships and aeroplanes, who create our motors and turbines, who direct the workshops and yards, who are engaged in the distribution of capital and in accountancy, who do the purchasing of goods in the colonies or from the factory, who put forth so many articles in the Press on the modern production of so much that is noble and horrible, who record as on a chart the high-temperature curve of a humanity in labour, in perpetual labour, at a crisis – sometimes in delirium. All human material passes through their hands. In the end their observation must lead them to some conclusion. These people have their eyes fixed on the display of goods in the great shops that man has made for himself. The modern age is spread before them, sparkling and radiant ... on the far side of the barrier! In their own homes, where they live in a precarious ease, since their remuneration bears no real relation to the quality of their work, they find their uncleanly old snail-shell, and they cannot even think of having a family. If they do so there will begin the slow martyrdom that we all know. These people, too, claim their rights to a machine for living in, which shall be in all simplicity a *human* thing.

Both the worker and the intellectual are precluded from following their deepest instincts in regard to the family; each and every day they make use of the brilliant and effective tools that the age has provided, but they are not enabled thereby to use them for themselves. Nothing could be more discouraging or more irritating. Nothing is prepared. We may well say: Architecture or Revolution.

Though modern society does not recompense its intellectuals judiciously, it still tolerates the old arrangements as to property which are a serious barrier in the way of transforming the town or the house. Established property rests on inheritance and its highest aim is a state of inertia, of no change and of maintaining the *status quo*. Although every other sort of human enterprise is subject to the rough warfare of competition, the landlord, ensconced in his property, escapes the common law in a princely fashion: he is a king. On the existing principle of property, it is impossible to establish a constructional programme which will hold together. And so the necessary building is not done. But if existing property arrangements were changed, and they are changing, it would be possible to build; there would be an enthusiasm for building, and we should avoid Revolution. [...]

Le Corbusier, extract from *Vers une architecture* (Paris, 1923); trans. Frederick Etchells, *Towards a New Architecture* (New York: Dover Publications, 1985) (Oxford: Architectural Press, 2000) 276–81.

Robert Smithson
A Tour of the Monuments of Passaic, New Jersey//1967

> He laughed softly. 'I know. There's no way out. Not through the Barrier. Maybe that isn't what I want, after all. But this – this – ' He stared at the Monument. 'It seems all wrong sometimes. I just can't explain it. It's the whole city. It makes me feel haywire. Then I get these flashes'.
> – Henry Kuttner, *Jesting Pilot*

> Today our unsophisticated cameras record in their own way our hastily assembled and painted world.
> – Vladimir Nabokov, *Invitation to a Beheading*

On Saturday, September 30th 1967, I went to the Port Authority Building on 41st Street and 8th Avenue. I bought a copy of the *New York Times* and a Signet paperback called *Earthworks* by Brian W. Aldiss. Next I went to ticket booth 21 and purchased a one-way ticket to Passaic. After that I went up to the upper bus level (platform 173) and boarded the number 30 bus of the Inter-City Transportation Co.

I sat down and opened the *Times*. I glanced over the art section: a 'Collectors', Critics' and Curators' Choice' at A.M. Sachs Gallery (a letter I got in the mail that morning invited me 'to play the game before the show closes October 4th'),

Walter Schatzki was selling 'Prints, Drawings, Watercolours' at '33 1/3 per cent off', Elinor Jenkins, the 'Romantic Realist', was showing at Barzansky Galleries, XVIII – XIX Century English Furniture on sale at Parke-Bernet, 'New Directions in German Graphics' at Goethe House, and on page 29 was John Canaday's column. He was writing on *Themes and the Usual Variations.* I looked at a blurry reproduction of Samuel E.B. Morse's *Allegorical Landscape* at the top of Canaday's column; the sky was a subtle newsprint grey, and the clouds resembled sensitive stains of sweat reminiscent of a famous Yugoslav watercolourist whose name I have forgotten. A little statue with right arm held high faced a pond (or was it the sea?). 'Gothic' buildings in the allegory had a faded look, while an unnecessary tree (or was it a cloud of smoke?) seemed to puff up on the left side of the landscape. Canaday referred to the picture as 'standing confidently along with other allegorical representatives of the arts, sciences, and high ideals that universities foster'. My eyes stumbled over the newsprint, over such headlines as 'Seasonal Upswing', 'A Shuttle Service', and 'Moving a 1,000 Pound Sculpture Can Be a Fine Work of Art, Too'. Other gems of Canaday's dazzled my mind as I passed through Secaucus. 'Realistic waxworks of raw meat beset by vermin' (Paul Thek), 'Mr Bush and his colleagues are wasting their time' (Jack Bush), 'a book, an apple on a saucer, a rumpled cloth' (Thyra Davidson). Outside the bus window a Howard Johnson's Motor Lodge flew by – a symphony in orange and blue. On page 31 in Big Letters: THE EMERGING POLICE STATE IN AMERICA SPY GOVERNMENT. 'In this book you will learn ... what an Infinity Transmitter is'.

The bus turned off Highway 3, down Orient Way in Rutherford.

I read the blurbs and skimmed through *Earthworks*. The first sentence read: 'The dead man drifted along in the breeze.' It seemed the book was about a soil shortage, and the *Earthworks* referred to the manufacture of artificial soil. The sky over Rutherford was a clear cobalt blue, a perfect Indian summer day, but the sky in *Earthworks* was a 'great black and brown shield on which moisture gleamed'.

The bus passed over the first monument. I pulled the buzzer-cord and got off at the corner of Union Avenue and River Drive. The monument was a bridge over the Passaic River that connected Bergen County with Passaic County. Noon-day sunshine cinema-ized the site, turning the bridge and the river into an over-exposed picture. Photographing it with my Instamatic 400 was like photographing a photograph. The sun became a monstrous light bulb that projected a detached series of 'stills' through my Instamatic into my eye. When I walked on the bridge, it was as though I was walking on an enormous photograph that was made of wood and steel, and underneath the river existed as an enormous movie film that showed nothing but a continuous blank.

The steel road that passed over the water was in part an open grating flanked by wooden sidewalks, held up by a heavy set of beams, while above, a ramshackle network hung in the air. A rusty sign glared in the sharp atmosphere, making it hard to read. A date flashed in the sunshine ... 1899 ... No ... 1896 ... maybe (at the bottom of the rust and glare was the name Dean & Westbrook Contractors, NY). I was completely controlled by the Instamatic (or what the rationalists call a camera). The glassy air of New Jersey defined the structural parts of the monument as I took snapshot after snapshot. A barge seemed fixed to the surface of the water as it came toward the bridge, and caused the bridge keeper to close the gates. From the banks of Passaic I watched the bridge rotate on a central axis in order to allow an inert rectangular shape to pass with its unknown cargo. The Passaic (West) end of the bridge rotated south, while the Rutherford (East) end of the bridge rotated north; such rotations suggested the limited movements of an outmoded world. 'North' and 'South' hung over the static river in a bipolar manner. One could refer to this bridge as the 'Monument of Dislocated Directions'.

Along the Passaic River banks were many minor monuments such as concrete abutments that supported the shoulders of a new highway in the process of being built. River Drive was in part bulldozed and in part intact. It was hard to tell the new highway from the old road; they were both confounded into a unitary chaos. Since it was Saturday, many machines were not working, and this caused them to resemble prehistoric creatures trapped in the mud, or, better, extinct machines – mechanical dinosaurs stripped of their skin. On the edge of this prehistoric Machine Age were pre- and post-World War II suburban houses. The houses mirrored themselves into colourlessness. A group of children were throwing rocks at each other near a ditch. 'From now on you're not going to come to our hide-out. And I mean it!' said a little blonde girl who had been hit with a rock.

As I walked north along what was left of River Drive, I saw a monument in the middle of the river – it was a pumping derrick with a long pipe attached to it. The pipe was supported in part by a set of pontoons, while the rest of it extended about three blocks along the river bank till it disappeared into the earth. One could hear debris rattling in the water that passed through the great pipe.

Nearby, on the river bank, was an artificial crater that contained a pale limpid pond of water, and from the side of the crater protruded six large pipes that gushed the water of the pond into the river. This constituted a monumental fountain that suggested six horizontal smokestacks that seemed to be flooding the river with liquid smoke. The great pipe was in some enigmatic way connected with the infernal fountain. It was as though the pipe was secretly sodomizing some hidden technological orifice, and causing a monstrous sexual organ (the fountain) to have an orgasm. A psychoanalyst might say that the landscape displayed 'homosexual tendencies', but I will not draw such a crass anthropomorphic conclusion. I will merely say, 'It was there.'

Across the river in Rutherford one could hear the faint voice of a PA system and the weak cheers of a crowd at a football game. Actually, the landscape was no landscape, but 'a particular kind of heliotypy' (Nabokov), a kind of self-destroying postcard world of failed immortality and oppressive grandeur. I had been wandering in a moving picture that I couldn't quite picture, but just as I became perplexed, I saw a green sign that explained everything:

YOUR HIGHWAY TAXES 21
AT WORK

Federal Highway Trust Funds 2,867,000	US Dept. of Commerce Bureau of Public Roads State Highway Funds 2,867,000

New Jersey State Highway Dept.

That zero panorama seemed to contain *ruins in reverse*, that is – all the new construction that would eventually be built. This is the opposite of the 'romantic ruin' because the buildings don't *fall* into ruin *after* they are built but rather rise into ruin before they are built. This anti-romantic *mise-en-scène* suggests the discredited idea of time and many other 'out of date' things. But the suburbs exist without a rational past and without the 'big events' of history. Oh, maybe there are a few statues, a legend, and a couple of curios, but no past – just what passes for a future. A Utopia minus a bottom, a place where the machines are idle, and the sun has turned to glass, and a place where the Passaic Concrete Plant (253 River Drive) does a good business in STONE, BITUMINOUS, SAND and CEMENT. Passaic seems full of 'holes' compared to New York City, which seems tightly packed and solid, and those holes in a sense are the monumental vacancies that define, without trying, the memory-traces of an abandoned set of futures. Such futures are found in grade B Utopian films, and then imitated by the suburbanite. The windows of City Motors auto sales proclaim the existence of Utopia through 1968 WIDE TRACK PONTIACS – Executive, Bonneville, Tempest, Grand Prix, Firebirds, GTO, Catalina and LeMans – that visual incantation marked the end of the highway construction.

Next I descended into a set of used car lots. I must say the situation seemed like a change. Was I in a new territory? (An English artist, Michael Baldwin, says: 'It could be asked if the country does in fact change – it does not in the sense a traffic light does.') Perhaps I had slipped into a lower stage of futurity – did I leave the real future behind in order to advance into a false future? Yes, I did. Reality was behind me at that point in my suburban Odyssey.

Passaic centre loomed like a dull adjective. Each 'store' in it was an adjective unto the next, a chain of adjectives disguised as stores. I began to run out of film, and I was getting hungry. Actually, Passaic centre was no centre – it was instead a typical abyss or an ordinary void. What a great place for a gallery! Or maybe an 'outdoor sculpture show' would pep that place up.

At the Golden Coach Diner (II Central Avenue) I had my lunch, and loaded my Instamatic. I looked at the orange-yellow box of Kodak Verichrome Pan, and read a notice that said:

> READ THIS NOTICE:
> This film will be replaced if defective in manufacture, labelling or packaging, even though caused by our negligence or other fault. Except for such replacement, the sale or any subsequent handling of this film is without other warranty or liability. EASTMAN KODAK COMPANY DO NOT OPEN THIS CART'RIDGE OR YOUR PICTURES MAY BE SPOILED – 12 EXPOSURES – SAFETY FILM – ASA 125 22 DIN.

After that I returned to Passaic, or was it the *hereafter* – for all I know that unimaginative suburb could have been a clumsy eternity, a cheap copy of *The City of the Immortals*. But who am I to entertain such a thought? I walked down a parking lot that covered the old railroad tracks which at one time ran through the middle of Passaic. That monumental parking lot divided the city in half, turning it into a mirror and a reflection – but the mirror kept changing places with the reflection. One never knew what side of the mirror one was on. There was nothing *interesting* or even strange about that flat monument, yet it echoed a kind of cliché idea of infinity; perhaps the 'secrets of the universe' are just as pedestrian – not to say dreary. Everything about the site remained wrapped in blandness and littered with shiny cars – one after another they extended into a sunny nebulosity. The indifferent backs of the cars flashed and reflected the stale afternoon sun. I took a few listless, entropic snapshots of that lustrous monument. If the future is 'out of date' and 'old fashioned', then I had been in the future. I had been on a planet that had a map of Passaic drawn over it, and a rather imperfect map at that. A sidereal map marked up with 'lines' the size of streets, and 'squares' and 'blocks' the size of buildings. At any moment my feet were apt to fall through the cardboard ground. I am convinced that the future is lost somewhere in the dumps of the non-historical past; it is in yesterday's newspapers, in the *jejune* advertisements of science-fiction movies, in the false mirror of our rejected dreams. Time turns metaphors into *things*, and stacks them up in cold rooms, or places them in the celestial playgrounds of the suburbs.

Has Passaic replaced Rome as The Eternal City? If certain cities of the world were placed end to end in a straight line according to size, starting with Rome, where would Passaic be in that impossible progression? Each city would be a three-dimensional mirror that would reflect the next city into existence. The limits of eternity seem to contain such nefarious ideas.

The last monument was a sand box or a model desert. Under the dead light of the Passaic afternoon the desert became a map of infinite disintegration and forgetfulness. This monument of minute particles blazed under a bleakly glowing sun, and suggested the sullen dissolution of entire continents, the drying up of oceans – no longer were there green forests and high mountains – all that existed were millions of grains of sand, a vast deposit of bones and stones pulverized into dust. Every grain of sand was a dead metaphor that equalled timelessness, and to decipher such metaphors would take one through the false mirror of eternity. This sand box somehow doubled as an open grave – a grave that children cheerfully play in.

> ... all sense of reality was gone. In its place had come deep-seated illusions, absence of pupillary reaction to light, absence of knee reaction – symptoms all of progressive cerebral meningitis: the blanketing of the brain ... (Louis Sullivan, 'one of the greatest of all architects', quoted in Michel Butor's *Mobile*)

I should now like to prove the irreversibility of eternity by using a *jejune* experiment for proving entropy. Picture in your mind's eye the sand box divided in half with black sand on one side and white sand on the other. We take a child and have him run hundreds of times clockwise in the box until the sand gets mixed and begins to turn grey; after that we have him run anti-clockwise, but the result will not be a restoration of the original division but a greater degree of greyness and an increase of entropy.

Of course, if we filmed such an experiment we could prove the reversibility of eternity by showing the film backwards, but then sooner or later the film itself would crumble or get lost and enter the state of irreversibility. Somehow this suggests that the cinema offers an illusive or temporary escape from physical dissolution. The false immortality of the film gives the viewer an illusion of control over eternity – but 'the superstars' are fading.

Robert Smithson, 'The Monuments of Passaic', *Artforum* (December 1967) © Artforum, 1967; reprinted under the full title 'A Tour of the Monuments of Passaic, New Jersey', in *Robert Smithson: The Collected Writings*, ed. Jack Flam (Berkeley and Los Angeles: University of California Press, 1996) 68–74. Text © Estate of Robert Smithson/Licensed by VAGA, New York.

Andreas Huyssen
Authentic Ruins//2006

[...] If in the late twentieth century, as Lyotard has claimed, architecture and philosophy lie in ruins, leaving us only with the option of a 'writing of the ruins' as a kind of micrology, then the question arises whether the tradition of modernist thought all the way into postmodernism is overshadowed by the catastrophic imagination and imaginary of ruins that has accompanied the trajectory of modernity since the eighteenth century.[1] Architecture in a state of decay or destruction seems to be an indispensable topos for this tradition. Real ruins of different kinds function as screens on which modernity projects its asynchronous temporalities and its fear of and obsession with the passing of time. Benjamin says that allegories are, in the realm of thought, what ruins are in the realm of things; this implies a production principle of modern art, literature and architecture which is *a priori* directed toward the ruinous.[2] For Adorno, in analogous fashion, the most authentic works of modernity are those which are objectively and formally determined by the ruinous state of the present. The architectural ruin seems to hover in the background of an aesthetic imagination that privileges fragment and allegory, collage and montage, freedom from ornament and reduction of the material. Perhaps this is the secret classicism of modernism which, however different from eighteenth-century classicism in its coding of temporality and space, is still predicated on an imaginary of ruins. Classicism in the eighteenth century defined itself through the ruins of antiquity, but aimed at a totality of style and symbolic representation rather than privileging montage, dispersion and fragmentariness as modernism did. One doesn't have to be a metaphysician of history in order to see from today's perspective, the field of classical modernism as an oscillating landscape of ruins left from a failed attempt to create an alternative kind of totality that in architecture was called International Style.[3]

As a product of modernity rather than a phenomenon from a deep pre-modern past, authenticity is analogous to Benjamin's aura. Originality and uniqueness, which characterize the auratic work of art in Benjamin, were made into privileged categories in an earlier age that was already flooded by reproductions, translations and copies of all kinds. Analogously, the ideological value of authenticity rose in proportion to mass culture's inherent tendency toward reproduction and repetition. Even in the transition from a Fordist to a post-Fordist mode of production, we can detect the attempt to return the semblance of authenticity and uniqueness to commodities by means of customization. Aura and authenticity are analogous to each other. Both have to be framed historically rather than ontologically. Modernist decisionism declared both of them dead and gone, but both have proved to be resistant to ideological critique. The desire for the auratic and the authentic always reflected the fear of inauthenticity, the lack of existential meaning, and the absence of individual originality. The more we have learned to understand all images, words and sounds as always already mediated, the more it seems we desire the authentic and the immediate. A gap opens up between intellectual insight into the obsolescence of authenticity and the life world's desire for the authentic – cuisine, clothing, identity. This longing can be seen as a media culture's romantic longing for its other. Reality TV is its pathetic expression. As we know from the critique of the concept, the positing of stable origins and a historical telos are never far when the authenticity tune is being played. The same is true for the discourse of ruins, which has played such a central role in legitimizing the claims to power of modern nation-states.

Indeed, romantic ruins seem to guarantee origins. They promise authenticity, immediacy and authority. However, there is a paradox. In the case of ruins, what is allegedly present and transparent whenever authenticity is claimed is present only as an absence. It is the imagined present of a past that can now be grasped only in its decay. Any ruin posits the problem of a double exposure to the past and the present. If the modern ruin is not exhausted by the semantics of pastness, its temporality, which points to past glory and greatness, is clearly different from the claims of plenitude and presentness invariably at stake in the discourse of authenticity. Yet authenticity claims are often contaminated by doubts which then have to be alleviated by further mythmaking. Thus some would claim that authentic authenticity was only possible in the past when the world was allegedly still *übersichtlicher* and not under the shadow of media representation and distortion. We know what kind of ideological phantasms such projections of authenticity have caused in the humanities and social sciences – from the authenticity of the archaic and primitive to the privileging of authentic community as opposed to the anomy and artificiality of modern societies. Especially in the post-Enlightenment discoveries of origins and national identities, the present of modernity appeared – more often than not – as a ruin of authenticity and a better and simpler past. Against this idea of a deep authenticity embodied in the ruins of a glorified past, I posit the idea of the authentic ruin as a product of modernity itself rather than as a royal road toward some uncontaminated origin.

Nostalgia is never very far when we talk about authenticity or romantic ruins. The political critique of ruin nostalgia simply as regression corresponds to the philosophical critique of authenticity as a phantasm grounding stable identities. But such a critique misses the fundamental ambiguity of the ruin and the authentic. However justified it may be to criticize the ideological instrumentalization of authenticity claims, it will not do simply to identify the desire for authenticity with nostalgia and dismiss it as a cultural disease, as Susan Stewart argues in *On Longing*. Neither will it do to understand the modern imagination of ruins and its link with the sublime as expressing nothing but fantasies of power and domination, though that is the case for Albert Speer's theory of ruin value. The dimension present in any imaginary of ruins but missed by such reductive critiques is the hardly nostalgic consciousness of the transitoriness of all greatness and power, the warning of imperial hubris, and the remembrance of nature in all culture.

At stake in the authentic ruin of modernity is not simply the genuineness or *Echtheit* of specific ruins, nor is it some superhistorical *memento mori*. Genuineness as naturalness in opposition to artificiality and the fake – a topos central to eighteenth-century aesthetics and middle-class culture – is an empirically verifiable criterion of the ruin, and the *memento mori* dimension is not limited to modernity. We can speak of the modern authenticity of ruins only if we look at the ruin aesthetically and politically as an architectonic cipher for the temporal and spatial doubts that modernity always harboured about itself. In the ruin, history appears spatialized, and built space temporalized. My thesis is that an imaginary of ruins is central for any theory of modernity that wants to be more than the triumphalism of progress and democratization, or the longing for past greatness. In contrast to the optimism of Enlightenment thought, the modern imaginary of ruins remains conscious of the dark side of modernity, what Diderot described as the inevitable 'devastations of time' visible in ruins. It articulates the nightmare of the Enlightenment that all history might ultimately be overwhelmed by nature. [...]

1 See Jean-François Lyotard, *Heidegger and 'the Jews'*, trans. Andreas Michel and Mark Roberts (Minneapolis: University of Minnesota Press, 1990) 43.

2 Walter Benjamin, *The Origins of German Tragic Drama* (1928), trans. John Osborne (London: Verso, 1977) 178.

3 For a compelling account of modernism as ruin, see Clark, *Farewell to an Idea: Episodes from a History of Modernism* (New Haven and London: Yale University Press, 1999).

Andreas Huyssen, extract from 'Authentic Ruins', in *Ruins of Modernity*, ed. Julia Hell (Durham, North Carolina: Duke University Press, 2009) 19–22.

Anthony Vidler
Architecture Dismembered//1992

> My body is everywhere: the bomb which destroys my house also damages my body in so far as the house was already an indication of my body.
> – Jean-Paul Sartre, *Being and Nothingness*

The idea of an architectural monument as an embodiment and abstract representation of the human body, its reliance on the anthropomorphic analogy for proportional and figurative authority, was, we are led to believe, abandoned with the collapse of the classical tradition and the birth of a technologically dependent architecture. With the isolated exception of Le Corbusier's vain attempt to establish the modulor as the basis for measurement and proportion, the long tradition of bodily reference from Vitruvius through Alberti, Filarete, Francesco di Giorgio and Leonardo seems to have been definitively abandoned with the rise of a modernist sensibility dedicated more to the rational sheltering of the body than to its mathematical inscription or pictorial emulation.

In this context it is interesting to note a recent return to the bodily analogy by architects as diverse as Coop Himmelblau, Bernard Tschumi and Daniel Libeskind, all concerned to propose a reinscription of the body in their work, as referent and figurative inspiration. But this renewed appeal to corporeal metaphors is evidently based on a 'body' radically different from that at the centre of the humanist tradition. As described in architectural form, it seems to be a body in pieces, fragmented, if not deliberately torn apart and mutilated almost beyond recognition. Further, this 'body' is advanced, paradoxically enough, precisely as a sign of a radical departure from classical humanism, a fundamental break from all theories of architecture that pretend to accommodation and domestic harmony. Evoked as referent and as generator of an architecture that stands, as Coop Himmelblau has insisted since the late 1960s, against 'Palladian' humanism and Corbusian modernism alike, this body no longer serves to centre, to fix or to stabilize. Rather, its limits, interior or exterior, seem infinitely ambiguous and extensive; its forms, literal or metaphorical, are no longer confined to the recognizably human but embrace all biological existence from the embryonic to the monstrous; its power lies no longer in the model of unity but in the intimation of the fragmentary, the morselated, the broken.

On first inspection, this cutting of the architectural body might appear to be no more than an obvious reversal of tradition, an almost too literal transcription of the idea of 'dismembering classicism'. But a closer examination of the diverse sources of this new bodily analogy reveals a more complex relationship to previous 'embodiments' from the Renaissance to modernism than that of simple pictorial caricature. Following the long history of the anthropomorphic analogy, these projects exhibit all the traces of their origins in classical and functional theory, while at the same time constituting an entirely different sensibility.

The history of the bodily analogy in architecture, from Vitruvius to the present, might be described in one sense as the progressive distancing of the body from the building, a gradual extension of the anthropomorphic analogy into wider and wider domains leading insensibly but inexorably to the final 'loss' of the body as an authoritative foundation for architecture. Three moments in this successive transformation of bodily projection seem especially important for contemporary theory: these might be described concisely as (1) the notion that building is a body of some kind; (2) the idea that the building embodies states of the body or, more importantly, states of mind based on bodily sensation; and (3) the sense that the environment as a whole is endowed with bodily or at least organic characteristics.

For the purposes of argument, these themes may be roughly identified with historical periods, although, as will be obvious, such a chronological 'progression' is more useful for clarity than it is historically accurate.

In classical theory the (idealized) body was, so to speak, directly projected onto the building, which both stood for it and represented its ideal perfection. The building derived its authority, proportional and compositional, from this body, and, in a complementary way, the building then acted to confirm and establish the body – social and individual – in the world. The principles of Vitruvius traced the origins of proportion to the Greek canons of bodily mathematics, to be incorporated by the architect-sculptor in the column and in the relations of the different parts of the order to the whole, and thence to the building; his ideal of unity was described by the celebrated figure of a man with arms outstretched inscribed within a square and a circle, navel at the centre. The theorists of the Renaissance from Alberti to Francesco di Giorgio, Filarete and Leonardo subscribed to this analogy, which determined the search for centralization in all its aspects.

Such an analogy, indeed, took on more than metaphorical meaning: in a real sense the figural expression of anthropomorphic form, from the column to the plan and façade, buildings were bodies, temples the most perfect of all, as were cities, the seat of the body social and politic. Alberti's proposition that 'the building is in its entirety like a body composed of its parts' – the relations of part to whole leading to his definition of beauty as the state where nothing can be added or taken away without destroying this delicate balance – was extended to embrace all animal bodies. Francesco di Giorgio showed a figure superimposed literally on the plan of a cathedral and of a city, while Filarete compared the building's cavities and functions to those of the body, its eyes, ears, nose, mouth, veins and viscera. Indeed, like a body, buildings and cities may fall ill: a building may, he hazarded, become sick and die, whence it needs a good doctor, the architect, to cure it. In a metaphor that established the full force of his analogy, Filarete compared the architect to a mother, carefully nurturing her child from conception to maturity.

As we know, the attraction of these formulations lasted well into the eighteenth century – and even, in the sheltered enclave of the École des Beaux-Arts, much longer. The body, its balance, standards of proportion, symmetry and functioning, mingling elegance and strength, was the foundation myth of building.

But beginning in the eighteenth century, there emerged a second and more extended form of bodily projection in architecture, initially defined by the aesthetics of the sublime. Here, the building no longer simply represented a part or whole of the body but was rather seen as objectifying the various states of the body, physical and mental. Edmund Burke, followed by Kant and the Romantics, described buildings not so much in terms of their fixed attributes of beauty but rather in their capacities to evoke emotions of terror and fear. Burke himself recognized, presciently enough, that the very definition of the sublime he was advancing, an aesthetic based on experience rather than artifice, would have the effect of rendering the premises of classical organicism null and void, if not vaguely ridiculous. Arguing against the idea that the proportions of a building should be derived from those of the human body, he made fun of the Vitruvian canon:

> To make this forced analogy complete, they represent a man with his arms raised and extended at full length, and then describe a sort of square ... But it appears very clearly to me, that the human figure never supplied the architect with any of his ideas. For in the first place, men are very rarely seen in this strained posture; it is not natural to them; neither is it at all becoming. Secondly, the view of the human figure so disposed, does not naturally suggest the idea of a square, but rather of a cross ... Thirdly, several buildings are by no means of the form of that particular square ... And certainly nothing could be more unaccountably whimsical, than for an architect to model his performance by the human figure, since no two things can have less resemblance or analogy, than a man, and a house or a temple.[1]

In place of these specious doctrines emanating from 'the patrons of proportion', Burke outlined an aesthetics founded on primary sensation. If any bodily attributes remained in the building, they were the result of projection, rather than of any innate qualities.

In architectural terms, the sensibility to the object as mirroring the states, rather than the aspect, of the body was theorized for the first time in the emerging psychology of empathy of the late nineteenth century. Thus the art historian Wölfflin, seeking to determine the change in style from the Renaissance to the baroque, following his thesis of 1886, 'Prolegomena to a Psychology of Architecture', applied the new discipline of psychology to reintroduce the body into the argument, but now in an active and entirely transformed manner:

> We judge every object by analogy with our own bodies. The object – even if completely dissimilar to ourselves – will not only transform itself immediately into a creature, with head and foot, back and front; and not only are we convinced that this creature must feel ill at ease if it does not stand upright and seems about to fall over, but we go so far as to experience, to a highly sensitive degree, the spiritual condition and contentment or discontent expressed by any configuration, however different from ourselves. We can comprehend the dumb, imprisoned existence of a bulky, memberless, amorphous conglomeration, heavy and immovable, as easily as the fine and clear disposition of something delicate and lightly articulated.[2]

What had previously been a foundation of classical design theory, a principle of making as well as a standard of judgement, was now entirely placed in the service of perception, and that of objects that in the classical sense were not in any way beautiful; the qualities of the architectural object, no matter what the intentions of its makers, were now those of all inanimate nature, only to be understood by a process of projection. 'We always', continued Wölfflin, 'project a corporeal state conforming to our own; we interpret the whole outside world according to the expressive system with which we have become familiar through our own bodies'. Such a transference of bodily attributes, such as 'severe strictness', 'taut self-discipline', or 'uncontrolled heavy relaxation', takes its place within what Wölfflin calls a 'process of unconscious endowment of animation', in which architecture, as an 'art of corporeal masses, relates to man as a corporeal being'.

Inevitably this process is historicized in Wölfflin's scheme. There is, he claims, a 'Gothic deportment' with 'tense muscles and precise movements' that, together with the Gothic nose 'which is sharp and thin', endows Gothic architecture with its quality of sharpness, its precisely pointed forms without relaxation or flabbiness – 'everything sublimates itself completely in energy.' Similarly, the Renaissance liberates these hard, frozen forms to express a state of well-being, vigorous and animated. In contrast, the baroque manifests itself in weight, the slender bodies of the Renaissance replaced 'by massive bodies, large, awkward, with bulging muscles and swirling draperies'. Light-heartedness has given way to heaviness, flesh is softer and flabbier, limbs are not mobile but imprisoned.

Movement becomes less articulated but more agitated and faster, in dances of restless despair or wild ecstasy. And so with architecture, the violence of which is best expressed in Michelangelo's *terribilità*. Quoting Anton Springer, Wölfflin notes the combination of 'mute massiveness' and unevenly distributed vitality in the sculptor's 'unresisting victims of inner compulsion'. Beyond this, indeed, the baroque moves away from the point at which it can even be seen in terms of the human body, or at least in terms of the articulated body invented by the Renaissance. Image, noncorporeal and atmospheric, has replaced defined plastic form, in a counterreformation dominated by yearning and spiritual ecstasy. Here Wölfflin stops; but not before he has himself projected this baroque spirit well into the eighteenth and nineteenth centuries:

> Carl Justi's description of Piranesi as a 'modern, passionate nature', whose 'sphere is the infinite, the mystery of the sublime, of space and energy', has a more general application. One can hardly fail to recognize the affinity that our own age in particular bears to the Italian Baroque. A Richard Wagner appeals to the same emotions ... His conception of art shows a complete correspondence with those of the Baroque.[3]

This led Wölfflin to draw the line; for, always sensible of the lost Renaissance body, he would insist that in architecture there were limits, where in music there were not; the 'restraining of the finished and rhythmic phrase, the strict systematic construction and the transparently clear articulation which may be fitting and even necessary to express a mood in music, signify in architecture that its natural limits have been transgressed'. Wölfflin's message is clear: the sublime in architecture, which necessitates the 'half-closed eyes' that see lines more vaguely in favour of unlimited space and the 'elusive magic of light', signals the end of bodily projection in its formed and bounded character, and perhaps the end of architecture itself. For Wölfflin, the end of the Renaissance body signifies a dangerous moment from which architecture must draw back.

For the modernists, however, this moment was one of opportunity, allowing for a universalizing abstraction and a psychology of sensation and movement; embodied in architecture that mirrored all the states of a regenerated and healthy body but corresponded as well to a similarly healthy mind. Cubist and post-cubist attempts to dismember the classical body in order to develop an expressive model of movement were thus dedicated not so much to its eradication but to its reformulation in modern terms. From Duchamp's *Nude Descending a Staircase*, based on Étienne-Jules Marey's careful studies of movement, to Balla's *Woman with a Dog on a Leash*, there seems to be no fear that the body is entirely lost: rather the question is one of representing a higher order of truth to perception

– of movement, forces and rest. Even in that primal scene, the 'Overture' to Proust's *Remembrance of Things Past*, where Marcel, on awakening, figures the parts of his body according to their 'successive positions' during the night, as if seen on a bioscope – the instrument invented by Muybridge to analyse the running positions of the horse – even this fragmented body is ready at any instant to be recomposed, as Proust observes, into the 'original components of the ego'. Analytical science, for many avant-garde modernists, was the necessary and prophetic armature of a new awareness but not a total dispersion of the body. Le Corbusier, as we know, even tried to restate it in a newer and more fundamental way, balanced between sensation and proportion: the *promenade architecturale*, the modulor, and the very plan of the *ville radieuse* unabashedly recreate Vitruvian man for the twentieth century.

This sense of the city as a bodily organism, one still tied to the classical tradition in its modernist versions, has led more recently to a third and final extension of the body outside itself: a kind of animism, which, through an even more generalized work of projection, refuses any one-to-one ascription of body and building. The projects of Coop Himmelblau, for example, seem calculated to extend far beyond actual identification with specific body parts or whole bodies; rather they are seen like machines for the generation of a whole range of psychological responses that depend on our faculty of projecting onto objects states of mind and body. 'We want ... architecture that bleeds, that exhausts, that whirls and even breaks', claimed Himmelblau in 1980 in conjunction with the 'Hot Flat Project', 'cavernous, fiery, smooth, hard, angular, brutal, round, delicate, colourful, obscene, voluptuous, dreamy, alluring, repelling, wet, dry, throbbing. An architecture alive or dead. Cold – then cold as a block of ice. Hot – then hot as a blazing wing.' This uncomfortable body is subsequently stretched to include the entire city, a city that 'throbs like a heart' and 'flies like breath'.[4] 'The Skin of This City' (1982, Berlin) proposed a form whose 'horizontal structure is a wall of nerves from which all the layers of urban skin have been peeled away'.

Such a literal biomorphism, akin to many similar but less threatening science fiction images of the Archigram era, has in recent years been extended by Coop Himmelblau's apparent desire to merge the body completely with the design and its context. In a revealing interview with Alvin Boyarsky, Himmelblau described their experiments into design as a kind of automatic writing that, operating through blind gesture translated into line and three-dimensional form, works literally to inscribe the body language of the designer onto the map of the city. Projects for Paris, Vienna and New York emerged from their sense that 'the face and body of these cities' was clearly readable; then they literally superimposed face and plan, so that 'our eyes became towers, our foreheads bridges, the faces became landscapes and our shirts the plans'.[5] In this way, photographic collages of Himmelblau's portraits, merged by reproductive processes into the texture of city plans, dramatically illustrate the urge to dissolve the authoritarian body of the architect into the world that receives its designs. In this procedure, in much the same way that Cindy Sherman has photographed herself almost buried amidst garbage-filled soil, Himmelblau hovers between narcissism and its opposite, in a strangely powerful celebration of the will to lose power. As they wrote in the prose poem 'The Poetry of Desolation', architecture's lyrical qualities now stem not from its organically conceived life but from its evident death:

> The aesthetic of the architecture of death in white sheets. Death in tiled hospital rooms. The architecture of sudden death on the pavement. Death from a rib-cage pierced by a steering shaft. The path of the bullet through a dealer's head on 42nd street. The aesthetic of the architecture of the surgeon's razor-sharp scalpel. The aesthetic of the peep-show sex in washable plastic boxes. Of the broken tongues and the dried-up eyes.[6]

Calling for an 'architecture of desolation', with its own 'fascinating landmarks', Himmelblau refuses all notions of a comfortable city where one might be safe and sound, while fully embracing the 'solitude of squares, the desolation of the streets, the devastation of the buildings'.[7]

But in this evocation of futurist and expressionist images, we sense none of the positive aspirations of the first avant-garde. For side by side with the continuity and gradual extension of the bodily metaphor, from the corporeal to the psychological, we can also detect, starting in the early nineteenth century and emerging with greatest force in the later years of the twentieth, a decided sense of loss that seems to accompany the move away from the archaic, almost tactile projection of the body in all of its biological force.

This perceived 'loss' of the body began, as I have noted, with the romantic sublime; under the influence of Kant and the German Romantics, it became the stimulus for a vision of a lost bodily unity fragmented by time and sense experience. The body became more an object of nostalgia than a model of harmony, manifested in art as a series of irreconcilable fragments: the 'parts', for example, in Mary Shelley's story of Frankenstein, that never could be assembled into anything but a monster. Similar retellings of classical myths of the ideal body – of Pygmalion and Galatea, of Apelles and Protogenes – and new stories of the creation of the unknown 'monstrous' double of man in art, exemplified in Balzac's short story 'Le Chef-d'oeuvre inconnu', reinforced the romantic tragic sense of loss.

In psychoanalytical terms it was Jacques Lacan, in his classic essay of the late 1930s 'The Mirror Stage', who proposed the model of a pre-mirror stage body, a 'corps morcelé' or 'morselated body' that participated, at the moment of the mirror stage, in a sort of drama impelled towards a spatial identification of the self with regard to its reflection. In this model the mirror is construed as a lure that in Lacan's terms 'machines' the fragmented phantasms of the pre-narcissistic body into what Lacan calls 'a form that [is] orthopaedic of its totality'. Deprived of its previous status by the reflection of the whole, this morselated body is repressed to the unconscious, where it shows up regularly in dreams or 'when the movement of psychoanalysis touches a certain level of the aggressive disintegration of the individual':

> It then appears in the form of disjointed limbs, or of those organs represented in exoscopy, growing wings and taking up arms for intestinal persecutions – the very same that the visionary Hieronymus Bosch has fixed, for all time, in painting, in their ascent from the fifteenth century to the imaginary zenith of modern man. But this form is even tangibly revealed at the organic level, in the lines of 'fragilization' that define the anatomy of phantasy, as exhibited in the schizoid and spasmodic symptoms of hysteria.[8]

Lacan's structuralist notion of a repressed fragmentation of the body finds its poststructuralist analogue in Roland Barthes' own fragmented text 'Fragments of a Lover's Discourse', where Barthes describes a body that, subjected to the gaze of desire, is so to speak transformed into a corpse. For Barthes, the very gaze of a hypothetical lover projected onto the body of the sleeping beloved is as analytical and dissecting as that of a surgeon in an anatomy class. Like Proust's Marcel as he watches Albertine asleep, the watcher searches, scrutinizes; takes the body apart, as if to find out what is inside it, 'as if the mechanical cause of my desire were in the adverse body'. Barthes concludes, 'Certain parts of the body are particularly appropriate to this observation: eyelashes, nails, roots of the hair, the incomplete objects.' This process, Barthes observes, would be the opposite of desire, and rather like 'fetishizing a corpse'.[9]

Barthes illustrates this kind of fetishization by reference to Balzac's romantic version of the Pygmalion myth, *Sarrasine*, where the central character falls in love with the transvestite singer La Zambinella. Before seeing La Zambinella, Sarrasine loves only 'fragmented woman' – 'divided, anatomized, she is merely a kind of dictionary of fetish objects. This sundered dissected body (we are reminded of boys' games at school) is reassembled by the artist (and this is the meaning of his vocation) into a whole body ... in which fetishism is abolished and by which Sarrasine is cured.' A 'unity' discovered in 'amazement', this body will of course be returned to its previous fetishized state when Sarrasine realizes the trick that his projected desire has played on him. Barthes remarks on the list of anatomical details that make up La Zambinella's body – a 'monotonous inventory of parts' that leads to the crumbling of what is being described: 'language undoes the body, returns it to the fetish.'[10]

This fetishization of the lost object of desire might well be extended to the interpretation of contemporary architectural fragmentation and 'morselation'. For behind what seem to be superficial and 'pictorial' attempts literally to dismember the classical body, we sense a deliberate attempt to address the question of the status of the body in postmodern theory, not just in the outward appearance of the work but in its inner procedures.

In a first instance, the body, rather than forming the originating point of a centred projection, is itself almost literally placed in question. Confronting the architecture of Himmelblau or, less dramatically, of Tschumi, the owner of a conventional body is undeniably placed under threat as the reciprocal distortions and absences *felt* by the viewer, in response to the reflected projection of bodily empathy, operate almost viscerally on the body. *We* are contorted, racked, cut, wounded, dissected, intestinally revealed, impaled, immolated; we are suspended in a state of vertigo, or thrust into a confusion between belief and perception. It is as if the object actively participated in the subject's self-dismembering, reflecting its internal disarray or even precipitating its disaggregation. This active denegation of the body takes on, in the postmodern world, the aspect of an autocritique of a modernism that posited a quasi-scientific, propaedeutic role for architecture. The body in disintegration is in a very real sense the image of the notion of humanist progress in disarray.

But these deliberately aggressive expressions of the postmodern corporeal also operate in another register, that of the strangeness evoked – as Freud noted with regard to the feeling of the uncanny – by the apparent 'return' of something presumed lost but now evidently active in the work. In this context it would be, so to speak, the return of the body into an architecture that had repressed its conscious presence that would account for our sense of disquiet.

As we have noted, Freud identified two causes of the uncanny, both founded on the movement between prior repression and unexpected return. The first stems from the return of something that was thought to be definitively repressed, such as ideas of animism, magic, totemism and the like, which, no longer believed in as real, throw into doubt the status of material reality when they reoccur. Examples of such a form of the uncanny would be the return of the infantile belief in omnipotence of thoughts (coincidence leading to the fear that one has killed someone after speaking idly of their death); or the seeming return of magical properties to things long since divested of their magical significance, as in a story Freud recounts from *The Strand Magazine* where a house furnished with a table carved with crocodiles is the setting for a night of faint terror, when smells and forms begin to move through the rooms as if some ghostly crocodiles were haunting the place. The second cause of the uncanny stems from the return of repressed infantile complexes, those of castration or womb fantasies for example, which, on returning, throw into question not so much the status of reality – such complexes never were thought to be real – but rather the status of psychical reality. Freud gives as an example of such causes 'dismembered limbs, a severed head, a hand cut off at the wrist ... feet which dance by themselves', evidently uncanny because of their proximity to the castration complex. The temptation is strong to ascribe our sense of destabilization in the face of Himmelblau's constructions to such an uncanny, now embodied in the dancing forms of a building once a body.

Such an interpretation is in fact reinforced by Himmelblau's own consistent opposition to the domestic, the *heimlich* in any form. Their passionate appeal, expressed in explosive performances, for a deliberately non-accommodating architecture has been tied, from the outset, to a resolute refusal of domesticity. 'Our architecture is not domesticated', they stated in 1982, 'it moves around in urban areas like a panther in the jungle. In a museum it is like a wild animal in a cage.'[11] Thence the beam that, like a backbone and head, rises and sinks like a panther, in the exhibit 'Architecture Is Now' installed at Stuttgart in 1982. This animal-like play, perhaps a recasting in terror of Alberti's benign vision of a 'building like a horse', was at the same time allied to a more direct exploration of that more elusive manifestation of the anti-domestic, the uncanny. Here the haunting absence of the body became as much a preoccupation as its physical presence. Speaking of the Red Angel Bar in Vienna of 1980–81, Himmelblau asked: 'Who knows what an angel's body really looks like?'[12] The bodiless object and the bodily agent, modelled in steel and wire, play together in a literally cutting fantasy. Finally, the Hot Flat (Vienna, 1978), a 'permanent' monument to an architecture that burns, or the Haus Meier-Hahn (Dusseldorf, 1980), otherwise titled Vektor II, with its impaled roof, illustrates almost too directly, but uncomfortably enough, the will to destroy the house of classical architecture and the society it serves. The latter project, indeed, encapsulates didactically, if not architecturally, the twin ambitions of Himmelblau to drive a stake at once through the house and through the specifically humanist body it represents.

This didactic and dramatic example of the house impaled takes its place, in the postwar period, within that discourse concerned to reveal the existential limits of what Gaston Bachelard has termed 'the coefficient of adversity'. This calculus of threat was explored by Sartre in *Being and Nothingness*, itself written in the aftermath of the war, where the definition of the self and its body is described, as a function of the perception of resistance that objects in the world have to the self. Thus, 'the bolt is revealed as too big to be screwed into the nut; the pedestal too fragile to support the weight which I want to hold up, the stone too heavy to be lifted up to the top of the wall'. In other cases, objects will be threatening to an already established instrumental complex – the storm to the harvest, the fire to the house. Step by step, these threats will gradually extend to the body, the centre or reference indicated by all these instruments; this centre will in turn indicate the centre of reference to them. Thence Sartre's proposition with regard to the body: the body is indicated firstly by an instrumental complex, and secondarily by a threat posed within this context:

> I live my body in danger as regards menacing machines as well as manageable instruments. *My body is everywhere: the bomb which destroys my house also damages my body in so far as the house was already an indication of my body.* [my emphasis.] This is why my body always extends across the tool which it utilizes: it is at the end of the cane on which I lean against the earth; it is at the end of the telescope which shows me the stars; it is on the chair, in the whole house; for it is my adaptation to these tools.

In this way Sartre rejects a classical notion of embodiment that then projects itself into the world as a mode of apprehension or control of the external environment. Instead, he poses our original relation to the world as the foundation of the revelation of the body: 'far from the body being first for us and revealing things to us, it is the instrumental – things which in their original appearance indicate our body to us.' 'The body', he concludes, 'is not a screen between things and ourselves; it manifests only the individuality and the contingency of our original relation to instrumental-things.'[13]

In this context, any initial interpretation of Sartre's formulation of the 'body in the house' as resonating with all the power of a long classical tradition, a tradition that posed the body as the essential model for all other created instruments, the body as *a priori* a foundation for the recognition and apprehension of all other objects, suffers a defeat. Sartre's body participates in a world within which it has to be immersed and to which it has to be subjected even before it can recognize itself as a body. It knows itself precisely because it is defined in relation to instrumental complexes that themselves are threatened by other instruments, understood as 'destructive devices'. The body knows itself to be by experiencing a 'coefficient of adversity'. Thus where, in classical theory since Alberti, the house is a good house only in so far as it is constituted analogically to the body, and the city a good city for the same reasons, in Sartrean terms the body is only seen to exist by virtue of the existence of the house: 'it is only in a world that there can be a body.' The bomb that destroys the house does not destroy a model of the body, but the body itself, because the house is needed for the body to project it. We are at once precipitated into a world of absolute danger and at the same time made to understand that this threat exists only in so far as we are in this world. It is, no doubt, the shiver of this world that Coop Himmelblau wishes us to experience.

1 [footnote 3 in source] Edmund Burke, *A Philosophical Enquiry into Our Ideas of the Sublime and the Beautiful* (1757), ed. J.T. Boulton (Notre Dame: University of Notre Dame Press, 1968) 100.

2 [4] Heinrich Wölfflin, *Renaissance and Baroque*, trans. K. Simon (Ithaca: Cornell University Press, 1966) 77.

3 [5] Ibid., 78–87.

4 [6] Coop Himmelblau, *Die Faszination der Stadt/The Power of the City* (Darmstadt and London, 1988) 95; 72.

5 [7] Ibid., 14.

6 [8] Ibid., 93.

7 [9] Coop Himmelblau, *Architecture is Now: Projects*, (Un)buildings, Statements, Sketches, Commentaries, 1968–1983 (New York: Rizzoli, 1983) 106.

8 [10] Jacques Lacan, *Écrits: A Selection*, trans. Alan Sheridan (New York: W.W. Norton, 1977) 4–5.

9 [11] Roland Barthes, *A Lover's Discourse: Fragments*, trans. Richard Howard (New York: Hill & Wang, 1978) 71.

10 [12] Roland Barthes, *S/Z*, trans. Richard Miller (New York: Hill & Wang, 1974) 112.

11 [13] Coop Himmelblau, *Architecture is Now*, op. cit., 11.

12 [14] Ibid., 73.

13 [15] Jean-Paul Sartre, *Being and Nothingness*, trans. Hazel. E. Barnes (New York: Philosophical Library, 1956) 323–5.

Anthony Vidler, 'Architecture Dismembered', *The Architectural Uncanny* (Cambridge, Massachusetts: The MIT Press, 1992) 69–84.

Jean Baudrillard
The Anorexic Ruins//1989

[...] Suddenly, I stand before [the Berlin Wall] without perceiving myself. It has a long series of graffiti running from one end to the other like those in the New York subway, like the decal of the West. All at once I have lost the historical imagination of this wall, of this divided city, divided like a head divided into two hemispheres by an artificial scalpel. The adjacent buildings bear charred traces of a hot history – while the cold history feeds on cold, transparent signs that drive the imagination to despair (and the graffiti, too, are cold signs – the only humorous signs are the rabbits scurrying around between the barbed wire entanglements of no-man's land).

It is impossible to recapture the tremor of terror. Everything is insignificant –here, at the pinnacle of history self-exposed by its violence, everything is eerily quiet like an abandoned November field. Every other abandoned urban zone offers the same spectacle. The most amazing thing is that history is being antiquated as *terrain vague*. One can remember it like some nightmare, that is, like fulfilling a desire, but the signs have long since become a true battlefield. They are the true conductors of lethal energy, the electrodes of electrocution. Today, it is the circular flows that burn, those of the head, those of the sensorial and beloved machines that we ourselves are. It is no longer the buildings that go up in flames and the cities that collapse; it is the Hertzian relays of our memories that crackle.

I view this wall with astonishment, and I no longer manage to remember anything. It is no different with me than it will be with those who in two thousand years might view this wall, which by that time will have only historical significance for them. By closing my mind's eye, I can see it like Christo's wall, that gigantic curtain of material stretched across the hills of California ... Whence this passion for unrolling bandages, walls – here, for example, the historical concrete closure; elsewhere, the magnetic strips? Whence among scientists, for example, this contrived development of chromosome chains or DNA spirals? Things are packaged in their own innermost reaches, in their inner coils, and this imbroglio need not be untangled. Here, the labyrinth of a city and the Gordian knot of history are destroyed at the same time in one stroke by a murderous incision. [...]

Jean Baudrillard, extract from 'The Anorexic Ruins', in *Looking Back on the End of the World*, ed. Dietmar Kamper and Christoph Wulf (New York: Semiotext(e), 1989) 35–6.

Svetlana Boym
Obscene Homes//2001

Kabakov's *Toilets* (1992) were criticized for the betrayal of Russia, for selling out to the West, as well as for obscenity. The obscenity charge haunts many twentieth-century works that were often produced by exiles, from Vladimir Nabokov's *Lolita* to Chris Ofili's *The Holy Virgin Mary* (1996), incorporating elephant dung, that created a scandal at the Brooklyn Museum of Art in 1999. Somehow obscenity is connected to the transposition of sacred and profane from one culture to another. The word obscene has an obscure etymology: it can be related to the Latin *ob* (on account of) plus *caenum* (pollution, dirt, filth, vulgarity); but it can also be related to *ob* (tension) plus *scena* (scene, space of communal ritual enactment, sacred space). In this sense, obscene doesn't suggest anything vulgar, sexually explicit or dirty, but simply something eccentric, offstage, unfashionable or antisocial. It is similar to profane (outside but in proximity of the temple). *Toilets* is Kabakov's most obscene installation thus far, responsible for a scandal, but it is difficult to figure out what exactly is 'off' about it.

In 1992 Kabakov constructed a replica of a provincial Soviet toilet – the kind one encounters in bus and train stations. He placed it behind Documenta's main exhibition building, the Museum Fridericianum in Kassel – just the right place for the outdoor toilets. Kabakov describes Soviet toilets of his youth as 'sad structures with walls of white lime turned dirty and shabby, covered by obscene graffiti that one cannot look at without being overcome with nausea and despair'.[1] They did not have stall doors. Everyone could see everyone else 'answering the call of nature' in what in Russian was called 'the eagle position', perched over 'the black hole'. Toilets were communal, as were ordinary people's residences. Voyeurism became nearly obsolete; rather, one developed the opposite tendency. One was less tempted to steal glances than to close one's eyes. Every toilet goer accepted the conditions of total visibility.

To go to the *Toilet*, visitors had to stand in a long line. Expecting to find a functional place to take care of one's bodily needs, or an artfully profane exhibit where one could flash a fashionable black outfit, visitors were inevitably shocked by the toilet's interior design. Inside was an ordinary, Soviet two-room apartment inhabited by 'some respectable and quiet people'. Here, side by side with the 'black hole', everyday life continues uninterrupted. There is a table with a tablecloth, a glass cabinet, bookshelves, a sofa with a pillow, and even a reproduction of an anonymous Dutch painting, the ultimate in homely art. There is a sense of a captured presence, of an arrested moment: the dishes have not yet been cleared, a jacket has been dropped on a chair. Children's toys frame the black hole of the toilet, which has lost its smell with the passage of time. Everything is proper here; nothing appears obscene.

The toilet, of course, is an important stopping point for the discussion of Russia and the West. Travellers to Russia and Eastern Europe, from the Enlightenment to our day, have commented on the changing quality of personal hygiene as a marker of a stage of the civilizing process. The 'threshold of civilization' was often defined by the quality of toilets. *Perestroika* started, in many cases, with *perestroika* of public and private toilets. Even the British Prince Charles pledged to donate a public toilet to the Pushkin Institute in Petersburg. In the major cities, paid toilets decorated by American advertisements and Chinese pin-up girls replaced public toilets like the ones reproduced by Kabakov, and the *nouveau riche* prided themselves on their 'euro-repairs', which included toilet and bath. In the cultural imagination, the toilet stands right on the border between public and private, Russia and the West, sacred and profane, high and low culture.

In the Russian press, Kabakov's work was reviewed very negatively as an insult to the Russian people and to Russian national pride. Many reviewers evoked a curious Russian proverb: 'Do not take your trash out of your hut' (*ne vynosi sor iz izby*), meaning do not criticize your own people in front of strangers and foreigners. The proverb dates back to an ancient peasant custom of sweeping trash into a corner behind a bench, and burying it inside instead of taking it outside. There was a widely held superstition that evil people could use your trash for casting magic spells.[2] This is a peculiar superstition against metonymic memory, especially when exhibited in an ambiguous foreign context. Kabakov's evocative domestic trash of the Soviet era was regarded as a profanation of Russia.

The artist shunned this symbolic interpretation. He recreated his toilets with such meticulousness – working personally on every crack on the window, every splash of paint, every stain – that the inhabited toilet turned into an evocative memory theatre, irreducible to univocal symbolism. Russian critics expropriated the artist's toilets and reconstructed them as symbols of national shame. National mythology had no place for ironic nostalgia.[3]

In the 'West', as Kabakov observed, there was also a curious tendency to see the toilet as a representation of Russia, only this time a literal one. The ethnographic 'other' is not supposed to be complex, ambivalent and similar to oneself. The museum guard in Kassel told the artist how much he liked the exhibit, and asked him what percentage of the Russian population lived in toilets after *perestroika*. The guard was right on the mark. Kabakov teases his viewer with almost ethnographic literalism. His art does not follow the modernist prescription of examining material and medium as such, nor does it employ the postmodern device of placing everything in quotation marks. The objects have an aura not owing to their artistic status, but because of their awkward materiality, outmodedness and otherworldliness – not in any metaphysical sense, but merely in the sense of being fragments of a vanished (Soviet) civilization.

Kabakov leaves his toilet at the crossroads of conflicting interpretations. He tells two tales, relating two points of the project's origin: the autobiographical and art historical. Both are told in the voice of a wistful storyteller who shares his secrets with a kind stranger on a long train journey, with whom he develops a deep but transient intimacy. The first tale is about the artist's and his mother's many stories of inner exile within the Soviet Union, and the early loss of a place called home.

> The childhood memories date back to the time when I was accepted at the boarding school for art in Moscow and my mother decided to abandon her work [in Dniepropetrovsk] to be near me and to participate in my life at school ... She became a laundry cleaner at school. But without an apartment [for that one needed special resident permits] the only place she had was the room where she arranged the laundry – tablecloths, drapes, pillowcases – which was in the old toilets. My mother felt homeless and defenceless vis-à-vis the authorities, while, on the other hand, she was so tidy and meticulous that her honesty and persistence allowed her to survive in the most improbable places. My child psyche was traumatized by the fact that my mother and I never had a corner to ourselves.[4]

In contrast with this affectionate memory of past humiliation, the tale of the project's conception is a tongue-in-cheek story of a poor Russian artist summoned to the sanctuary of the Western artistic establishment, Documenta, much to his embarrassment and humiliation:

> With my usual nervousness I had the impression that I had been invited to see the Queen who decides the fate of the arts. For the artist this is a kind of Olympic Games ... The poor soul of a Russian impostor was in agony in front of these legitimate representatives of great contemporary art ... Finding myself in this terrifying state, on the verge of suicide, I distanced myself from those great men, approached the window and looked out ... 'Mama, help' – I begged in silence. It was like during the war ... At last, my mother spoke to me from the other world and made me look through the window into the yard – and there I saw the toilets. Immediately the whole conception of the project was in front of my eyes. I was saved.[5]

The two origins of the toilet project are linked – the mother's embarrassment is reenacted by her artist son, who feels like an impostor, an illegal alien in the home of the Western contemporary art establishment. The toilet becomes the artist's diasporic home, an island of Sovietness, with its insuppressible nostalgic smell that persists – at least in the visitor's imagination – even in the most sanitized Western museum. Yet the museum space is not completely alien to the artist; it is a space where he can defamiliarize his humiliating experience. Panic and embarrassment are redeemed through humour.

Another origin of Kabakov's toilet is to be found in a Russian and Western avant-garde tradition: Kabakov ironically suggested a resemblance between his black hole' and Malevich's black square and hinted at 'toiletic intertextuality' between this project and Marcel Duchamp's *Fountain* (*La Fontaine*). Duchamp purchased a mass-produced porcelain urinal, placed it on a pedestal, signed the object with the pseudonym R. MUTT, and proposed to exhibit it at the American Society for Independent Artists.[6] A hung jury rejected the project, judging that while the urinal is a useful object, it is 'by no definition, a work of art'. In twentieth-century art history, this rejection has been seen as the birth of conceptual art and of an artistic revolution, which happened to take place in 1917, a few months before the Russian Revolution.[7] Subsequently, the original 'intimate' urinal splashed with the artist's signature has vanished under mysterious circumstances. What survived was the artistic photograph by Alfred Stieglitz made from the 'lost original', which has added an aura of uniqueness to a radical avant-garde gesture. A contemporary wrote that the urinal looked 'like anything from a Madonna to a Buddha'. In 1964, Duchamp himself made an etching from Stieglitz's photograph and signed it with his own name. The permutations of the best-known toilet in art history are a series of defamiliarizations, both of the mass-reproduced everyday object and of the concept of art itself, and challenge the cult of artistic genius. Yet, paradoxically, by the end of the twentieth century, we witness an aesthetic reappropriation of Duchamp's readymades. Duchamp's cult imbued everything he touched with an artistic aura, securing him a unique place in the modern museum.

In comparison with Kabakov's toilet, Duchamp's urinal really does look like a fountain; it is clean, characteristically Western and individualistic. Scatological profanity became a kind of avant-garde convention – part of early twentieth-century culture as represented by Bataille, Leiris and others. Kabakov's installation is not merely about radical defamiliarization and recontextualization but also, more strikingly, about inhabiting the most uninhabitable space – in this case, the toilet. Inhabiting the toilet doesn't make it a cosy, nostalgic refuge. Yet it seems that only by attempting to inhabit can the artist confront the incommensurability of loss and estrangement. Instead of Duchamp's sculpture-like readymade, we have here an intimate environment that invites walking through, storytelling and touching. (Visitors are allowed to touch objects in Kabakov's installations.) The artist's own artistic touch is visible throughout. Kabakov took great care in arranging the objects in the inhabited rooms around the toilet, those metonymical memory triggers of everyday Soviet life.

Duchamp questioned the relationship between high art and the mass-reproduced object, and played with the boundaries of the museum; yet he could afford to transgress museum conventions, because he took for granted the museum's survival, as well as the role of art and artists in society. In Kabakov's work, one gets a sense of the fragility of any artistic institution. The artist's installation is a surrogate museum as well as a surrogate home; it is as much a memory museum as it is a museum of forgetting. In his readymades, Duchamp was concerned with the context and aura of the object, but not so much with its temporality. Kabakov works with the aura of the installation as such, and with the drama of captured, or constipated, time; this temporal and narrative excess of the old-fashioned toilet makes it new and nostalgic at the same time.

Kabakov writes that his total installations have more to do with narrative and temporal arts than with plastic and spatial ones, such as sculpture and painting. He insists that his installations are not based on a model based on a picture, but rather on the world as a picture. In other words, the visitor walks into the installation and for a brief period inhabits it as an alternative, multidimensional universe; the fourth dimension is provided by texts. There are no symbols here, nothing personifies time à la Dalí; time hides in the configurations of objects. The past is embodied in fragments, ruins, trash and vessels of all sorts – chests of drawers, cupboards, rugs and worn-out clothes. The future is suggested in texts, frames, white walls, cavities, cracks and openings. The installations incorporate other temporalities, and cheat linear time and the fast pace of contemporary life.[8]

There is almost an excess of narrative potentiality in Kabakov's works. They intrigue the visitor with their mystery, like detective stories, and offer many controversial clues. Where indeed are the hosts of the toilet-duplex? What made them leave in a rush without even clearing the table or washing the dishes, as 'nice, orderly people' would do? Are they standing in line for toilet paper? Was it fear of invasion, or of a strange encounter with aliens or natives? Has it already happened or is it imminent? What kinds of skeletons are we about to discover in the closet?

Kabakov's toilet is not about the 'shit of the artist' – to name another conceptual readymade [Manzoni's *Merda d'artista*] – nor is it even about the metaphysical shit of Milan Kundera or Georges Bataille. It is by no means pornographic; some clothes are left on the chair, but unclothed people are nowhere in sight. The toilet is about panic and fear, not erotic fantasies. Yet the perverse toiletgoer cannot stop herself from a far-fetching exploration of the invisible shit. In the choice of subject matter, Kabakov clearly appeals to scatological sensationalism as well as to Russian and Soviet exoticism, even if in the end he does not 'deliver'. One is reminded that the success of another émigré, Vladimir Nabokov, was related to *Lolita*'s scandalous topic. Nabokov insisted that the novel was not pornographic, because pornography resides in the banal and repetitive narrative structure, not in the subject of representation. Similarly, Kabakov's toilet does not offer us the conventional satisfaction of a single narrative, but leaves us at a loss in a maze of narrative potentials and tactile evocations.

Yet what is obscene in Kabakov is neither the vulgar nor the sexual, but rather the ordinary, the all too human. 'There is a taboo on humaneness in contemporary art', Kabakov said in one of our conversations, sounding a bit like a disgruntled Russian writer of the nineteenth century complaining about the coldness of the West. At the same time, one is struck by this insight. Humaneness is not really a subject of contemporary art, which prefers body, ideology or technology to outmoded affect. Roland Barthes has observed the paradoxical nature of contemporary obscenity. He says that in high culture affection has become more obscene than transgression; the story of affections, frustrations and sympathies is more obscene than Georges Bataille's shocking tale of the 'pope sodomizing the turkey'. Affection and surprise have become outmoded even in the lover's discourse.

> Whatever is anachronistic is obscene. As a (modern) divinity, History is repressive, History forbids us to be out of time. Of the past we tolerate only the ruin, the monument, kitsch, what is amusing; we reduce this past to no more than its signature.
>
> The lover's sentiment is old-fashioned, but this antiquation cannot even be recuperated as a spectacle.[9]

Kabakov's nostalgic obscenity does not simply refer back in time, but rather sideways. In his artistic quest, Kabakov moves away from the much explored verticality of high and low towards the horizontality of the banal and its many invisible dimensions. Kabakov is an archaeologist and collector of banal memorabilia. The black hole of the toilet is surrounded by found objects from a Soviet child's world. This appears to be an inverse framing: objects frame the black hole, but the black hole gives them their uncanny allure. When another passionate collector of modern memorabilia, Walter Benjamin, visited Moscow in 1927, he abstained from direct ideological metaphors and theoretical conclusions, and instead offered a detailed and seemingly literal description of everyday things. In a letter from Moscow he wrote, 'factuality is already theory'. In other words, a narrative collage of material objects tells an allegory of Soviet reality. The same principle is at work in Kabakov's installations, where objects are on the verge of becoming allegories, but never symbols.

The toilet is embarrassing, not shocking. It does not contain the excrement of the artist, but his emotion. The toilet's black hole does not allow the artist to rebuild the perfect home of the past; leaving an unbridgeable gap in the archaeology of memory. The black hole of the toilet is the opposite of Malevich's avant-garde icon, the 'black square', which Kabakov loves to hate. The black hole of the toilet might be equally mystical, but its power lies on the border between art and life. The toilet becomes one of the artist's diasporic homes, a home away from home, a home in the museum, which 'offstages' the predictable narrative of Russian and Soviet shame and Western experimental eschatology.

1 Ilya Kabakov, *Installations 1983–1995* (Paris: Centre Georges Pompidou, 1995) 162; and *The Toilet* (Kassel: Documenta 11, 1992).
2 Vladimir Dal', *Tolkovyi slovar zhivogo velikorusskogo iazyka*, vol. 4 (St Petersburg, 1882) 275.
3 It is hard to imagine Duchamp's urinal being interpreted as an insult to French culture, in spite of its provocative title, *La Fontaine*. Yet the insults that Kabakov endured are part of being a 'Soviet artist' – a role Kabakov chose for himself, not without inner irony and nostalgic sadomasochism.
4 Kabakov, *Installations*, op. cit,, 162-63. Translation mine.
5 Ibid., 163.
6 For an insightful discussion of Duchamp, see Dalia Judovitz, *Unpacking Duchamp: Art in Transit* (Berkeley and London: University of California Press, 1996) 124–35.
7 See Marjorie Perloff, lecture at Harvard University, November 1998.
8 Ilya Kabakov, *On the Total Installation* (Cantz, 1992) 168.
9 Roland Barthes, *A Lover's Discourse: Fragments*, trans. Richard Howard (New York: Hill and Wang, 1978) 177–8. See Svetlana Boym, 'Obscenity of Theory', *Yale Journal of Criticism*, vol. 4, no. 2 (1991): 105–28.

Svetlana Boym, extract from *The Future of Nostalgia* (New York: Basic Books, 2001) 313–20.

Geoff Dyer
Leptis Magna//2004

[...] The entrance to the ruins was indicated by the arch of Septimius Severus: scaffold-clad, in the process of some kind of renovation – and therefore disappointing. Reminding us that the past's survival is not due entirely to its own stored reserves of longevity, scaffolding is fatal to the spell of antiquity. It gets – mediates – between the clean lines of ancient stone and the framing timelessness of the sky. I moved on, to the *palaestra*, an expanse of grass and scattered columns. Immediately there was the sense – which I've had in only a few places in the world – of entering not so much a physical space as a force field, a place where time has stood its ground. I first experienced it on the Somme, at Thiepval, and perhaps I've never felt it quite as powerfully anywhere else. Other people get a similar feeling when they step into a great cathedral, into Chartres or Canterbury, or just a church even. I assumed I'd never been able to feel it in such places because of a lack of – even a profound aversion to – the faith that inspired them. But equivalent places – mosques, synagogues – leave me cold also. (I feel more comfortable in Buddhist or Hindu temples, where the faith is so all-embracing that you could, if you feel like it, leave a cuddly Donald Duck at the altar without encroaching on the holiness – let alone the aesthetic harmony – of the place.). Then, in the Rothko Chapel at Houston, Texas, I had a revelation. In that famously non-denominational environment – a place designed to provide a setting for the contemplation of the spirit by those who, like myself, did not feel at home in any of the more traditional places of worship – I felt ... nothing. Not a thing. If anything, it all felt slightly bogus. Pious even. I had plenty of time, was in no hurry. I sat there for a good while, surrounded by those impenetrable menus of the artist's soul, waiting for something to happen, willing on the blood-and-pigment epiphany. But there's no faking these things: either you have the great experience or you don't. I knew it was not going to happen. And then it did happen, in the sense that I realized it could never happen indoors.

D.H. Lawrence experienced a sense of arrival, of 'something final', at Taos Pueblo. Some places felt temporary on the face of the earth, but Taos, Lawrence thought, retained 'its old nodality'. It was the same here, at Leptis. It was not a place I had entered, but the dream space of the past. I was in the Zone.

I always know when I'm in the Zone. When I'm in the Zone I don't wish I was anywhere else. Whereas when I'm not in the Zone I'm always wishing I was somewhere else, wishing I was in the Zone.

A narrow-gauge railroad track wound its way through the site (part, now, of the ruin whose excavation it had been designed to facilitate). The Hadrianic Baths were flooded by the recent rain. The surface of the waters was stirred by the wind. A few tins rusted at the bottom of the baths. Weeds writhed over broken tiles.

It was not surprising that these details came straight out of [the film] *Stalker*: I got the idea of the Zone from Tarkovsky but the Zone in *Stalker* is not the only Zone. If it weren't for *Stalker* I'm not sure I would ever have realized that the place I wanted to be – and the state I wanted to be in – was the Zone. Before I saw *Stalker* I only had the need, the longing. In some sense I might have been in the Zone prior to seeing *Stalker*, but part of being in the Zone is realizing you're in the Zone, and since I didn't know there was such a thing as the Zone, I was not really in it. That is the thing about the Zone, that is one of the things I love about it: I know when I'm there, and I knew I was in it in the Severan Forum. [...]

Geoff Dyer, extract from 'Leptis Magna', in *Yoga For People Who Can't be Bothered to Do It* (London: Abacus, 2004) 185–6.

Giuliana Bruno
Modernist Ruins, Filmic Archaeologies//2003

Lost Sites of Power

Jane and Louise Wilson's excavation into the psychology of architecture, deep into the way it sounds, reacquaints us with a particular use of archaeology. As an archaeology of the modern, *A Free and Anonymous Monument* represents the culmination of the artists' 'sound' meditation on architectural ruins and technological obsolescence. It is a mature articulation of many of the themes that have emerged in the past work of the pair, and its suspended, mnemonic design reinforces the affinity for mental architectures present in their earlier work.

Take *Stasi City* (1997) and *Gamma* (1999), for example, each of which consists of two pairs of screen projections on walls meeting at two 90-degree angles, diagonally opposite from each other. The architectural layout of these installations – two points of view shown simultaneously and bound together – mirrors a psychic architecture. This architecture of vision reveals the kind of double-vision characteristic of the bond that connects these artists, who are identical twin sisters. Conceived in a double frame, a Wilson installation is almost never a single work but most often pairs up, as happens with both *Gamma* and *Stasi City*, double works that are linked.

Gamma was shot in the former US Air Force base at Greenham Common, a cold war operation that housed nuclear weapons and which is now a decommissioned site. The installation inspects spaces of inspection and surveils control rooms and security zones, taking us off-limits into 'untouchable' spaces of power. Exhibiting the same vision, *Stasi City* was also shot in abandoned buildings. Since these buildings are the former East-German secret police headquarters in Berlin and a former Stasi prison, one might describe the work itself as interrogating places of interrogation.

In powerful and subtle ways *Stasi City* feels, as do other of the twins' works, like a set. The installation in fact restages situations that were themselves 'staged' in order to instil anxiety or fright. Figures 'hang' in the space, evoking perhaps a deadly fear of death by hanging. Or maybe they are just suspended, pending judgement – suspended, that is, in that zero gravity of lengthy bureaucratic time. The space is carefully choreographed. Devoid of human presence, with the closed doors that once imprisoned the investigated subject now pushed wide open, the 'construction' of the very space of fear is revealed. We can now see the cheapness, even the fakeness, of the psychic mechanism that was staged here – the mechanism that runs a theatre of terror.

The technique of revealing the internal mechanism of a disused architecture recurs in the work of the Wilson twins. For example, in different yet related ways, the open doors of the British Houses of Parliament in *Parliament* (1999) also question power this way, enabling us to get a glance at the mechanism that regulates social domination as we peer into the system of authority and legality. However, we can only be there when the place is not active, precisely because it is not functioning. Jane and Louise Wilson are endlessly attracted to places of power and control, but only when those in command have left the site. They are interested in accessing emptied, evacuated places to explore what is no longer in control there. They fancy a place out of control. Or, rather, they are interested in what happens when a place has lost control. Or, else, when a place is simply lost.

In this respect, the Wilsons' work recalls that of another architectural artist, Robert Polidori. In his photographic portraits, especially in his vision of Chernobyl and Pripyat, Polidori puts himself in the same position.[1] He, too, investigates the leftovers, picturing the ruins of power and the effects of industrialization, and does so also with an explorative architectural eye. His camera also travels through spaces that bear traces of destruction. Redolent with the patina of time, abandoned places are shown, or rather laid bare, in Polidori's photographs – their intestines wide open to view. In many ways, his renderings of Chernobyl and Pripyat parallel the Wilsons' *Home/Office* (1998), an installation that re-presents rescued footage from London's fire brigade. Their memory loops let us into the ravages of destruction, enabling us to inhabit what are now uninhabitable spaces.

Archaeological Journeys

A Free and Anonymous Monument shares with many other works the pair has made the form of a meditation on matters of desuetude, post-industrial ruins and technological waste. In fact, these artists have long shown a predilection for visionary, 'machinic' installations – mental architectures that are barren landscapes and deserts of the mind. Take, for example, the desolate spatial layout of *Proton, Unity, Energy, Blizzard* (2000). Four screens simultaneously track the space of a Russian cosmodrome, introducing us to the engineering mechanism of a proton rocket factory. We hang in a barren hanger, visit empty offices and medical facilities. We follow a narrative sequence of telephones that no longer ring. We try to decipher signatures – traces of life – left on doors, now left 'hanging', doors no longer opening or closing for anyone. Camels inhabit the literally deserted space. As they walk away from what were launch-site towers, they lead us out of this human desert.

In a similar vein, *Dreamtime* (2001) examines the rituals of rocket launching and space travel with monumental, military solemnity. It parallels *Star City* (2000), also devoted to the once futuristic, now bygone, art of travel out-of-space. In this lost' city', we architecturally explore the kinetic form of rockets and spaceships as the artists let us travel inside and out of off-limits space. Here, again, we are impressed by the presence of absence. Empty astronaut suits, empty dressing rooms, empty capsules and offices. Suits and rooms both voided of presence. In this way, the Wilsons' acute, observant camera connects architecture to clothing. It equates them as spaces of the body, both inhabited by flesh. It shows what happens when bodies leave and places are evacuated of life. With the inhabitants that 'suited' these spaces now departed, only empty shells are left, melancholically drifting lifeless on screen.

Gardens of the Post-Industrial Era

Jane and Louise Wilson constantly return to what is left of a place, left out or even left over, and this return extends to the industrial landscape that makes up *A Free and Anonymous Monument*. Turning to a regional geography marked by the problems of post-industrialization, the installation looks at a place in ruin. Ruinous is, indeed, the state of Victor Pasmore's pavilion. Once a pristine structure, a utopian monument to the idea of enacting social transformation by way of urban design, the Apollo Pavilion is now a shadow of its former self. What we see over and over again in the installation is a building that is badly maintained, dilapidated, partly dismantled and even locked up.

In July 2000, the *Sunday Telegraph* happily announced the potential success of a campaign to demolish the Apollo Pavilion, despite its status within English Heritage as 'an internationally important masterpiece'. The *Telegraph* labelled the Apollo Pavilion a 'concrete bungle'. Less than charmed by its modernist material, the paper reported that 'people around here think of it as just a heap of dirty, slimy concrete which youths climb up to have sex and urinate on passers-by'.[2] Indeed, the space has been 'consummated' by the younger population's way of using the lonely concrete structure.

This never seemed to bother Victor Pasmore, who died in 1998. When the artist returned to the Newcastle region to visit Peterlee, he witnessed the murals with which he had decorated the pavilion defaced. Graffiti covered the crumbling façade of his concrete building. He was not disturbed by what others saw as a state of desolation. On the contrary, he found the graffiti to be an improvement. He mentioned that this intervention ameliorated the architecture of his building more than he himself could have done and believed this act of appropriation to have humanized the building,

A cinematic inscription of pavilion architecture, Jane and Louise Wilson's *A Free and Anonymous Monument* is a metaphoric graffito. It is itself an act of appropriation, not only of the Apollo Pavilion as an artistic matrix but of the entirety of its post-industrial region. It is furthermore an intimate appropriation, since it is an act of love for the place of the artists' youth. It is not irrelevant that Jane and Louise Wilson were born in Newcastle, in this nineteenth-century centre for coal export, shipbuilding and heavy engineering, and that Jane studied at Newcastle Polytechnic.

In some way, the mnemonic structure of their monument is a moving monument to their own past and to the crumbling nature of the region's post-industrial landscape.

Victor Pasmore's post-industrial pavilion made an artificial garden out of the urban industrial zone in the North East of England where Jane and Louise Wilson grew up. Its modernist design was a utopic attempt to create recreation where there was industrialization. His restorative gesture addressed what continues to be a problem today. Urban regeneration is now a social and political issue at a global level. As artists brought up in a place that faced this issue early, the Wilson sisters are particularly sensitive to this landscape.

In their art, Jane and Louise Wilson make continual attempts to investigate, and intervene in, sites that bear the texture of their region and of Pasmore's own site of urban intervention. Completing the collection of their previous projects of recollected landscapes, their latest venture is a work shot on location in New York, on Governor's Island. An island off the coast of Manhattan, this was home not only to the Governor but also to marine, penitential and military structures. A place of residence for nearly 5,000 people who worked in those infrastructures, it is now totally evacuated of life. It is no wonder that this – the largest and most attractive site of potential urban regeneration in the New York region – has attracted the Wilsons for another filmic intervention. It is sited precisely along their path of creative, lost urban geography.

Our Modernist Ruins

The installation of *A Free and Anonymous Monument* ultimately places on exhibit Jane and Louise Wilson's relentless, recurring fascination with the ruins of modernity. Although their approach to this mental architecture is so personal and intimate here that it exudes traces of a psychogeographic return, one can see throughout their work a personal interest in the environmental history of the aftermath of industrialization and the cold war, which formed them as modern artistic subjects.

With respect to a specific engagement with the vicissitudes of modern architecture, their act of re-engineering Victor Pasmore's design tackles a particular issue in the demise of modernity – the ruins of modernism. In this regard, their intervention joins that of other contemporary artists for whom the legacy of modernism is a present history to contend with. In a similar way, for example, Gabriel Orozco has taken upon himself to reconstruct Carlo Scarpa's once pristine and now crumbling 1952 modernist architecture, in a work presented at the 2003 Venice Biennale [*Shade between Rings of Air*, 2003].

But what do we mean by intimately revisiting this legacy? Can we really speak of a modernist ruin? Unlike the porous, permeable stone of ancient building, the material of modernism does not 'ruin'. Concrete does not decay. It does not slowly erode and corrode, fade out or fade away. It cannot monumentally disintegrate. In some way, modernist architecture does not absorb the passing of time. Adverse to deterioration, it does not age easily, gracefully or elegantly.

Modernism, after all, had an issue with history. It was an art of the present. Modern architecture looks good in its own present. It wears itself in the now, and does not wear out. It shines when recently constructed or freshly painted. It looks at its best dressed in white. It wears only pure 'coats' of paint and pristine fashions. It looks outstanding when freshly made-up. Its façade is a face that cannot bear age marks, does not like to 'wear' them. With concrete, there no longer can be lines emerging gently on the face of a building, line drawings on the map of time past. With concrete come only cracks, the breaking up of the façade.

If the façade is a face, then the problem of modernism is skin. Modernist architecture was, after all, an architecture of the surface. This modern epidermics has the same issue with time that we do. We modern subjects, too, have an increasing issue with the deterioration of our skin. Refusing to age gracefully, we seek the radical fix. Plastic surgery is perhaps itself a measure, if not quite an invention, of modernist time and its passing. It is the sign of our times.

As we live in an age in so many ways repelled by ruination, what kind of archaeology can we now create? In answering this question, we can take one last look at Jane and Louise Wilson's archaeology, and ponder in yet one more way their fascination with post-industrial ruins. We should recognize that our history is made up of different ruins. In modern times, different architectures bear the mark of time. Time passing is not simply etched on the surface of stone. It is marked on the skin of celluloid. It is impressed on other kinds of architecture – the translucent screens of moving-image installations. Pictures in motion write our modern history. They can be the living, moving testimony of the effects of duration. Moving images are modernity's ruins. They are our kinds of monuments. A Free and Anonymous Monument.

1 Robert Polidori, *Zones of Exclusion: Pripyat and Chernobyl* (Göttingen: Steidl, 2003).

2 Nigel Burnham, *Sunday Telegraph*, (16 July 2000).

Giuliana Bruno, extract from 'Modernist Ruins, Filmic Archaeologies', in *Jane and Louise Wilson: A Free and Anonymous Monument* (London: Film & Video Umbrella/Lisson Gallery/Newcastle upon Tyne: BALTIC, 2003) 20–24.

Barbara Clausen
Dorit Margreiter//2008

The film *10104 Angelo View Drive*, made in 2004 by Vienna and Los Angeles-based artist Dorit Margreiter, is a portrait of the Sheats/Goldstein residence in Beverly Hills. Designed by celebrity architect John Lautner in 1963, the building is one of California's most futuristic homes, literally anchored to its furniture in a way that radically overturns architectural hierarchies: Sofas, beds, dining room tables, and the like, are set into concrete, while the walls, generally made of glass, are movable and can be remotely controlled. As is typical of warmed-over, commercial depictions of modernism, the house has a quasi-bachelor-pad ethos – indeed, it is probably most familiar as the home of bad guys and psychos in a series of Hollywood blockbusters, including *The Big Lebowski* (1998), *Charlie's Angels* (2000) and *Mullholland Drive* (2001).

The identification of this modernist building with masculinity in the Hollywood unconscious is key to Margreiter's film, which investigates the intertwined artificial worlds of film sets and 1960s architecture – and, in doing so, reconceptualizes 'reality' as an overlap of history and theatricality. In the more commonly seen of the film's two versions, Margreiter splices classic documentary style shots of the building's moving parts with a series of briefly glimpsed *tableaux vivants*, in which the queer Los Angeles-based performance group the Toxic Titties depict charged scenarios, including a rock'n'roll-style orgy in the master bedroom and a sci-fi laboratory scene in the kitchen. These static visual flashes counter the dynamic activity of the house's design and serve to point up and disrupt the fantasy of male domination that the building seems to embody in both its technological sophistication and its setting high above Los Angeles. The distinction between the real and the imagined is also exploited, more subtly, in scenes depicting stacks of literature aimed at women, including novels, homemaking manuals, comics, and classics of feminism: *La Femme soviétique*, *Amazon Odyssey*, *The Betty Betz Career Book*, *Lesbo* and *Twisted Sisters* are casually displayed alongside memorabilia owned by the home's current owner, real estate investor and basketball fanatic James Goldstein.

Margreiter's exhibitions have likewise focused on the social construction of architectural space, playing out the fictional and the documentary along the blurred boundary of popular and high culture. When *10104 Angelo View Drive* was presented at the Museum Moderner Kunst Stiftung Ludwig Wien in 2004, it was screened as part of an installation in which a model of the home's television set – which is seen ascending out of a concrete base in the film – was incorporated as a sculptural element. (The credits for the film ran in a loop on this monitor, while the 16 mm film itself was projected on an adjacent screen.) This partial reconstruction of the house (and film set) within the exhibition extended the work's premise that the Sheats/Goldstein residence is equally fictional and real. Moreover, by covering the gallery walls and ceiling with black paint and using theatrical spotlights to guide the viewer through the installation, Margreiter physically enforced the interplay between illusion and reality – thus making the image politics of her film equally applicable to the representational and architectural context of the art institution. As MUMOK curator Matthias Michalka argued in his catalogue text for this exhibition, 'through the act of reproduction ... the conditions of reproduction [themselves] are ... "retroactively" fictionalized and redefined.'

The concurrent disappearance and glorification of modernism's former utopias are at the core of this time-travelling practice. The artist's recent video *Exquisite Function* (2007), for instance, centres on the politics of interior design during the economic boom in 1950s West Germany, investigating the history of the Hansaviertel, a modernist model city district built in Berlin between 1957 and 1961. The cultural mission of the Hansaviertel's architects – who included Alvar Aalto, Walter Gropius and Oscar Niemeyer – was to look to the future and to forget the monstrosities of the past. Margreiter in turn bypasses the district's classically modernist exteriors and instead places her emphasis on the intimacy of the interior. As a voice-over in the form of a narrated film script describes scenarios of 1950s domestic life, a series of tables, chairs, lamps, books and even plants are filmed individually and dramatically lit against a black background, with the camera seeming almost to touch the surfaces of its isolated prey. Exposed like precious antiques in a museum – or, alternatively, like objects for sale at IKEA – these objects reflect not only the marketability of a nostalgically desired past but also the accompanying loss of its political origins and implications.

Margreiter's preoccupation with modernism's contingent relationship to politics is most fully evident in a sequence of works made for a 2006 exhibition at the Galerie für Zeitgenössische Kunst in Leipzig, Germany, all based on a neon sign affixed to the Brühlzentrum, a modernist housing project in the East German city. The building and the sign bearing its name date from 1963, the heyday of the GDR's neon craze (which was allegedly sparked by General Tito's having remarked on the dreary impression made by the cities of East Germany). But times change: The impending demolition of the Brühlzentrum had already been announced when Margreiter made her film *zentrum* (2006), in which we see the hundreds of neon tubes that give the round-edged, full-bodied letters their shapes light up one last time.

In seeking to situate the aesthetics of socialist modernism in the twenty-first century, Margreiter reveals and perpetuates modernity's ongoing relationship with the moving image: *zentrum* is also an ode to her fascination with early cinema about the city. In films such as Charles Sheeler and Paul Strand's *Manhattan* (1921) or Walter Ruttmann's *Berlin: Symphony of a Great City* (1927), modernism's complexity and social dynamism are given form through lighting, *mise-en-scène*, editing and cinematography. In her filmic reconstruction of the neon sign, Margreiter likewise pays homage to technical ingenuity: the work is often shown in conjunction with a video documentary depicting the elaborate preparations for the night-time shoot, which reveals that the sign was not in fact illuminated – the tubes were merely wrapped in white tape that reflected the light of hand-held spots. Moreover, although the piece was shot on digital video, it is projected in grainy, black-and-white 16 mm stock. In using the digital to reproduce the aesthetics of the analogue, she highlights the historical counterflow in her work, as her deployment of technology points up the shifting social relevance of design and its status as cultural memory. The fleeting moment when the letters light up in the dark appears as the past revived in the present, and so Margreiter marks the constitutive time gap between an event and its reproduction, emphasizing their ontological distance.

Margreiter documents and redeploys the remnants of modernism before they disappear and, subsequently, keeps them 'alive'. In this case, the artist saved the

Brühlzentrum sign from its complete amnesiac erasure in more ways than one: She also designed a typeface, called *zentrum* (2005), using the modular components of the sign's letters. This font resonates throughout the history of twentieth-century design: In its mode of construction as well as in appearance, it is strongly reminiscent of Josef Albers' *Kombinationsschrift* (Combination Type), a stencil-based typeface he designed for the Bauhaus at Dessau, Germany, in the late 1920s. Margreiter thus suggests a third phase for the familiar historical trajectory of modernism. After the initial utopian impulse and the revival of its forms in the fashions of mainstream culture several decades later, there is still the possibility of a new lease on life: as a piece of art that can shift its medial character from image to text to sculpture. Since the *zentrum* font is neither a homage to the original nor an imitation of its 1960s copy, but rather a graphic set of modules existing between the two- and three-dimensional, the typeface regains presence.

This font will be used in yet another medium in a project for the website of the Dia Art Foundation [*alphabeth*, 2009–]. Margreiter's proposal involves channelling the written information released by the institution into an endless graphic code made up of the modular components of the *zentrum* font. What we see on the Web is two frames – one, running in a loop, presents the typographic system in which all the letters of the alphabet are combinations of one or more rectangular or curved elements. In an adjacent frame, a selection of Dia's outgoing press materials and public announcements will be presented in this code, as an endless feed of text – which looks, it turns out, much like Oskar Fischinger's early twentieth-century experiments in animation. The speed of the image sequence in the streaming text screen determines the level of abstraction: the faster the signs follow one another, the more potentially legible the words, as the constituent parts of each letter follow one another more quickly. Still, Margreiter's channelling of public information defies the intelligibility demanded by the press release as a format by transforming it into something difficult – if not impossible – to understand. The piece relies on the tension between abstraction and information, a dichotomy that spans history from the font's Bauhaus roots to its encoding of press materials detailing future events.

If Margreiter's films and installations usually reflect the social function and representational politics of art within the context of modernist aesthetics and its influence on urban identity, image production and exhibition making, both the Dia project and a commission for the European Kunsthalle in Cologne mark her shift to a direct engagement with the aesthetic and logic of art's interaction with the public. Margreiter designed a temporary outdoor exhibition space, European Kunsthalle c/o Ebertplatz, which opened this past August [2008] – three years after the kunsthalle's founding as a 'field of activity' unattached to any physical site. Ebertplatz itself is a public square typical of 1970s urban planning, with angular, semi-green concrete islands, stadium-style stairways and a giant sculpture of bent nails: elements that come together as a bleak hybrid of pedestrian park, busy street crossing and subway entrance, Yet Margreiter's proposal does not beautify or cover up the existing site: It involves adding a projection screen, a vitrine, an exhibition wall, a pavilion and a cubic pedestal to the pre-existing architecture. These 'architectural modules' are not held together by an outside shell but unified through their formal interaction with passers-by. At the same time, however, European Kunsthalle c/o Ebertplatz is itself a sculptural intervention, shifting between public art and exhibition display. In contrast with Margreiter's previous emphasis on media-constructed spaces, her own intervention into architectural terrain avoids the imposition of an alternative reality onto what already exists.

Barbara Clausen, 'Dorit Margreiter', *Artforum* (September 2008) 443–7.

Mark Lewis
Is Modernity Our Antiquity?//2006

> Art, considered in its highest vocation, is and remains for us a thing of the past.
> – G.W.F. Hegel, *Aesthetics: Lectures on Fine Art.*[1]

> By 'modernity' I mean the ephemeral, the fugitive, the contingent, the half of art whose other half is the eternal and the immutable.
> – Charles Baudelaire, *The Painter of Modern Life.*[2]

For five years now, every time I am back in Vancouver, I have been taking pictures of a small modernist apartment building that sits very close to Stanley Park, the large and beautiful urban park that borders the centre of the city. I have been taking pictures because one day I imagine that I might make a film there. I am not sure what this film will be: if it should be 'about' the building, or whether the building will simply feature as a part of a larger landscape. Regardless, it's the building that I have been drawn to. And even though I have taken hundreds of photographs and hours of video footage, I still am not sure if I am any closer to knowing what to do with this building than I was when I first saw it five years ago. When I lived in Vancouver I must have walked or cycled past the building hundreds of times without ever noticing it. It seems mildly significant that my fixation or compulsion should begin only after I moved away to a country (England) where modernist architecture is not only hard to find, but its reputation, until recently at least, has been rather battered and neglected. Is it this relative absence at 'home', I wonder, that compels me to notice this form elsewhere?

Now that I'm a foreigner in my own town, Vancouver is exotic and unknown to me in a way that it never was before. But the question remains as to what it is that continues to draw me to this modernist form, and why I continue to feel that I can make a work from it or about it. This question has made me reflect more generally on the whole idea of taking identifiably modernist forms as the subject, in one way or another, of a contemporary work. Why, for instance, are so many artists drawn to modernist forms and landmarks that are slowly crumbling and disappearing, in Vancouver and everywhere else? And if they are not crumbling and disappearing, then often they are being lovingly restored and transformed into museum pieces of the period; on the face of it, just a part of the same phenomenon.

In some regards it is composition that the Vancouver building foregrounds: the volumes, shapes, curves and complex juxtapositions when looking at it from certain viewpoints. For me this phenomenon is strongest and most compelling on the peripheral edges of the building: the rear exterior and the 'visitor's parking' area. This building, then, presents compositional opportunities. Similar to many other buildings like it, it is almost already an image in both complicated and simple ways. Point your camera at any 'good' modernist building and the blocking, the cubic forms, the mixed and contradictory volumes that are created through compelling and vital montage – this is what these buildings already articulate against their respective backgrounds.

The apartment block in Vancouver carries on its surface the recognizable signs of a modernist history. In terms of architectural history we might want to call it a modest example of the high modern. Its modesty is achieved, I think, because although attention is certainly what it demands (all modernist forms do this, in one way or another) its function as a middle-sized apartment block built in the early 1960s in the then small coastal city of Vancouver means that it cannot have expected too much. Today other, newer buildings that cry out for much more attention surround it: the latter are brash, loud and bullish in their demand for 'exclusive' views of the surrounding ocean and mountains. They have been built in front of the simpler modern structures of the 1950s and 1960s, often destroying or occupying their old grounds. 'My' building, of course, remains standing, and it has resisted (temporarily) any contemporary 'remodelling', though it has started to look more than a little neglected: its paint is peeling; the concrete has started to crumble here and there, softening the building's hard angular edges; and the 'visitor's parking' area is no longer level but slopes rather aimlessly towards its northern perimeter.

Alarmingly, it occurs to me that this disintegration and decay might be the real reason why I am drawn to this building, and why I continue to think that it may have something to reveal (don't I secretly pray each time I visit the location that some massive renovation and/or restoration has not taken place?) The idea of a modernist ruin in the making, while compellingly seductive, seems depressingly elegiac and tautological at best. Didn't the images and forms of modernism already have ruin, decay and obsolescence written into them? Was this not meant to serve as an inbuilt apotropaic function, all the better to protect against the future romantic appeal of their ruining? And do I really want to make an elegy to something like 'modernism's forgotten promise'? There's the rub. For today it is fundamentally a question of our relationship to these recently past forms, a question of what is to be done as the artistic signs and images of emerging and developing modernity are rapidly becoming historical. It can be quite disconcerting, I think, to recognize just how fast this has happened, to acknowledge that high-modernist forms have become historical ones.

By this I mean that we can no longer fully identify with them, as they belong to a different time, to a different knowledge, and finally, of course, to a different ambition. On the other hand, it may be important to recognize that this impression we have that our modern forms are rapidly accruing a sense of 'pastness' is in part the result of our contemporary cult of the past. Bruno Latour wants to argue that this cult of the past – this need, at one and the same time, to conjure the past, revere it, excise it and destroy it – extends to the very heart of modernism and is in the end what undermines modernism from within, in fact what makes modernism not modern at all.[3] I want to touch on this in a moment, but suffice it to say here that the massive building worldwide of new museums of contemporary art, presumably to provide for and continue the historicization of objects, forms and ideas from where the museums of modern art have only recently left off, suggests that this obsession with 'instant antiquity' is not entirely imaginary.

The real problem, I suppose, is how to represent this passage (from modern to historical) without succumbing to a melancholic reverie; and, moreover, how to try and give form to this when by its very name, modernism came to stand for those artistic forms where, metaphorically at least, the present waged a perpetual war on the past. The name we give to this war is iconoclasm, and while modernism may have more or less banned the pre-modern tradition of the actual material destruction of works, iconoclasm was internalized as a metaphorical *a priori* of modernism. A sense of iconoclasm gave fuel to the latter's sense of invention and history, and in particular to how many of its leading practitioners conceived of their own work: 'Previously a picture was a sum of additions. With me a picture is a sum of destructions' (Picasso); and 'the destruction of old forms was a condition for the creation of new, higher forms' (Mondrian). Following Adorno, we perhaps need to think of the categories of decline (of old forms) less as categories of destruction, but rather as categories of transition. If modernism is indeed now historical, then this surely raises the question of transition as a return to the question of the end of art, the very condition for art that Hegel had already announced in the 1820s. But is this necessary state of transition, knowing and acknowledging that things are changing rapidly and that the promise of yesterday is no longer (nor ever will be) the realization of today – is this the same thing as assuming an antiquity for our immediate past? Adorno opened his *Aesthetic Theory* with the now-famous declaration, 'It is self evident that nothing concerning art is self evident any more, nor its inner life, nor its relation to the world, nor even its right to exist.'[4] Art, says Adorno, takes refuge in its own negation, hoping to survive through its death. This negation must extend, *a fortiori*, to the idea of art's relationship to its past forms, no matter how immediate or far away.

If we accept that we are modern and that we continue to live in the time of modernity, then we know that modernist representational forms have staked their legibility and 'success' in the figuring of other futures, necessarily utopian, in the possibilities of modernity. The building in Vancouver is rather modest in this regard. At the same time I acknowledge that to think about modesty as part of the ambition of modernism is almost paradoxical. But sometimes I think modesty is, quite perversely, smuggled in, not noticed at first (a modesty not noticed is a strange tautology, in fact a modest modesty). And maybe that modesty is only recognizable now, some fifty years after the building was completed. If the latter is true, this speaks to how an archaeology of the modern might reveal unexpected, perhaps inexplicable results – we look to the (monumental) history of modernism to tell us something about the conflicts at the heart of the modern, about the latter's failure to make us free, its failure to provide us with a future that we might recognize ourselves in. In the end, this may not be so very different from the desire to find the truth in the classical past. Paradoxically, a building or form not noticed (too much) with regards to the large ambitions for future change and organization may be one that has failed to become properly past, failed to become historical.

In a struggle to define the feeling and form of a future modernity, modesty is just one contemporary retrospective sign that speaks to the inscrutability of the former ambition. In other words: do we really know what this building has wanted, when its formal propositions now seem so modest? And for me, in order to proceed it is important to keep 'its' desire in the present imperfect, to acknowledge that it might just continue 'wanting'. Its modesty is perhaps just another way of saying that we do not yet understand its relationship to the future. [...]

1 G.W.F Hegel, *Aesthetics: Lectures on Fine Art* (1831), trans. Malcolm Knox (Oxford: Oxford University Press, 1975); quoted in T.J. Clark, *Farewell to an Idea: Episodes from a History of modernism* (New Haven and London: Yale University Press, 1999) 371.

2 Charles Baudelaire, *The Painter of Modern Life* [1863] *and Other Essays*, trans. Jonathan Mayne (New York: Da Capo Press, 1986) 13.

3 See Bruno Latour, *We Have Never Been Modern*, trans. Catherine Porter (Cambridge, Massachusetts: Harvard University Press, 1993).

4 Theodor W. Adorno, *Aesthetic Theory* (1970) (London: Athlone Press, 1997) 1.

Mark Lewis, extract from 'Is Modernity Our Antiquity?', *Afterall* (Autumn/Winter 2006) 109–11.

Martin Herbert
Sifting Defunct Modernity in Search of Something Useful//2009

Here is your narrow room, floors and ceiling swathed with black-and-white stripes, V-shaped constructivist protrusions spiking every surface. Here is your assumedly pre-World War II abstract painting, a harlequinade of interknitted mauve/azure/tangerine polyhedra. Here is your blocky black post-minimalist sculpture. Here, really, are thumbnail sketches of recent art by Esther Stocker, Anselm Reyle and Tom Burr, and if you squint, it is 1921 or 1935 or 1969, and if you don't squint, it is very much the present moment.

New modernism is rampant. In 2005 at a symposium in east London gallery The Showroom entitled 'New Moderns?', French curator/theorist Nicolas Bourriaud characterized 'altermodernism' – a term borrowed from Croatian poet Filip Erceg – as 'a reloading of modernism according to twenty-first-century issues', particularly the homogenizing effects of globalization. In 2006 Tomma Abts won the Turner Prize with her austere painterly revisions of modernist geometries for an age of abiding doubt. (On the Turner Prize shortlist last year was Goshka Macuga, another artist deeply invested in modernism.) In 2007, lecturing at the Frieze Art Fair, American critic Dave Hickey asked whether anybody had noticed that 9/11 had killed off postmodernism. Pretty hard to talk about the end of history under such circumstances, Hickey suggested. But the defensive language of postmodernism, with its lockstep ironies and bricolage of aesthetic pastiches, had already for some time been proving itself incommensurate with the persistence of pesky hardwired stuff in the human psyche: desires for a better world, regret at the one we've got, refusal to accept that progress is impossible (even PoMo's pioneers got to feel as if they were actively closing a door, seemingly presuming that everyone afterwards would just stare sombrely at it), nostalgia, emotion in general and curiosity about babies and bathwater.

This refreshed attention to modernism's potentials might be considered a classic generational response to a bequest of obsolete tools. Though increasingly prevalent in recent exhibitions – the [2008] Berlin Biennial, for example, which pointedly sited its contents in modernist venues – it has been swelling for some time. The aforementioned Tom Burr, for one, has been repurposing minimalist and post-minimalist aesthetics since the mid 1990s, conflating that art's emphasis on the viewer's body (and an otherwise assiduous muteness) with, on occasion, that of the gay cruiser, and more generally the policing of social space. Perhaps never more memorably than in *Deep Purple* (2000), his two thirds-scale, 82 metre-long remake of a former landmark in his home city of New York: Richard Serra's contentious sculpture *Tilted Arc* (1981), here given a camp purple makeover, ostentatiously propped – like a stage, or something to consort behind – and with the curve returned as a signifier of the divisional 1980s, replete with reminders of Dionysian rock music and sexual politics. More recently, Burr has laced featureless black shiny boxes with wine glasses and brimful ashtrays (2003's *Black Out Bar*), and adopted a spacious scatter aesthetic involving bulletin boards and photographic references (to, among others, Jim Morrison, Frank O'Hara and visionary curator 'Chick' Austin) alongside hinged sculptures resembling collapsed bodies. A modified modernism that admits to bodily pleasure and casualties and decries the unspoken and closeted, Burr's rigorous and poignantly commemorative art is an outrider in the continuum of the altermodern, whose proponents sift defunct modernity in search of what retains the potential for use.

Martin Boyce, meanwhile, likes to characterize his artworks as 'undead', and in his scuffed and plywood-patched examples of Charles and Ray Eames' mid-century modern design furniture, such as *Now I've Got Worry (Storage Unit)* (1997), modernism returns ghostlike, trailing philosophic counsel about how things slip inexorably in and out of style, looking bruised but unbeaten by the ravages of transit and offering instruction in disharmonious sentiment: nostalgia, threat, loss, revivification. In conversation, the Glaswegian artist denies that he's 'playing in the ruins' of the modern era. For him, installations such as *Our Love is Like the Flowers, the Rain, the Sea and the Hours* (2002) – with its skeletal trees made of strip lights, fragments of Mies van der Rohe-like furniture and bins bent dreamily into isomorphic perspective, all wrapped in a cyclone fence enclosure – are intentionally productive, compounding an admonition that everything must change with the potential to trigger miniature Proustian rushes that summon memories of one's own personal, probably youthful, adventures amid cold modernist urbanism.

If Boyce rehearses and finds compensation in the destined diminishing and potential return of the modern in general, other artists have attended closely to specifics, treating quadrants of the modernist past as chapters to be rewritten or sedulously edited. Paulina Olowska has in recent years used an increasingly ramified aesthetic – paintings, photo-collages, videos, tapes of self-written stories, performance and installations – to sketch an imaginary feminist-modernist bohemia, a world of bob-haired strong women interwoven with visual cues (neon signs, film posters) from 1960s Poland, pointedly a period of relative freedom under the communist yoke. The Gdansk-born Olowska has, for example, convened provisional salons of modernist women, arranging, in 2004, her large fragmentary canvases of Djuna Barnes, Vanessa Bell, Virginia Woolf, Charlotte Perriand and more on wheeled supports so that they confronted each other, their conversation almost audible, in the salubrious environs of the Kunstverein Braunschweig. It's a vision of a strong, connected female avant-garde within the modern, one that never really transpired: the sustaining of this dream cadre, and what the example might mean in the present, is what counts here. That Olowska recognizes the fragility as well as the necessity of what she's doing, however, was reaffirmed by her 2006 show at Warsaw's Foksal Gallery.

The key element was a looped presentation of Wolfgang Peterson's 1984 film *The Never-ending Story*, concerning a fantasy world that exists only so long as people believe in it: the free presentation of the movie itself, exploiting a loophole in Polish copyright laws, stood meanwhile as a testament to inventiveness over restriction.

Note that such art is reflexive, querying itself even while moving gingerly forward, fighting shy of certainty. Mai-Thu Perret's ongoing project *The Crystal Frontier* (begun in 1999) similarly redrafts modernist histories in the service of a vigilant though provisional communitarian feminism. Its narrative spine is seemingly this: a group of Palm Springs women have quit the birdcage of housewifery for life as New Ponderosa Year Zero, a community seeking to get back to nature and hands-on craft in the New Mexico desert, where their collective life – an extension of twentieth-century idealist communes – refracts through those diary entries and objects the Swiss artist presents in galleries and museums. But this is an uneasy, deliberately unresolved, anti-industrial romanticism. Perret's displays, particularly in their mixture of faceless mannequins (seemingly representing the women) and handmade objects (seemingly bulletins from their world of production), weirdly elide the functional and the commodified aesthetic, and the artist evidently relishes this irresolution. Indeed her whole approach, dusted with Bauhaus and constructivist references, clouds her stance on modernist communitarians, who've historically imploded melancholically, but, again, tended not to organize along female-only lines. It's a possible future wrapped in a possible past, harshly illuminating real futures and pasts; if it only spurs a think-through of its own achievement's conditionals, then Perret's work is likely done. The new modernism's ethos would frequently seem to involve being a believer and an agnostic simultaneously. Writing recently on Courbet for *Artforum*, the German painter Michael Krebber described one strand of contemporary painting as 'practising Kandinskian formalism in the full knowledge that it cannot possibly work out, but sticking with it all the same'. True enough of, say, Victoria Morton and Joanne Greenbaum, but it needn't be Kandinskian. Consider Anselm Reyle's accelerated rush, in recent years, through a boggling range of postwar styles: Yves Kleinesque chromatic reduction, gestural and lyrical abstraction, colour-field, Minimalism, post-Minimalism. The Berlin-based painter's canvases enact a kind of double-imaging, being hot, sensual, engaging and insincere. Reyle will crumple coloured foil, wrap it around canvas and seal it in a shallow Perspex box, and the result is both unarguably gorgeous and blatantly cheap (at least to make). He'll arrange a changeably glowing spaghetti of multicoloured neon tubes in a darkened gallery and fulfil the conditions of 'drawing in space', while refusing any of the momentum, the will-to-newness, of high modernist experiment. His art, much of which originates in everyday found objects that Reyle liked the look of, is beautifully belated and a tribute to what continues to move us when it shouldn't.

Not that it can't be equally desirable to numb the heart as warm it. US painter Wade Guyton filters motifs through impersonal technologies, enacting a cold reprising of geometric abstraction. Behind his accretions of coloured grids and displaced stand-alone objects is time spent leafing through an immensity of books, particularly volumes on modern art. But closer to the surface there are the unlikely potentialities of flatbed scanners and industrial-size Epson printers, which, with their tendency to create unpredictable blurs and dribbles, scratches and pops when bolts of folded canvas are fed into them, have become Guyton's distaff paintbrush, simulating expressivity in a way that tickles residual nostalgia for the artist's hand (Reyle, too, paints his dribbles on afterwards) before we realize that we're looking at mindless contingency. Confliction seems close to the heart of Guyton's art: his recent 'paintings' of large black Xs on unprimed canvas, for instance, are geometric abstraction reprised as muscular inaction, their motif halfway between a kiss (feeling) and a cross-out (refusal). They feel dead, but there's something paradoxically bracing, even potentially redemptive, about seeing painting purge itself so thoroughly of humanism.

Looking at Guyton's art, one can seem to be zooming backwards, watching the discredited enthusiasm and willpower that fired the modern era shear away like so much dead skin. In the case of Esther Stocker's paintings, photographs and installations, which similarly root themselves in abstraction, we're plunged into another kind of ground-zero uncertainty – one concerning a relation to physical space and distance. The Italian-born Stocker has been overt about this. Her recent show at London's Museum 52 was entitled 'What I Don't Know About Space', and, aside from black-and-white paintings in which grids fracture quietly along their axes and resemble distorting eight-bit graphics, its main stretch was a single, immersive installation. This was a room-filling riot of differently sized, predominantly V-shaped pieces of wood, covered in black gaffer tape and bursting forth from walls, floor and ceiling into the airspace, demarcating and seemingly measuring distances and angles; but, particularly when considered in tandem with the title, apparently doing so in a chaotic manner resembling a paranoid reflex action. We have been too bold, Stocker suggests, taken too much for granted that remains irresolute. We might need to start again from first principles; we might find that we cannot move forward from that. Again, modernism here presents itself as a temporal continuum to be entered at any point: a fossil field, of the sort implied by Goshka Macuga's installations. The Polish artist is perhaps best known for her pioneering collapse of the roles of artist and curator: since early in her career, she's presented cabinets and constructed environments devoting space to the practices of others, both living and dead, and to objects pulled from different cultural strata. But her work of late has increasingly overlaid theological and spiritualist concepts on to modernism, positing it as a spirit field – a land of ghosts – in, for instance, a carved sculpture of theosophist Madame Blavatsky levitating between two chairs (*Madame Blavatsky*, 2007). Her large-scale 2006 show at A Foundation in Liverpool, 'Sleep of Ulro', meanwhile, took the acclaimed sets of Robert Wiese's 1919 expressionist movie *The Cabinet of Doctor Caligari* as its starting point, setting mini-exhibitions, performances and theatrical tableaux within an architectural psychosphere.

Macuga, for all her increasingly dreamlike concepts of reanimation, appears devoted to a conception of the modern as sheer simultaneity: all its moments existing at once, quantum physics-style, in some accessible elsewhere, amenable to recombination. If this simultaneity descends from postmodernism, the contradistinctive issue for artists working today is what one does with the knowledge of it. In this regard it's not hard to see why, aside from its surpassingly cool Möbius-strip narrative structure, Robert Zemeckis's 1980s cinematic trilogy *Back to the Future* has been increasingly saluted of late by young artists and curators. (M/M Paris, the artist partnership, arguably got there first, lifting its typeface when designing the logo for the 2003 Lyon Biennial, 'It Happened Tomorrow'.) Working on the basis that hindsight is 20/20, today's take on modernism might be considered a fantasy of going back, Marty McFly-like, into vanished moments and tweaking them before they explode. Or, perhaps more accurately, of dragging past into present – 'reloading it', as Bourriaud would have it – hymning its potentials, exposing its failings for careful repair; and, in the process, tentatively resurrecting something that feels like hope.

Martin Herbert, 'Sifting Defunct Modernity in Search of Something Useful', *TATE etc.*, no. 15 (Spring 2009) 62–8.

Gilda Williams
It Was What It Was: Modern Ruins//2010

A word close to 'ruin' is 'derelict', yet these two terms prompt opposite reactions – a ruin inspiring poetry, the other calling for demolition. What exactly is the difference between them? London is host to a thriving sub-city of derelict architectures – abandoned pubs, boarded terraces, trails of vacated shops – but, arguably, few real ruins. Go to www.battersea-powerstation.com to see how one of London's most impressive and last remaining industrial ruins is on the verge of reclamation, to be swamped by the usual crop of high-rise residential blocks. Watch the words 'Pruitt' and 'Igoe' form as if by magic before your very eyes. The demolition begun on 16 March 1972 of the doomed Pruitt-Igoe residential towers of St Louis – whose dark, deserted, concrete 'streets in the sky' proved ideal hunting ground for a flourishing community of muggers – was claimed by postmodernist architectural historian Charles Jencks as 'the day modernism died'.

Weirdly, the successive era, our contemporary period, probably also began with a ruin: the collapse of the Twin Towers in 2001, which ushered in a whole new (and still unresolved) world order. Weirder still, both Pruitt-Igoe and the Twin Towers were built by the same architect, Minoru Yamasaki, giving him the dubious title of the most significant architect of cataclysmic ruins of the late twentieth- and early twenty-first centuries. He died in 1986, and was thus spared having to watch, for the second time, another of his architectural achievements spectacularly razed to the ground. We might, however, keep an eye on his other, still-standing edifices (for example, King Fahad International Airport in Saudi Arabia) in case another should perish and take the rest of the world down with it.

For almost two decades after it closed as a power station in 1981, Bankside stood like a ruin on London's Southbank, eventually to be reborn in 2000 as a testament to the unexpected mass appeal of modern art [Tate Modern]. Art and ruins have entered into a close alliance, with artists regularly called in to 'do something' with unused yet still viable places that nobody else seems either foolhardy or imaginative enough to cope with. Back in the recession of the early 1990s, in 'Project Unité' curator Yves Aupetitallot invited artists including Jim Isermann, Philippe Parreno and Dominique Gonzalez-Foerster to 'do something' with Le Corbusier's crumbling masterwork, Unité d'Habitation, near Marseilles. At the time, Le Corbusier's twelve-storey social experiment stood half-empty; now it boasts a thriving community of modernist aficionados. In the summer of 2009, New York City's vacated Governor's Island, a former military site abandoned in 1995, hosted 'This World & Nearer Ones' curated by Mark Beasley and featuring 32 international artists; can the developers be far behind? On this site heading towards ruin, Teresa Margolles imported another ruin: *Shot-up Wall* (2008), a segment of cinderblock wall scarred with bullet holes and flecks of blood – the actual backdrop for a gang execution in the artist's home city of Culiacán, Mexico. In a work that is, one could say, the deserted ruin of the wall behind *The Execution of Emperor Maximilien* (1868–69), after Manet's exquisitely painted firing squad have all gone home and the heap of bodies been cleaned up, Margolles' brief length of wall returns us to one of Romanticism's most beloved paradoxes: as a fragment, a ruin is more loaded with meaning than when it was part of a whole.

Artists have traditionally demonstrated a remarkable willingness to live and work inside ruins too. Artist squats like those at Tacheles in Berlin and RAMPart in London save urban architecture from decay only to face eviction or, as Svetlana Boym describes Tacheles residents, to be reduced to playing bohemian extras in semi-dilapidated neighbourhoods, 'where Bavarian bus tours stop for a taste of exotic Berlin radicalism'. Artists have been upgrading peripheral London squalor into profitable building stock since at least the days when Constable moved to the then semi-rural, now posh area of Hampstead, or the 'young British artists' colonized Hoxton. But in our current, exponential world population boom, estimated to hit eight billion by 2025 – that's twice as many people as inhabited the earth in 1974 – where are artists leading us?

Wherever there's space. For example, beneath bridges, like the one where Ian Davenport's colourful *Poured Lines* (2006) now makes the grey underbelly of the Western Bridge in Southwark more hospitable. Or we may follow Conrad Shawcross' *Chord* (2009) – his complex, rainbow-like rope-weaving machine – underground, into an abandoned railway line complete with shreds of World War II-era travel posters (actually 1990s-era copies, pasted up during a filmshoot) and situated in the heart of London's City where aboveground office rentals start at £40 per sq ft. Ruins have always been replete with nostalgia; how much more so in the twenty-first century, when cities like London just can't afford them? In future, real ruins may be replaced only by their memory. Albert Speer lamented that European modern architecture would produce deeply disappointing ruins; in fact we seem destined to produce few locally at all, just endless lost ruins.

Invisible ruins are the subject of Florin Tudor's *Vacaresti* (2006), in which the Romanian artist traces with sticks, wire and string the outlines of the once magnificent eighteenth-century Vacaresti monastery outside Bucharest, which Ceausescu demolished in 1985. Tudor's performance – as he walks in straight lines, abruptly turning corners, across a barren field – is a 'nonument' to a mistreated, absent ruin. In *Kant Walks* (2005), Danish artist Joachim Koester retraces the legendary strolls of the philosopher through his beloved Königsberg, renamed Kaliningrad by the Soviets in 1945 after the Nazis had burned down the synagogues and RAF bombs had flattened most of the old town. Koester drifts through Kantian psychogeographies in this unrecognizable city, surrounded by battered Pruitt-Igoe-like tower blocks and the vast and crumbling communist cultural centre, built in 1970 over the ruins of the former Königsberg castle and hopelessly sinking into the castle's former dungeons: one doomed ideology replaced by another.

Ever since Italian Renaissance writers fantasized about reviving the glories of Ancient Rome evidenced in their grand and broken antiquities, ruins have been put to work for politico-cultural causes. In summer 2009, the *New York Times* ran a lengthy piece titled 'Ruins of the Second Gilded Age', a cautionary visual essay on the greed and waste of the collapsed US building industry. Featuring splendid colour photographs by Portuguese photographer Edgar Martins of unfinished homes and abandoned building sites, the article revealed a generation of twenty-first-century US ghost towns, lost in capitalist limbo between boomtown prosperity and quiet devastation. It turned out, to the dismay of some, that the photographs had been digitally altered to enhance their sense of emptiness and drama, resulting in (semi-)artificial ruins constructed via the miracles of Photoshop. Nothing new there: Martins, like his Romantic counterparts over 200 years ago, had adopted artificial ruins for aesthetic pleasure but also to drive home a political point. In the same way, late eighteenth-century English architects of false ruins were commissioned to erect fragments of monasteries and mediaeval castles in pleasure gardens not only for their beauty, but also because their patrons delighted in seeing the outmoded institutions behind these half-buildings – the papacy and feudal aristocracy – in visible collapse. The artificial ruins announced to visitors their owners' liberal politics – not unlike the Liberal Democrat sticker in your neighbour's front window.

Robert Kusmirowski's *Bunker* (2009), is another artificial ruin: a reconstructed World War II bolt-hole staged in fetishistic detail (built by a professional forger and artist) that points to a longing for both old-fashioned war and future apocalypse, though without the visionary exuberance of Dominique Gonzalez-Foerster's *TH.2058*, commissioned for Tate Modern's Turbine Hall in 2008. Her mass sleeping quarters, stocked and ready for emergency action in a future London evidently on the verge of catastrophe, seemed to return Bankside to the empty, bunker-like ruin it once was, erasing its brief history as a museum and visualizing Benjamin's idea of ruins as offering a 'prophetic' picture, one in which 'all that lies in store for us has become the past'. This before-and-after effect performed by ruins was also apparent in Jeremy Deller's *It Is What It Is: Conversations about Iraq* of 2009. Here, after a series of talks on the Iraq experience held at New York's New Museum, Deller went on a road show across the US with two vehicles: a massive, top-of-the-line, shining RV 'Chalet'; and the husk of a rusted and crumpled, bombed-out car exported from Baghdad. Here, Deller updates one of Pop art's most treasured subjects, the American automobile, by parading before ambivalent citizens the before-and-after effects of US excess and its petrol-reliant romance with the open road.

A ruin is said to result from some man-made or natural disaster – an earthquake in Lisbon; Reformationist zeal in St Andrews; a dioxin spill in an abandoned town in Ohio. So much human failure and misery from the recent past is tied up with ruins: postwar Hiroshima, post-meltdown Chernobyl, post-communist Eastern Bloc, post-Katrina New Orleans. The remains of Berlin in 1945, or Detroit and Beirut today. Which exactly is the calamity that has determined contemporary artists' interest in ruins? The simple answer would be the collapse of modernist ideals, and the nagging sensation that it was all just an elaborate, late-Enlightenment folly whose optimism, moreover, we have lost forever. This was literally staged in *The Philosophy of Time Travel* (2007), an installation by Edgar Arceneaux, Rodney McMillian and others at Harlem's Studio Museum, wherein Brancusi's *Endless Column* (1938) is replicated as a ruin – having finally reached its announced end and, toppling under the weight of its own sky-high ambitions, crashed through the roof. In Cyprien Gaillard's *Belief in the Age of Disbelief* (2005), the artist presented Le Corbusier's Unité flourishing in an arcadia of greenery; in fact this is just how the architect first imagined it, surrounded by Bois de Boulogne-type overgrowth and not the stubble of ugly low-rise housing surrounding the Marseillaise monument today – hinting at the closet Romantic Le Corbusier actually was. Postmodernist architectural theorist Colin Rowe surmised that the carefree, perfectly contented beings whom Le Corbusier drew occupying his clean sparse flats and tending his jungle-like balcony gardens were just the modernist equivalents of the Romantics' noble savage: want-free beings relocated in idealized forest homes in the sky (the same ideological creatures recently seen, ten feet tall and tinted blue, in James Cameron's *Avatar* [2009]).

The parallel between the state of the house and the state of the inhabitants' frame of mind has been the leitmotif of so many gothic tales centring on ruins, from Poe's *The Fall of the House of Usher* (1839), to *Grey Gardens* (1975), Albert and David Maysles' documentary of the long-declined high-society Beale family (socialite mother Edie and daughter Edith, relatives of Jaqueline Kennedy Onassis) who live in a spectacularly dilapidated villa on Long Island's southern Gold Coast, the fading backdrop for the pairs' own mental deterioration. In Ulla von Brandenburg's *Singspiel* (2009), filmed in Le Corbusier's single-family masterpiece Villa Savoye outside Paris, built in 1931, the now abandoned home becomes a set for family melodrama. To populate Villa Savoye with a singing and performing family is to contradict its very spirit; theatricality and modernism do not mix, as Michael Fried once emphatically made clear. Vintage photographs of the house never show any human residents, who probably would have looked gaudy and out of place there. Apparently the house began falling into ruin almost immediately; the victim of experimental building techniques, Villa Savoye was shabbily built, leaky and poorly insulated. According to von Brandenburg, the Savoye family was not happy there. A tense, eight-year correspondence between Madame Savoye and the architect sees her endlessly complaining about the detrimental effects that the cold house is having on her frail young son, whose pneumonial condition was made worse by the draughty architectural masterpiece. Le Corbusier eventually grows impatient – what is one child's health in the face of the world's finest architecture? The villa was eventually abandoned in the 1940s and virtually ignored until around 1963, when Corbusier himself insisted on its preservation. If we can finally define a ruin as an architectural site whose inhabitants were forced out, whereas the derelict site is a place so unwelcoming its residents packed up and left voluntarily, Villa Savoye, one of the twentieth century's purest and most emblematic architectures, was by this definition just another derelict building, not a ruin.

For Georg Simmel, writing in 1911 ['*Die Ruine*'], a ruin is a site where nature and humankind work together to form a collaborative work, a vision evoked in Robert Smithson's lecture/performance *Hotel Palenque* (1973). There the artist verbalized humankind's side of Simmel's bargain by reading grand architectural efforts into this modest, abandoned cinderblock shell. In Smithson's words and 43 colour slides, the Hotel is forever preserved, reborn as legendary jungle shrine to some Aztec god of entropy. Shifting in tone throughout – from satirist to poet, explorer, dumb American tourist – Smithson effectively follows in the footsteps of the many novelists and dreamers who, since the dawn of modernity, envisioned a depopulated world reclaimed to beauty by nature. From Mary Shelley's *The Last Man* (1826), to Richard Jefferies' *After London, or Wild England* of 1885, to J.G. Ballard's *The Ultimate City* in 1978, artists and writers have fantasized about the entirety of humankind perishing by some happy magic, leaving our cities to collapse into what Benjamin called 'irresistible decay'. William Morris, remembering with fondness the imagined end of London described by Jefferies, wrote of the 'absurd hopes that curled around my heart' as he read of the imagined cataclysmic end of the city. Why was Morris so comforted by the possibility of mass extermination? How can mankind, as Benjamin once asked, 'experience its own destruction as an aesthetic pleasure of the first order'?

Of course, any problem plaguing humankind – war, global warming, economic instability, unrequited love, thinning hair – would be miraculously washed away under a powerful carpet of weed vegetation, wild dogs and spectacular rodents. In *Dead Cities* (2005), Mike Davis updates Jefferies' nineteenth-century vision based on the evidence presented in *New Scientist* in 1996, which set out to describe, with scientific accuracy, how long it would take for all traces of mankind to be swept away once nature got the upper hand. The answer: 500 years – tops – with almost everything disappearing in well under a hundred. How pleasing to imagine kestrels and red-tailed hawks occupying the immense owlery of Canary Wharf, all its windows long blown-out and towering over a forest of buddleia, an imported plant to Britain so rapacious it penetrates into mortar to extract its moisture and is able to grow out of rooftops, pavements and empty swimming pools. The return to nature in the evacuated city of Pripyat, Ukraine, adjacent to Chernobyl, has been even hastier than scientists predicted; in 25 short years the city has been almost fully reclaimed. The football pitch, for example, is now a thriving little oval-shaped forest, flanked by decrepit bleachers: a mysterious ruin where a lonely visitor might sit and watch it grow.

Gilda Williams, 'It Was What It Was: Modern Ruins', *Art Monthly*, no. 336 (May 2010) 1–4.

Within an industrial framework, time has

a completely different dimension than

it does in architecture, where

structures can last for over

a thousand years. In the

industrial sector

history speeds

by

–

a

dragonfly

that lives for one day

Bernd and Hilla Becher, 'Industrial Landscapes: In Conversation with Suzanne Lange', 2002

THE MILITARY-INDUSTRIAL SUBLIME

J.G. Ballard
A Handful of Dust//2006

Few people today visit Utah beach. The sand seems colder and flatter than anywhere else along the Normandy coast where the Allies landed on D-day. The town of Arromanches – a few miles to the east and closer to Omaha, Gold and Sword beaches – is a crowded theme park of war museums, cemeteries and souvenir shops, bunkers and bunting. Guide books in hand, tourists edge gingerly around the German gun emplacements and try to imagine what it was like to stare down the gun sights at the vast armada approaching the shore.

But Utah beach, on the western edge of the landing grounds, is silent. A few waves swill over the sand as if too bored to think of anything else. The coastal land seems lower than the sea, and fails to echo the sounds of war inside one's head.

Walking along the beach some years ago, I noticed a dark structure emerging from the mist ahead of me. Three storeys high, and larger than a parish church, it was one of the huge blockhouses that formed Hitler's Atlantic wall, the chain of fortifications that ran from the French coast all the way to Denmark and Norway. This blockhouse, as indifferent to time as the Pyramids, was a mass of black concrete once poured by the slave labourers of the Todt Organization, pockmarked by the shellfire of the attacking allied warships.

A flight of steps at its rear led me into the dank interior with its gun platforms and sinister letterbox view of the sea. Generations of tramps had dossed here, and in the stairwells were the remains of small fires, piles of ancient excrement and a vague stench of urine.

At first sight, the blockhouse reminded me of the German forts at Tsingtao, the beach resort in north China that my family visited in the 1930s. Tsingtao had been a German naval base during the first world war, and I was taken on a tourist trip to the forts, a vast complex of tunnels and gun emplacements built into the cliffs. The cathedral-like vaults with their hydraulic platforms resembled Piranesi's prisons, endless concrete galleries leading to vertical shafts and even further galleries. The Chinese guides took special pleasure in pointing out the bloody handprints of the German gunners driven mad by the British naval bombardment.

Years later, in that Utah beach blockhouse, I was looking at similar stains on the concrete walls, but the scattered rubbish and tang of urine made me think of structures closer to home in England – run-down tower blocks and motorway exit ramps, pedestrian underpasses sprung from the drawing boards of enlightened planners who would never have to live in or near them, and who were careful never to stray too far from their Georgian squares in the heart of heritage London.

From the rooftop barbette I looked along Utah Beach towards an identical blockhouse 800 yards away, and beyond that to the faint silhouette of a third. The Atlantic wall was only part of a huge system of German fortifications that included the Siegfried line, submarine pens and huge flak towers that threatened the surrounding land like lines of Teutonic knights. Almost all had survived the war and seemed to be waiting for the next one, left behind by a race of warrior scientists obsessed with geometry and death.

Death was what the Atlantic wall and Siegfried line were all about. Whenever I came across these grim fortifications along France's Channel coast and German border, I realized I was exploring a set of concrete tombs whose dark ghosts haunted the brutalist architecture so popular in Britain in the 1950s. Out of favour now, modernism survives in every high-rise sink estate of the time, in the Barbican development and the Hayward Gallery in London, in new towns such as Cumbernauld and the ziggurat residential blocks at the University of East Anglia.

But modernism of the heroic period, from 1920 to 1939, is dead, and it died first in the blockhouses of Utah beach and the Siegfried line. Yet in its heyday between the wars, modernism was a vast utopian project, and perhaps the last utopian project we will ever see, now that we are well aware that all utopias have their dark side.

Nazi Germany and Soviet Russia were two utopian projects that turned into the greatest dystopias the world has known. Modernism briefly survived them both, but lost its nerve in the 1960s when the municipal high-rise estates in St Louis, Missouri, were deemed social catastrophes and dynamited. However, I sometimes think that social catastrophe was what the dirt-poor residents secretly longed for.

Modernism's attempt to build a better world with the aid of science and technology now seems almost heroic. Bertolt Brecht, no fan of modernism, remarked that the mud, blood and carnage of the first world war trenches left its survivors longing for a future that resembled a white-tiled bathroom. Architects were in the vanguard of the new movement, led by Le Corbusier and the Bauhaus design school. The old models were thrown out. Function defined form, expressed in a pure geometry that the eye could easily grasp in its entirety. Above all, there should be no ornamentation. 'Less is more', was the war cry, to which Robert Venturi, avatar of the tricksy postmodernism that gave us the Sainsbury wing of the National Gallery, London, retorted: 'Less is a bore.'

But the modernists maintained that ornamentation concealed rather than embellished. Classical columns, pediments and pilasters defined a hierarchical order. Power and authority were separated from the common street by huge flights of steps that we were forced to climb on our way to law courts, parliaments and town halls. Gothic ornament, with all its spikes and barbs, expressed pain, Christ's crown of thorns and agony on the cross. The Gothic expressed our guilt, pointing to a heaven we could never reach. The Baroque was a defensive fantasy, architecture as aristocratic playpen, a set of conjuring tricks to ward off the Age of Reason.

So modernism was a breath of fresh air and possibility. Housing schemes, factories and office blocks designed by modernist architects were clear-headed and geometric, suggesting clean and unembellished lives for the people inside them. Gone were suburban pretension, mock-Tudor beams and columned porticos disguising modest front doors.

Hitler and Stalin were intrigued by modernism, which seemed part of a new world of aviation, radio, public health and mass consciousness. But the dictators were nervous of clear-headed people who thought for themselves. The Nazis promptly closed the Bauhaus when they came to power and turned it into an SS training school.

Modernism saw off the dictators, and among its last flings were Brasilia, the Festival of Britain and Corbusier's state capital buildings at Chandigarh in India. But it was dying on its pilotis, those load-bearing pillars with which Corbusier lifted his buildings into the sky. Its slow death can be seen, not only in the Siegfried line and the Atlantic wall, but in the styling of Mercedes cars, at once paranoid and aggressive, like mediaeval German armour. We see its demise in 1960s kitchens and bathrooms, white-tiled laboratories that are above all clean and aseptic, as if human beings were some kind of disease. We see its death in motorways and autobahns, stone dreams that will never awake, and in the turbine hall at that middle-class disco, Tate Modern – a vast totalitarian space that Albert Speer would have admired, so authoritarian that it overwhelms any work of art inside it.

Modernism was never popular in Britain – a little too frank for its repressed natives, except at lidos and the seaside, where people take their clothes off. The few modernist houses and apartments look genuinely odd. Why?

I have always admired modernism and wish the whole of London could be rebuilt in the style of Michael Manser's brilliant Heathrow Hilton. But I know that most people, myself included, find it difficult to be clear-eyed at all times and rise to the demands of a pure and unadorned geometry. Architecture supplies us with camouflage, and I regret that no one could fall in love inside the Heathrow Hilton. By contrast, people are forever falling in love inside the Louvre and the National Gallery.

All of us have our dreams to reassure us. Architecture is a stage set where we need to be at ease in order to perform. Fearing ourselves, we need our illusions to protect us, even if the protection takes the form of finials and cartouches, corinthian columns and acanthus leaves. Modernism lacked mystery and emotion, was a little too frank about the limits of human nature and never prepared us for our eventual end.

But all is not lost for admirers of modernism. They should visit the mortuary island of San Michele in the Venice lagoon, where many pioneers of modernism such as Igor Stravinsky, Serge Diaghilev and Ezra Pound are interred. After taking the ferry, you disembark at a gloomy landing stage worthy of Böcklin's Island of the Dead. This is a place beyond hope, of haunted gateways and melancholy statues.

But then, in the heart of the cemetery, there is a sudden lightening of tone, and you find you are strolling through what might be a modern suburb of Tunis or Tel Aviv. The lines of family tombs resemble cheerful vacation bungalows, airy structures of white walls and glass that might have been designed by Le Corbusier or Richard Neutra. One could holiday for a long time in these pleasant villas, and a few of us probably will.

So, there is one place where modernism triumphs. As in the cases of the Pyramids and the Taj Mahal, the Siegfried line and the Atlantic wall, death always calls on the very best architects.

J.G. Ballard, 'A Handful of Dust', *The Guardian* (20 March 2006) 16.

Paul Virilio
Bunker Archaeology//1975

[...] When calling to mind the reasons that made the bunkers so appealing to me almost twenty years ago, I see it clearly now as a case of intuition and also as a convergence between the reality of the structure and the fact of its implantation alongside the ocean: a convergence between my awareness of spatial phenomena – the strong pull of the shores – and their being the locus of the works of the 'Atlantic Wall' (*Atlantikwall*) facing the open sea, facing out into the void.

It all started – it was a discovery in the archaeological sense of the term – along the beach south of Saint-Guénolé during the summer of 1958. I was leaning against a solid mass of concrete, which I had previously used as a *cabana*; all the usual seaside games had become a total bore; I was vacant in the middle of my vacation and my gaze extended out over the horizon of the ocean, over the perspective of sand between the rocky massifs of Saint-Guénolé and the sea wall in the port of Guilvinec to the south. There were not many people around, and scanning the horizon like that, with nothing interrupting my gaze, brought me full round to my own vantage point, to the heat and to this massive lean-to buttressing my body: this solid inclined mass of concrete, this worthless object, which up to then had managed to martial my interest only as a vestige of the Second World War, only as an illustration for a story, the story of total war.

So I turned around for an instant to look at what my field of vision onto the sea had not offered up: the heavy grey mass where traces of planks lined up along the inclined ramp like a tiny staircase. I got up and decided to have a look around this fortification as if I had seen it for the first time, with its embrasure flush with the sand, behind the protective screen, looking out onto the Breton port, aiming today at inoffensive bathers, its rear defence with a staggered entrance and its dark interior in the blinding light of the gun's opening toward the sea.

I was most impressed by a feeling, internal and external, of being immediately crushed. The battered walls sunk into the ground gave this small blockhouse a solid base; a dune had invaded the interior space, and the thick layer of sand over the wooden floor made the place ever narrower. Some clothes and bicycles had been hidden here; the object no longer made the same sense, though there was still protection here.

A complete series of cultural memories came to mind: the Egyptian mastabas, the Etruscan tombs, the Aztec structures ... as if this piece of artillery fortification could be identified as a funeral ceremony, as if the Todt Organization could manage only the organization of a religious space ...

This was nothing but a broad outline, but from then on my curiosity would be quickened; my vacation had just come to an end, and I could guess that these littoral boundary stones were to teach me much about the era, and much about myself.

On that day I decided to inspect the Breton coasts, most often on foot along the high-tide line, further and further; by car as well, in order to examine distant promontories, north toward Audierne and Brest, southward to Concarneau.

My objective was solely archaeological. I would hunt these grey forms until they would transmit to me a part of their mystery, a part of the secret a few phrases could sum up: why would these extraordinary constructions, compared to the seaside villas, not be perceived or even recognized? Why this analogy between the funeral archetype and military architecture? Why this insane situation looking out over the ocean? This waiting before the infinite oceanic expanse? Until this era, fortifications had always been oriented towards a specific, staked-out objective: the defence of a passageway, a pass, steps, valleys or ports, as in the case of the La Rochelle towers; it had always been a question of 'guarding,' as easy to understand as the caretaker's role. Whereas here, walking daily along kilometre after kilometre of beach, I would happen upon these concrete markers at the summit of dunes, cliffs, across beaches, open, transparent, with the sky playing between the embrasure and the entrance, as if each casemate were an empty ark or a little temple minus the cult. It was indeed the whole littoral that had been organized around these successive bearings. You could walk day after day along the seaside and never once lose sight of these concrete altars built to face the void of the oceanic horizon.

The immensity of this project is what defies common sense; total war was revealed here in its mythic dimension. The course I had begun to run, over the banks of *Festung Europa* (Fortress Europe), was going to introduce me into the reality of Occidental geometry and the function of equipment on sites, continents and the world.

Everything was suddenly vast. The continental threshold had become a boulevard – the linearity of my exploration; sun and sand were now personal territory that I was beginning to like more and more. This continuous band of dunes and pebbles and the sharp crest of the cliffs along the coast fit into a nameless country where the three interchanges were glimpsed: the oceanic and aerial space along with the end of emerged land. The only bearings I had for this trip from the south to the north of Europe were these *stelae* whose meaning was still unsure. A long history was curled up here. These concrete blocks were in fact the final throw-offs of the history of frontiers, from the Roman limes to the Great Wall of China; the bunkers, as ultimate military surface architecture, had shipwrecked at lands' limits, at the precise moment of the sky's arrival in war; they marked off the horizontal littoral, the continental limit. History had changed course one final time before jumping into the immensity of aerial space.

My activities often led me into teeming ports, and what most surprised and intrigued me there was finding once again in the middle of courtyards and gardens my concrete shelters; their blind, low mass and rounded profile were out of tune with the urban environment. As I concentrated on these forms in the middle of apartment buildings, in courtyards and in public squares, I felt as though a subterranean civilization had sprung up from the ground. This architecture's modernness was countered by its abandoned, decrepit appearance. These objects had been left behind and were colourless; their grey cement relief was silent witness to a warlike climate. Like in certain works of fiction – a spacecraft parked in the middle of an avenue announcing the war of the worlds, the confrontation with inhuman species – these solid masses in the hollows of urban spaces, next to the local schoolhouse or bar, shed new light on what 'contemporary' has come to mean.

Why continue to be surprised at Le Corbusier's forms of modern architecture? Why speak of 'brutalism'? And, above all, why this ordinary habitat, so very ordinary over so many years?

These heavy grey masses with sad angles and no openings – excepting the air inlets and several staggered entrances – brought to light much better than many manifestos the urban and architectural redundancies of this postwar period that had just reconstructed to a tee the destroyed cities. The anti-aircraft blockhouses pointed out another lifestyle, a rupture in the apprehension of the real. The blue sky had once been heavy with the menace of rumbling bombers, spangled too with the deafening explosions of artillery fire. This immediate comparison between the urban habitat and the shelter, between the ordinary apartment building and the abandoned bunkers in the hearts of the ports through which I was travelling, was as strong as a confrontation, a collage of two dissimilar realities. The anti-aircraft shelters spoke to me of men's anguish and the dwellings of the normative systems that constantly reproduce the city, the cities, the urbanistic.

The blockhouses were anthropomorphic; their figures recalled those of bodies. The residential units were but arbitrary repetitions of a model – a single, identical, orthogonal, parallelepipedal model. The casemate, so easily hidden in the hollow of the coastal countryside, was scandalous here, and its modernness was due less to the originality of its silhouette than to the extreme triviality of the surrounding architectural forms. The curved profile brought with it into the harbour's quarters a trace of the curves of dunes and nearby hills, and there, in this naturalness, was the scandal of the *bunker*. [...]

Paul Virilio, extract from *Bunker Archéologie* (Paris: Centre Georges Pompidou and Centre de Création Industrielle, 1975); trans. George Collins, *Bunker Archaeology* (New York: Princeton Architectural Press, 1994) 10–13.

James Lingwood
The Weight of Time//2002

On a cold December day in 1968, Bernd Becher took the German gallery owner Konrad Fischer and the visiting American artist Robert Smithson on a field trip. They set off from Düsseldorf, where Fischer had recently opened his gallery, and headed for Oberhausen, some twenty miles away, one of the largest industrial complexes in the Ruhr district, itself one of the most concentrated areas of industrial production in Western Europe at that time.

The field trip was for the benefit of Smithson, who was scheduled to open his first one-person exhibition in Europe in Fischer's gallery in Andreastrasse in a couple of weeks' time. In the summer of 1968 Fischer had invited Smithson to show, perhaps as a consequence of his participation in the groundbreaking 'Minimal Art' exhibition at the Gemeentemuseum in The Hague in May 1968. Smithson accepted the invitation and wrote back in August

> I think I would like to do an 'indoor earthwork' (a nonsite) based on some rock or sand deposits in Germany – if you know of any quarries, we could collect the material when I get over there. Slag heaps, slate, coal, limestone, shale or other mining areas could be used. After I get the gallery plans, I'll send you my plans for the nonsite 'containers' – that hopefully you could have fabricated before I arrive in November. Some geological maps of German rock and mineral deposits would be a help ...[1]

Oberhausen was a site which Bernd and Hilla Becher already knew well. They had begun to work there in 1963 (photographing the blast furnaces at Gutehoffnungshütte West), and continued between 1967 and 1969, this time concentrating on the other blast furnace, Gutehoffnungshütte Ost. It was an area with which, for a very different reason, Fischer was intimately familiar, since his grandfather's family had owned the entire complex as part of one of the oldest and largest steel companies in Germany, Hanel & Lueg. Although Smithson had made several excursions to quarries and mining areas as well as distressed industrial sites in his native New Jersey, the journey to Oberhausen was his first prospecting visit to an industrial site in Europe.

The rolls of film which Smithson took with his Instamatic refract the Oberhausen site through the restless lens of Smithson's eye. There is no particular route or narrative development within these photographs. What appears to be the first roll follows a pathway into one of the entrances to the site and includes details of trodden down grass, stone and slag, mud imprinted with the tracks of heavy lorries, as well as photographs of Smithson with his fellow prospectors. The other rolls contain many more close-ups of industrial wreckage, pools of solidified asphalt, mounds of broken-up slag, and cracked earth. Smithson kept close to the elemental details of the site, though these photos are interspersed with occasional glimpses through the smog of the blast furnaces which had spewed out all this waste. The sequences of prosaic black and white snapshots do more than describe an industrial wasteland. They conjure up an almost apocalyptic vision of an exhausted world. Oberhausen isn't so much documented as subjected to a temporal transformation, characteristic of Smithson's penchant for dramatic mental leaps in time and space, from the prehistoric (before anything had emerged from the primordial soup) to the post-historic (when everything would return to a similarly undifferentiated state).

The wasted landscapes Smithson found at the edges of the Oberhausen site matched perfectly the exhortation of one of Smithson's favourite writers, T.E. Hulme: 'Great men, go to the outside, away from the Room, and wrestle with the cinders.'[2] By the late 1960s, Smithson was already clear that his operational zone of preference was away from 'the Room', at the periphery, where he could locate 'the memory-traces of an abandoned set of futures',[3] before bringing them back to the centre in the form of nonsites and displacements, films and writings which would collectively 'surmount the perimeters of the old sensibility'.[4]

Bernd and Hilla Becher saw the Oberhausen site differently. They knew the whole Ruhr district intimately, and had reconnoitred every industrial complex in the area, large and small. They had begun to photograph in the mining area around Siegen, where Bernd had grown up, in the early 1960s and quickly formulated working methods which remain essentially unchanged today. In the Robert Smithson papers in the Archives of American Art, there is a single black and white photographic print given to Smithson by the Bechers: a panoramic view of the industrial landscape of Oberhausen, with the coal mining complex Zeche Concordia in the foreground, and Gutehoffnungshütte Ost and West, the two huge steel-making factories, in the background. Many of the types of industrial buildings which were central to the photographic project of the Bechers feature in this panorama: winding-towers and water towers, coal silos, cooling towers, gas holders and blast furnaces, as well as factory buildings of many different kinds. This overview is reproduced on the first pages of their 1971 book *Die Architektur der Förder- und Wassertürme* in juxtaposition to an engraving of an industrial landscape from 1800, a comprehensive summary of forms of buildings clustered in a heavily industrialized landscape.

By the time of the trip, the Bechers had already conceived their immensely ambitious, open-ended project – nothing less than to create a quasi-encyclopaedic record of the vernacular buildings of the industrial age, first in their immediate region and then beyond. Since the end of the Second World War, photography in Germany had turned away from the shattered landscape towards manipulated 'subjective' worlds. The Bechers faced out again, picking up the disrupted (and at the time largely forgotten) approach of the Neue Sachlichkeit. Sander's photographs of German citizens were a revelation and Blossfeldt's book of close-ups of plants and flowers, *Urformen der Kunst*, provided them with a precedent of precise description and delineation of different forms.

The terrain of the Bechers' project was the industrial world. Both the Bechers and Smithson shared a mutual fascination for the sites of heavy industry and an interest in a certain aesthetic ambiguity which issued from their uses of photography. They shared many friends amongst the rapidly evolving international art milieu of the late 1960s, including most notably Carl Andre and Sol LeWitt, both of whom had already showed in Fischer's gallery. They exchanged works. The Bechers remember giving Smithson several photographs of cooling towers which apparently hung in his bedroom (a painting by Kosuth based on a blow-up of the dictionary entry for 'Entropy' was in the dining room). Smithson gave the Bechers a small nonsite in 1969, for which they gathered the slag themselves in Oberhausen. But the modus operandi of the artists could hardly have been more different. The photographic tool of the Bechers was a wieldy plate camera (first an old wooden plate camera, and then a Plaubel 13/18) which enabled them to make photographs with an exceptional degree of definition. Smithson on the other hand used an Instamatic camera in an apparently casual manner to produce small snapshots. The Bechers arrived to photograph at a particular site following detailed research and they methodically applied a predetermined formal system. Smithson arrived somewhere in a far less deliberate way, improvising on the themes he had coursing around his fertile mind. Where the Bechers saw forms and structures within a working industrial complex, Smithson sought out formlessness, disintegration and waste.

Oberhausen was a particularly rich seam for the Bechers to mine. Though they had already travelled extensively through Northern Europe as their project began to take shape, Oberhausen was one of the largest sites closest to home. They worked there extensively between 1968 and 1972, making as many visits as possible when the weather conditions were right (essentially a neutral and cloudless sky – nothing could be more different than the murky atmosphere in Smithson's snaps). At the time, they had begun to exhibit in Germany and to find their work placed within the context of conceptual art and they were building up groupings of buildings for their first book, *Anonyme Skulpturen*, published in 1970. The book enabled the Bechers for the first time to present many of the key types in their natural history of industrial buildings or objects. In the back of the book, they articulate with typical conciseness their intentions. 'In this book we show objects predominantly instrumental in character whose shapes are the results of calculation and whose processes of development are optically evident. They are generally buildings whose anonymity is accepted to be the style. Their peculiarities originate not in spite of, but because of the lack of design.'[5]

The objects the Bechers presented were organized into families of forms, sequenced to emphasize the way in which different vernacular forms evolved in response to different needs and developing technologies. The categories they chose to present in this first publication were lime kilns, cooling towers, blast furnaces, winding towers, water towers, gasholders and silos. The book included photographs from Oberhausen in several of these sections, amongst them portraits of many of the individual buildings which feature in the overview photograph of Oberhausen such as the cooling towers, winding towers, water towers and gasholders from Zeche Concordia and the blast furnaces at Gutehoffnungshütte.

The Oberhausen 'archive' gradually found its way into different families of types. The Bechers were more interested in showing how one form related to another in terms of form than in terms of function. But occasionally, the family of buildings on one particular site have also been shown together, as was the case with the Gutehoffnungshütte site which was the subject of an exhibition of photographs at Konrad Fischer's gallery in 1976.[6]

The first book by the Bechers already embodies their refined aesthetic of hard facts. Each building or structure has been photographed and presented in as clear, as frontal and as apparently unmediated a form as possible. Each seems to present itself directly to the camera, so that the character of each building is as clearly delineated as possible. They share similarities, but they are never precisely the same. As Hilla Becher has stated, 'You can only see the differences between the objects when they are close together, because they are sometimes very subtle. All the objects in one family resemble each other, they are similar. But they also have a very special individuality.'[7]

At the same time, the sequencing of the photographs expresses the relationship of the individual variations to basic, general forms in a vernacular equivalent to the development of different sculptural languages in mediaeval Europe. It may appear that the Bechers' work is cool, controlled and detached. But rarely can such apparent detachment have been allied to such enduring passion – in this case to attest to the endless variations of vernacular industrial form – and rarely can such apparent stylelessness have evolved into such a singular style. Their immersion in the overlooked and unaestheticized landscapes of the industrial era is not based on a mental projection of time, as it is with Smithson, but on a desire to engage the viewer in the mentality of a particular time – the era of heavy industrial production.

Days after their joint expedition to Oberhausen, Smithson's exhibition opened at the Galerie Konrad Fischer. He presented two works. The sculpture he had described to Fischer became the most ambitious articulation of his 'nonsite' idea to date: *Nonsite (Oberhausen)* (1968). In one of Smithson's characteristically laconic inversions, he deposited bits of slag, the waste product from the industrial process used to produce steel, in five steel bins, painted white. The slag, collected on the field trip, filled each container like specimens in a geological display. At the same time, protruding from the top bar of the stratified steel, they look like ranges of disrupted landmass.

On the wall to the side of the containers Smithson installed five panels. Each panel had the same detail of the map of the Oberhausen site, a description of the site written by Smithson, and five photographs from the rolls taken on the field trip.[8] Different kinds of evidence rubbed up against each other – hard geological facts, photographic impressions and cartographic description – in a display which mirrors Smithson's own restless mind as it oscillates between microcosm and macrocosm, scientific specimen and imaginative projection.

The second work Smithson exhibited in Düsseldorf in December 1968 was a lump of asphalt, picked up on site and deposited on the floor of the gallery without further artistic intervention and without any additional information. Asphalt is the residue from refining coal, just as slag is the by-product of steel-making. Nothing in Smithson's previous work quite prepares us for this radical gesture, except perhaps the playful, provocative tone of his writing. *Asphalt Lump* is a post-industrial readymade, an object of pure impurity, a black formless counterpoint to Duchamp's white shrine. No bin contained the lump, it was framed only by a white rectangle painted on the gallery floor. It just sits there, an absurd specimen of solidified formlessness, the very embodiment of entropy – that state of inert equivalence which fascinated Smithson and which was the polar opposite of the Bechers' interest in the differentiation of objects.

Smithson had been prospecting with friends and fellow artists in the US since the early 1960s. Usually accompanied by Nancy Holt, and most often in the hinterlands of New Jersey, Smithson made expeditions with, amongst others, Carl Andre, Donald Judd, Michael Heizer, Sol LeWitt, Robert Morris, (Andre and LeWitt were also close friends of the Bechers) as well as Virginia Dwan in whose New York gallery he would present a substantial nonsite exhibition in February 1969. In one of his first nonsites (*A Nonsite, Franklin, New Jersey*) realized in May 1968, Smithson juxtaposed an aerial photograph of the site cut up into five sections with five bins containing mineral deposits from Franklin. In a text which was part of the work, he wrote, 'The map is three times smaller than the nonsite. Tours to sites are possible. The five outdoor sites are not contained by any limiting parts – therefore they are chaotic sites, regions of dispersal, places without a Room - elusive order prevails, the substrata is disrupted (see snapshots of the five shots).'

During this period of intense development from his quasi-minimal sculpture, Smithson articulated the formulation of the site/nonsite dialectic in a key essay published in *Artforum* in September 1968, 'A Sedimentation of the Mind – Earth Projects'. The essay foregrounds more intensively than any of Smithson's previous writing his obsession with structures and their inevitable collapse: 'A bleached and fractured world surrounds the artist. To organize this mass of corrosion into patterns, grids and subdivisions is an aesthetic process that has scarcely been touched ... construction takes on the look of destruction; perhaps that's why certain architects hate bulldozers and steam shovels. They seem to turn the terrain into unfinished cities of organized wreckage ... The actual disruption of the earth's crust is at times very compelling, and seems to confirm Heraclitus' Fragment 124: "The most beautiful world is like a heap of rubble tossed down in confusion."' And then later: 'The strata of the Earth is a jumbled museum. Embedded in the sediment is a text that contains limits and boundaries which evade the rational order, and social structures which confine it. In order to read the rocks, we must become conscious of geologic time ...'[9]

Smithson's interest in 'geologic time' echoes the strata of time which the great French historian Fernand Braudel described as coexisting within the present. Braudel articulated three different temporal modes: the time of the individual, which he called 'biological time', the 'social time' of human cultures, their mental structures, beliefs, habits and customs and, finally, a much slower time of environmental, climatic and demographic change which he termed 'geographical time'. Smithson's interest in 'geologic time' echoes this final temporal mode of Braudel's but it also exceeds it, since geologic time was too slow and too deep to take any account of humankind at all. It stretched back to the cataclysmic movements of landmass and catastrophic shifts in temperature which preceded any signs of human life on earth.

His fascination with the elemental facts of geology had grown from his adolescent excursions to the Museum of Natural History in New York (a site to which he returned in the *Spiral Jetty* film) to the field trips with his co-artists until, by the end of 1968, he wanted to go further than the quasi-scientific observation and presentation of geologic time. He wanted not only to observe 'geologic' time but to imitate its vastness and depth: to play at being it. Informed by his research into landslides, avalanches and eruptions, he began to make drawings of these phenomena. The drawings projected imaginary flows of mud, asphalt and cement on to the landscape and a trilogy of actions emulating geological movements were performed in late 1969 and early 1970. *Asphalt Rundown* was realized in a quarry outside Rome in the autumn of 1969 (the location of the quarry on the run-down periphery of the epicentre of classical civilisation was particularly pleasing to Smithson), followed by *Concrete Pour* in a quarry near Chicago, and soon after a smaller scale work, *Glue Pour* in Vancouver.[10]

Smithson had stated in an interview: 'It is sort of interesting to take on the persona of a geologic agent where man actually becomes part of that process rather than overcoming it.'[11] In taking on that persona, he could play at escaping the constraining structures of aesthetic convention of his time – notably the preoccupation with the unity of the gestalt. In a letter from 1968 he wrote that 'geologic time has a way of diminishing "art history" to a mere trace'.[12] Similarly, following his encounter with the crumbling chaos of the slate quarries in Bangor in Pennsylvania, he rejoiced that 'All boundaries and distinctions lost their meaning in this ocean of slate and collapsed all notions of gestalt unity. The present fell forward and backward into a tumult of "de-differentiation".'[13] Smithson was not alone in co-opting the power of natural disaster in an assault on modernist aesthetics. In 1967 his friend Carl Andre had proposed to make a work of art which was an explosion, and Walter De Maria had earlier suggested that an earthquake was a work of art. Smithson however pushed further into the territory of the imagination with projects which specifically confronted the habitat of man – symbol of Braudel's social time – with the geologic time of earth movement

In April 1969 on a field trip with Nancy Holt and Virginia Dwan to the Yucatan, Smithson had initially thought to head for the famous Mayan ruins. Instead, he became preoccupied with a small hotel. Hotel Palenque was a site on which it was unnecessary to perform any action. It already epitomized the irreversible force of entropy. From a series of colour slides made in 1969, Smithson eventually invented a laconic travel guide (returning to the mode he had deployed in his earlier piece of writing and photography 'A Tour of the Monuments of Passaic, New Jersey', published in *Artforum* in December 1967) which he delivered to students at the University of Utah. Rather than relocating his project in the remnants of an earlier civilization, he located it in the ruins of his own. One part of the tourist hotel was in the process of being constructed, whilst other parts of the building were already in the process of falling apart. His drawing of the layout of the hotel noted areas of garbage, rubble and ruins as well as the rooms which had been finished, a dried-out swimming pool and a dance hall with a stuffed hawk.

Smithson was not, as were the Bechers, an observer by disposition. Standing at the threshold of awesome nature was insufficient. He wanted to cross that threshold and simulate that power himself. When invited to make a work at Kent State University, Ohio, in January 1970, he had initially proposed a mud flow. When that proved impossible, because it was too cold in Ohio in the winter for mud to flow, he rethought his project in relation to a small construction at the edge of the University campus. Photographs of destroyed human habitats had long fascinated Smithson – houses overwhelmed by lava or mud, villages destroyed by earthquakes or landslides.

On the Kent State campus, he again emulated the destructive force of nature by organizing a bulldozer to load earth onto an abandoned woodshed until the weight of earth had cracked the central supporting beam. At the point at which the central structure was destroyed, Smithson declared the work to be complete. *Partially Buried Woodshed* was a perfect embodiment of Smithson's equation of mental and physical de-construction. 'One's mind and the earth are in a constant state of erosion', he wrote, 'mental rivers wear away abstract banks, brain waves undermine cliffs of thought, ideas decompose into stones of unknowing, and conceptual crystallizations break apart into deposits of gritty reason. Vast moving faculties occur in this geological miasma, and they move in the most physical way. This movement seems motionless, yet it crushes the landscape of logic under glacial reveries.'[14]

Smithson's actions in the landscape – culminating in the vast *Spiral Jetty* which he realized later that same extraordinarily fertile year – contrast vividly with the testament of the Bechers. Smithson's work from this period is full of real or implied sound; the crash of huge earth-moving machines, the cracking of structures, the whirring of film, the torrent of words. The world of the Bechers' photographs, on the other hand, irrespective of whether the sites in which they photograph are active or obsolete, is muted and silent.

Because of the formal resolution and consistency of their work, it is tempting to call the Bechers' work timeless. But it is in fact full of time – a time which Braudel called 'social' but which in the case of the Bechers could be called 'historic' time, in distinction to the 'geologic' time of Smithson's projections. In their books and exhibitions, they invite first a concentrated scrutiny of their chosen objects, a meditation on their sameness and difference, form and function, and through this comparative reading, a reflection on the form of the society that produces them. The individual forms may be presented excised from context, but the Bechers remain acutely aware of the forces at work in the construction and ultimate obsolescence of these forms. The plants begin to die the moment they cease to produce, their instability masked by their massive physical presence. In their inevitable fate as much as their huge scale, these buildings embody, as Hilla Becher has remarked, 'the mentality' of the industrial age.[15]

To the Bechers it was already clear in the 1960s that these structures were essentially nomadic and had a comparatively short life compared with more classical or sacred architectural forms. Their first two books already presented many industrial sites which had closed down, particularly coal mines no longer productive in the 1960s. They present these objects in precisely the same way as any others, without comment and without sentiment. When they visited the

United States on a long working trip in 1973, they photographed extensively throughout the coal mining area of Pennsylvania, where a particular kind of winding tower, called coal mine tipples, had been constructed by small-scale coal mining enterprises. Strips of wood and bits of steel were fastened together with only the most functional aim in mind – to enable coal to be brought to the surface – and the Bechers hurried to photograph them in all their apparent frailty. These provisional wooden constructions apparently on the point of collapse or abandonment mirror the fragility of the simple woodshed which Smithson had overloaded.

On the same trip to the US, the Bechers also photographed huge steel mill complexes in Pennsylvania and Alabama. Amongst the portraits of blast furnaces and cooling towers, they made photographs of the landscape in which these sites were located. Perhaps inspired by the example of Walker Evans, who had also photographed in some of these areas, some of these photographs embody a less reserved description of the mentality of the age. The huge blast furnaces at Ensley, Alabama, for example, are juxtaposed with a large scrapyard of discarded automobiles: symbols of the quickening cycles of construction and production, usefulness and uselessness at the heart of the postwar economic miracle.

Smithson wanted his work to emulate the process of entropy. He wanted to play with time, to wrestle with it, to accelerate or decelerate it to a point of disintegration, to quicken the collapse of the belief systems and structures which underpinned this 'historic' time. Smithson, the great artist/entropologist of his generation projected his work into the greatest expanses of time and imagined its ultimate cooling down, to the point where nothing could be differentiated and everything would be formless.

By contrast the Bechers, his guides to the Oberhausen site and our guides to a 'historic' time, have built a structure to meditate on the difference of things. Theirs is a work of patient construction, as Smithson's is one of impatient de-construction. In their immense photographic project, their natural history of industrial form, the Bechers have slowed time down. It is almost as if the Bechers, the great artist/encyclopaedists of their generation, want us not simply to see the very singularity of every object, but to hold them, to feel their weight, and through them to feel the very weight of time.

1 Unpublished letter from Robert Smithson to Konrad Fischer (9 August 1968), Archives of American Art, Smithsonian Institute, Washington D.C.

2 T.E. Hulme, 'Cinders – A New Weltanschauung', *Speculations* (London, 1936) 236.

3 Robert Smithson, 'The Monuments of Passaic', *Artforum* (December 1967), reprinted under its full title in *The Writings of Robert Smithson*, ed. Nancy Holt (New York: New York University Press, 1979) 5.

4 Mel Bochner and Robert Smithson, 'The Domain of the Great Bear', *Art Voices* (Fall 1966). Also reprinted in *The Writings of Robert Smithson*, op. cit., 26.

5 *Anonyme Skulpturen* (Düsseldorf: Artverlag Press, 1970) n.p.

6 This exhibition is now in its entirety in the Crex Collection at Schaffhuasen. The photographs are also reproduced over 4 pages of the catalogue published by the Van Abbemuseum (Eindhoven, 1981) 38–41.

7 Hilla Becher, conversation with James Lingwood, 1995.

8 Smithson had the rolls of film developed in Düsseldorf for the exhibition. Twenty five were used in the *Nonsite (Oberhausen)* work, now in the Flick collection. The remaining photographs were retained at the Galerie Konrad Fischer. A group of 28 of these photographs subsequently entered first a private collection in Germany and then a private collection in the United States, which also has a further group of three photographs. The artists' widow, Nancy Holt, bequeathed the negatives as well as a series of 60 10 x 8" black and white prints to the Archives of American Art in Washington D.C.

9 'A Sedimentation of the Mind: Earth Projects' in *The Writings of Robert Smithson*, op. cit., 83.

10 *Concrete Pour* was realized for the exhibition 'Art by Telephone' at the Museum of Contemporary Art in Chicago, 1 November to 14 December 1969, and *Glue Pour* was realized as part of Lucy Lippard's exhibition '955,000' at the Vancouver Art Gallery from 14 January to 8 February 1970.

11 Conversation with Gianni Pettena, *Domus* (November 1972). Also reprinted in *The Writings of Robert Smithson*, op. cit., 187.

12 Unpublished letter to Martin Friedman (30 May 1968), Archive of American Art, Washington D.C.

13 'A Sedimentation of the Mind: Earth Projects', op. cit., 89.

14 Ibid., 82.

15 Hilla Becher, conversation with James Lingwood, 1995.

James Lingwood, 'The Weight of Time', in *Field Trips: Bernd & Hilla Becher/Robert Smithson* (Porto: Museu de Arte Contemporanea de Serralves, 2002) 70–79.

Tacita Dean
Sound Mirrors//1999

Dungeness

Dungeness has always been a place of significance to me: a bleak pebbled peninsula where we would go as children across the Romney Marshes to get to the sea. Wandering along the shingle beach, I once found a huge stone that barely had any weight at all. I coveted this 'trick' stone for some time in my collection, and only writing about it now do I suspect that my discovery was more likely radioactive debris from Dungeness power station: lit up at night in the middle distance beckoning and repulsive, and perpetually humming.

The land around Dungeness always feels old to me: a feeling impossible to explain, other than it is just 'unmodern'. It is flat, scruffy and waterlogged, full of herons and curlews and Martello towers, and defences built against every threat from the sea this nation has ever known. To me it feels 1970s and Dickensian, prehistoric and Elizabethan, Second World War and futuristic. It just doesn't function in the now.

Close by, Lydd Airport still operates, serving cream teas in the Biggles Restaurant and shuttling people across the Channel to Le Touquet. I remember standing as a child at a gate when the airport felt more like a field, and looking at the big-bellied silver planes taking cars to France. Lydd Airport was the closest I got to air travel for many years. I could have been standing at NASA for the intensity of the thrill it gave me. Chris Marker's *La Jetée* makes me think of Lydd Airport. Something to do with the nature of memory itself: a black and white place full of tableaux and whispering and in this case, aeroplanes.

And then Derek Jarman moved to Dungeness and it became his place too. A home for his imagination and charisma, and for his film *The Garden*. I met him on a train just after its première in London, and he was on his way back to Dungeness. Mrs Thatcher had just resigned and everyone felt an enormous sense of relief. It was a heady experience for me to meet Derek on that train. I was studying at the Slade at the time and had a new life in London. I was going back home to visit my parents but felt estranged from my life there. Derek gave me back Kent, and Dungeness. *The Garden* was so full of possibility and magic and metamorphosis, that it created a new conceptual place as well as reclaiming the old one.

I went there the Saturday after Derek died, and stood in his garden amongst his driftwood sculptures and resilient plants, watching the beam of the second lighthouse turn in the night sky. The power station twinkled; the shingle made huge banks down to the sea. Prospect Cottage stood black and yellow under the vast sky, still full of Derek, readying itself for the icon it was to become. I walked from his garden to the road: there are no gates or fences in Dungeness: nothing to divide one property from another or from the beach itself. It is an empty desolate place, and I'm sure it is this desolation that makes Dungeness so utterly attractive: that in its emptiness it can become so full.

Denge

The sound mirrors sit like big ears in the landscape at Denge by Dungeness in Kent. When they were built between 1928 and 1930, nothing stood between them and the sea, and between them and France. Now the ground where they stand has been flooded and turned into a gravel pit. The mirrors have begun to erode and subside into the mud: their demise now inevitable. A caravan park separates them from the sea, and a barbed wire fence divides the mirrors from the holidaymakers and the weekend ramblers. To get close to the site at Denge, you have to trespass.

The sound mirror scheme was conceived during the First World War when the concept of an air attack became the new danger to national security. The development of an early warning system became a matter of great urgency, and detection through acoustic methods seemed one possible solution. A series of listening stations were developed on the South coast using diverse methods of sound collection. Six varying sized mirrors were built on three different locations. Listeners would sit in chambers beneath the concrete structures, using stethoscopes to monitor the direction and strength of the sound. The idea was to catch the vibrations of planes taking off in France and to plot their course towards Britain, having first alerted London.

Only the mirrors were not discriminating enough. Although they caught the sound well, they would also pick up other noise, like the wind and the traffic and the propeller of a passing passenger liner, making any effective warning impossible. They persevered with them for a while, but soon they were abandoned in favour of the radar: an exciting new development with radio waves. An order to have them destroyed got lost with the outbreak of war, and these listening monoliths were spared and left to stand, solemnly eavesdropping on the sounds of Dungeness into the next century.

Tacita Dean, 'Sound Mirrors' (1999), *Selected Writings* (Göttingen: Steidl/Paris: ARC/Musée d'art moderne de la Ville de Paris, 2003) n.p.

Darian Leader
The Architecture of Life//2006

The title of Jane and Louise Wilsons' new installation at Haunch of Venison Zurich poses an immediate contradiction. *Sealander* (2006) contains both land and sea, as well as evoking an action or movement with its suffix, as if land and sea were not only nouns but verbs. This movement is evoked by the Wilsons' camera, as it cuts between images of decayed, abandoned World War II coastal bunkers and footage of a rare deep sea squid continuing its silent, repetitive trajectory.

The bunkers lie fractured and awry, at odds with the vast, empty beaches around them. They no longer have a purpose and have become repositories for litter, graffiti and the detritus of illicit activities. The bulky gigantic concrete blocks seem like debris from another world, spacecraft that have crashed into our planet millennia ago and now lie unattended and useless.

Even before they became relics, these structures possessed an alien quality as signs of an invader's presence. Built by an occupying army, they aimed to defend a territory that was never their own to start with. As defences, their status was ambiguous, since the very ground they stood on had been purloined. They were signs of both possession of a space and the fact that this possession was never secure. Signs, then, of both having and not having.

As their defensive function was lost, the ambiguity of these bunkers became an out-of-placeness. Their massive presence marks the beaches with no obvious use, yet the combination of this out-of-placeness with their spatial isolation produces an odd effect: it invites a comparison with ourselves. The solitary and ineffable structures evoke our own identity, or at least that part of it which remains mute and alone. The bunkers become an echo of our own out-of-placeness with the world, that side of human life which consists of brute, meaningless presence. The way that the artists film the bunkers, dwelling on their holes and apertures, strengthens this identification, bringing out the correspondence with human, bodily forms.

The footage of the vampire squid, so-named because of the sharp tooth-like fangs that line its arms, might seem an odd accompaniment to these concrete masses. *Vampyroteuthis infernalis* is a little studied cephalapod found in the deepest, darkest waters. Although its size is relatively humble – it averages between 15 and 30 cm – it possesses the largest eye proportional to its body of any known creature. Studding this body are small light-producing organs called photophores, which are turned on and off to ensure either invisibility or defensive flashes.

As the Wilsons' camera turns the bunkers into bodies, so the rather enigmatic presence of the squid becomes less baffling. Its juxtaposition with the bunkers draws out the comparison with organic form, with the body. The squid's massive eye is reflected in the gaping gun holes of the concrete structures, and the internal contradiction of the show's title becomes an explanation: the inorganic and formal is inhabited by the organic and vital. But perhaps this interpretation is too hasty. Perhaps the tension that the work explores is more complex.

Both the bunkers and the squid have something otherworldly about them. Just as the bunkers index a period that seems long past, so the squid remains suspended in an ancient, inaccessible time. We know that many deep-sea creatures resist categorization and capture, and some of them have survived relatively unchanged since prehistoric times. They embody a kind of time tunnel, a passage from this world to another, archaic one. The darkness that the squid swims in is not just the darkness of space, but of time.

The bunkers also pose the question of time, but their presence is predicated on culture, not nature. Like remnants of some lost civilization, they evoke the human work of creation, of building. Severed from their former use, they have been linked to a whole series of spaces in the Wilsons' work, from the old Greenham Common missile site to the derelict Stasi headquarters to the empty pavilion of Victor Pasmore. But is their function simply memorial? The artists have said that they aim, in fact, not to invite but to avoid nostalgia. The immersion of past in present is not the usual romantic one but concerned with symbolic and cultural value.

Like the Pasmore pavilion and the Greenham site, the bunkers have lost the symbolic value they once had: that of modernist precision, of imperialism, of protest and of military hindrance. These spaces have not only become uninhabited by people, but by symbolic value itself. They have become odd liminal spaces, filled with graffiti, piss, litter, condoms. But where we would expect these transformations to signify some kind of mortification and death, doesn't the artists' insistence on a dialogue with vital forms – from the children in the Pasmore Pavilion to the squid in *Sealander* – suggest not death but life? A strange kind of life perhaps, and one we might wish to avoid, but life all the same. Piss, excrement, condoms, obscene graffiti all testify to presence not absence, the side of human life that gravitates to the points where symbolic value has been extinguished or undermined.

This brings us back to the question of the organic and the formal. The architectural structures that so fascinate the Wilsons aren't just akin to bodies, but to bodies whose symbolic function has been checked or deleted. And this metamorphosis produces an effect on the experience of space itself. In her essay on the Wilsons, Giuliana Bruno quotes the idea of Victor Pasmore that 'urban space is interior like the interior of a house'.[1] Taken seriously, this means that what we might usually think of as an external space can be understood as an interior one, in the same way that at a certain historical moment, Byzantine church interiors were identified with the external space between the figures painted on their walls. Reality becomes like a glove turned inside out. And isn't this exactly what we see with the squid, as we watch it effortlessly turn itself inside out, like the topological space known as the Klein Bottle?

The dialogue that the Wilsons create in *Sealander* concerns this relation between interior and exterior. Just as we witness the squid's inversion of itself, so we are encouraged to think of the space surrounding the bunkers, the very space that we might think of as external and objective. As their roving cameras move along and across the bunkers' surface, distinctions between inside and outside become less apparent. And this is perhaps both a semantic theme and a formal technique that is explored uniquely in the work of the Wilsons. [...]

1 Giuliana Bruno, 'Modernist Ruins, Filmic Archaeologies', in *Jane and Louise Wilson: A Free and Anonymous Monument* (London: Film and Video Umbrella/Lisson Gallery/Newcastle on Tyne: Baltic, 2004) 7–24.

Darian Leader, 'The Architecture of Life', in *Jane & Louise Wilson: Sealander* (Zürich: Haunch of Venison Zürich, 2006) n.p.

Caoimhín Mac Giolla Léith
The Light Gleams an Instant//2008

> When you wet the bed first it is warm then it gets cold.
> – James Joyce[1]
>
> They give birth astride a grave, the light gleams an instant, then it's night once more.
> – Samuel Beckett[2]

To invoke two of Ireland's most celebrated writers of the last century in addressing the work of a contemporary Polish artist is, in the case of Miroslaw Balka, neither arbitrary nor inappropriate. For a start, the title of the earliest of Balka's sculptures included [in his exhibition at the Irish Museum of Modern Art, Dublin, 2008], alludes to the passage quoted above, which is from the beginning of James Joyce's *A Portrait of the Artist as a Young Man*. *When you wet the bed* (1987) is an important sculpture which anticipates a crucial moment in the formal development of Balka's art as it came to international prominence around 1990. This work heralded the abandonment of the relatively elaborate figurative tableaux that were typical of the artist's earlier work, for more elemental and abstracted forms, as invocational presence gave way to evocative absence in a manner that bears comparison with the evolution of the writing of Joyce's one-time amanuensis, Samuel Beckett. In fact, Balka's work as a whole might be read as a mediation between impulses epitomized, however schematically, by Joyce and Beckett.

Balka shares with early Joyce, in particular, a frequent recourse to autobiography, with a focus on the minutiae of childhood memory. They also have in common a fascination with the power and persistence of culturally embedded symbolism, and the working through of an uneasy relationship with a hegemonic Catholic church as well as the competing claims of alternative ideologies (atavistic nationalism for Joyce, Communist collectivism for Balka). Balka's affinities with Beckett are at once more superficially apparent and more universally resonant. They include the stark theatricality typical of his installations, his mature sculpture's formal tendency towards reductiveness and an 'art of impoverishment', alongside a fascination with debilitation and decay (as evidenced, for example, by the recurring motif of the rubbish bin).[3] There is also the contrast between the base materiality of bodily functions and evacuations, though these are often obliquely registered by Balka, and the metaphoric, if not metaphysical, implications of corporeal absence; and an emphasis on the inherent physical limitations of the isolated human body, as well as various constraints and indignities visited upon it (expressed in Balka by the body's abstracted sculptural surrogates, rather than by actors on a stage).

The mediation between 'Joycean' and 'Beckettian' modes may best be illustrated by comparing the two works which occupy the first rooms of this exhibition. *When you wet the bed* comprises three main elements, each of which is simply constructed from wood. The first of these is a bed-like structure with a thin, padded mattress and pillow. A small hose protrudes from the centre of the bed, spouting water into a rectangular hollow in the raised platform on which the whole ensemble stands. At the head of the bed, but to one side, is a stout, T-shaped cross. A second jet of water arcs from a hose poking from a triangular aperture close to the top of the two-panel door that constitutes the front of the cross's vertical section, commingling with the first stream as they splash into the rectangular font. The final element, a *prie-dieu* of similarly rudimentary construction, stands at the bottom of the bed, a little further to the side and facing the cross at an angle. The symbolism of the work is unambiguous and overpowering, as the all-seeing gaze of a forbidding deity (Balka has explicitly referred to the triangular opening in the cross as 'the eye of Providence') forcefully expresses tears in apparent response to the precocious incontinence of nascent adolescent sexuality.[4] While the two-part installation *2 x (55 x 23 x 27), 190 x 190 x 0,3* (1995) that occupies the room adjacent to *When you wet the bed* shares its simplicity of form and facture, it is quite different in other respects. This difference is most immediately signalled by the contrast between the works' titles. The earlier recourse to literary allusion is replaced by a title simply derived from the physical dimensions of this later work's two constituent elements. (In some ways, Balka's tendency to title works whose form is highly suggestive symbolically in the reductive and self-reflexive terms of their physical dimensions is the opposite of a strategy where an artist provides an abstract work of art with an evocative 'literary' title that is seemingly unmotivated by the work's manifest form.) The first element, a pair of empty old dirty brown linoleum boxes with handles, is mounted on short steel legs with felt pads underneath. The twinned boxes stand on the edge of a square field of ashes (measuring 190 cm by 190 cm) bounded by a narrow PVC border (3 mm thick) flush to the ash field. The linoleum was salvaged from Balka's studio in Otwock on the outskirts of Warsaw, which is also the house in which he spent his childhood years. The dimensions of the ash field were dictated by the artist's precise height and the width of his outstretched arms, as are the dimensions of many other works (the measurement 250 cm, which also recurs frequently, refers to that of the artist's body with his arms stretched overhead). Its depth corresponds more nebulously to what Balka describes as 'the thickness of touch'.[5] Despite the work's indexical link to the specifics of personal history and physical embodiment, its symbolic charge is notably more diffuse than that of the earlier work. The boxes are empty containers, seemingly designed to be readily portable. But what might they be imagined to carry, if not the ashes that are now spread out beside them? And from what origin to what destination? The ash conjures an equally indeterminate set of associations. It has comforting intimations of traditional domesticity and an open hearth. Yet these are overshadowed by the ominous suggestion of consumption by fire and charred remains, a reading accentuated by the evidence of other works, such as the series of 'burnt drawings', retrieved from a disastrous studio fire in 1993, which Balka continues to exhibit on occasion. The funereal echo of the phrase 'ashes to ashes' also resounds, incidentally amplified by the artist's observation, in another context, that after we die, 'eighty per cent of the water in our body disappears. What remains is about 2 kg of ashes'.[6]

Other materials repeatedly deployed by Balka are burdened by similarly conflicted connotations. First there is the wood, steel and felt, whose associations with traditional building and construction are often as insistent as any associations with the history of fine art. In addition to the sheets of PVC and scraps of linoleum already mentioned, there are also sundry other found materials whose real world decrepitude is transformed by the alchemy of artistic labour and redeemed by translation into the exalted context of the art gallery. The most visually arresting element in the relatively early work, *60 x 30 x 6,5; Penguin lamp; 200 x 60 x 162* (1990) is the large, battered metal container whose shape is comically reminiscent of a penguin. This 'penguin' was in fact a trash can in an earlier life, of a design familiar in Poland in the 1970s. Balka saved this redundant object from imminent extinction, giving it a new lease of life in the confines of the museum space, infusing it with new spirit in the form of the light bulb placed in its interior that illuminates it from within. Other superrannuated objects, however, have suffered a crueller fate. A flayed basketball hangs from a steel spike (*25 x 25 x 30*, 2000), salt heaped in the coil of skin that sits on the ground, suggesting the handiwork of some meticulous torturer. A deflated blue rubber ball with its top sliced off has likewise been filled with salt (*Untitled*, 2002). A string of used and discarded bars of soap, suspended from two points in the gallery ceiling, looks like a primitive, multicoloured necklace, while this work's title, *Hanging Soap Women* (2000), hints at some savage ritual. Salt is a mineral essential to life, associated with preservation and purification. But salt is also expelled from the body in the form of sweat or tears. When applied to a wound the effect can be excruciating. Soap is first and foremost a cleansing agent, associated with bodily hygiene. But it has other historical associations. Among the more vivid of these, and the most pertinent to Balka's work, is the widespread belief that during the Second World War the Nazis manufactured soap from the corpses of murdered Jews.

The fraught question of how an artist who is not Jewish, and who was born more than a decade after the end of the war, might address the horror of the Holocaust is an aspect of the wider debate concerning the ethical challenge to representation, memorialization and poesis posed by the most emblematically traumatic episode in twentieth-century history. Born in 1958, Balka is the grandson of a stonemason who made tombstones, which his father also engraved as a part-time occupation. He grew up in a deeply Catholic environment in communist Poland, in a place still haunted by the memory of wartime atrocities, including those perpetrated in nearby Treblinka. The traumatic history of the extermination camps has inspired various works over the years, including a large-scale outdoor sculpture in progress [*250 x 700 x 455, ø 41 x 41/Zoo/T*, 2007–8] based on the architecture of 'Treblinka Zoo'. In early 1943 the camp commandant, Franz Stangl, decreed that a zoo be built at Treblinka. At the lower level there was a cave for captured foxes and one for other animals trapped in the surrounding forest. There was a dovecote on the roof and the building was bordered by a decorative birch fence with rustic settees scattered around, providing a recreational area in which the SS might relax after their day's work. Balka's steel replica of the structure's basic armature, whose height is that of the artist's upstretched arms, with the zoo's original dimensions shrinking accordingly, exacerbates the ghastly irony of this prison-within-a-prison by effectively reducing it to a shrunken skeleton.

Another work explicitly addressing the history of the camps is the video *B* (2006). Balka's enthusiastic turn to video installation suggests that the video-loop was a form just waiting for his inevitable attention, in so far as the relentless cycle of narrative repetition and the strict rectilinear boundaries of conventionally projected moving images already had their respective formal correlatives in his sculpture. (While the linear time of classic narrative cinema may be related to the unfolding of history, the repetitive or cyclical time of contemporary video, as well as that of certain early cinematic forms, is more obviously related to ritual.) Various works present the viewer with looped footage of the agitated fluttering of a moth on the floor of a train carriage (*Tanz 190 x 250*, 2002), or the clustering of flies in a corner as the camera pans slowly and repeatedly up and down (*140 x 107 x 22/ Wydawaloby Sie [It Would Seem]*, 2005), or the endless tedium of staring at a blank studio wall (*210 x 280 x 40/ The Wall*, 2006). Such works are not so far in spirit from a sculpture such as *270 x 449 x 12* (2004) a white foam rubber wall with a cutaway door opening, which is isolated in space and turns interminably on its own motorized axis, the doorway leading everywhere and nowhere – not to mention several other works in which constant, mechanized rotation plays a part. The dimensions of the 'screen' onto which Balka's filmed images are projected are sometimes derived from the span of the artist's body, just as in many of the sculptures, with something akin to the cold ergonomic efficiency of a prison cell or a cemetery plot. *B* comprises close-up footage of the isolated letter 'B' in the first word of the infamous legend, '*ARBEIT MACHT FREI*', that greeted prisoners passing through the gates of Auschwitz. Shot amid flurries of snow from a position inside the camp, this reversed capital is isolated from the surrounding letters and words that gave it meaning. The camps are invoked more obliquely in *Kategorie* (2006), a six-metre long, two-metre high tunnel built from grey plasterboard, which is bisected along its central axis by a row of coloured threads suspended from rotating metal brackets spaced at one-metre intervals. Balka has indicated that the particular order of coloured threads – red, purple, black, pink and green – was designed so that, in general terms of colouristic associations, this austere procession ends with the colour green, 'which signifies hope'. Yet each of these colours once designated the identity of categories of prisoner in the camps: red for political prisoners, purple for Jehovah's Witnesses, pink for homosexual or bisexual men, black for 'asocial' elements such as Roma, alcoholics, vagrants, people with intellectual disabilities etc., and green for criminals.

Skirting the ethical issue of who is entitled to speak of the unspeakable, it might be tempting to view Balka's preoccupation with the history of the concentration camps as a morbid fascination that is explicable primarily in terms of the accidents of birth and upbringing, and perhaps compounded by a fundamentally melancholic nature. Yet to do so would be to imply that this preoccupation is not merely exceptional, but somehow marginal to the proper concerns of contemporary art at this particular historical moment. This is surely problematic. Zygmunt Bauman has warned against the danger of sidestepping the Holocaust as either a uniquely Jewish tragedy or a vile aberration in the history of modernity – an inexplicable resurgence of barbarism that briefly, if catastrophically, punctuated the progress of modern civilisation. For to do so is to ignore the many ways in which the Holocaust is deeply involved with the nature of modernity.[7] More recently, Giorgio Agamben has argued that the birth of the concentration camp, 'decisively signals the political space of modernity itself'. Its history may be charted from the camps created by the Spanish in Cuba during the Spanish-American War and the British during the Second Boer War, to their contemporary reflections in the ethnic rape compounds, refugee camps, airport *zones d'atteintes*, and even 'certain outskirts of our cities' today. For Agamben, in a world in which the 'state of exception' is fast becoming the rule, it is the camp, rather than the city, that is now 'the fundamental biopolitical paradigm of the West', a place where people are stripped of all political status, and power confronts bare life with little or no mediation.'[8] Miroslaw Balka's work is clearly more concerned with affect than with analysis, with a fidelity to the workings of memory as opposed to an assertion of the truths of history. This does not, however, make its continuing resistance to the anaesthetic of forgetting any less significant or timely.

1 James Joyce, *A Portrait of the Artist as a Young Man* (1914–15) (New York: Viking Press, 1964).
2 Samuel Beckett, 'Waiting for Godot', *Samuel Beckett: The Complete Dramatic Works* (London: Faber and Faber, 2006) 83.
3 See Leo Bersani and Ulysse Dutoit, *Arts of Impoverishment: Beckett, Rothko, Resnais* (Cambridge, Massachusetts: Harvard University Press, 1993).
4 Juan Vincente Aliaga, 'Danse Macabre: An Interview with Miroslaw Balka', in *Revision 1986–1997* (Valencia: IVAM, 1997) 146.
5 All quotations from the artist, unless otherwise indicated, are from a conversation with the writer in Dublin or from subsequent email correspondence, August to September 2007.
6 Aliaga, op. cit., 148.
7 Zygmunt Bauman, *Modernity and the Holocaust* (Ithaca, New York: Cornell University Press, 1989).
8 Giorgio Agamben, *Homo Sacer: Sovereign Power and Bare Life* (Stanford: Stanford University Press, 1998).

Caoimhín Mac Giola Léith, 'The Light Gleams an Instant', in *Miroslaw Balka: Tristes Tropiques* (Dublin: Irish Museum of Modern Art, 2008) 40–46.

Jörg Heiser
Susan Hiller: *The J. Street Project*//2005

My initial contact with this work was through its title *The J. Street Project* and a description of its realization: 'Over the past three years, Susan Hiller filmed and photographed all 303 streets, alleys and paths in Germany whose names refer to a Jewish presence.' Even before I had seen a frame of the film or a single photograph, these details gave a clear indication of the artistic approach involved. My attempt to work out the relationship between the work's title and the method used before turning to the relationship between that title and what is actually on show would, I hope, meet with Hiller's approval, reducing as it does the likelihood of lazily mixing up the theme of the piece and its concrete artistic form. For any discussion of *The J. Street Project* cannot simply be taken as an opportunity or excuse carelessly to add just one more item to the long list of works and publications dealing with the history, trauma, repression and destruction of Jewish life in Germany. Instead, it must first examine what artistic approaches in general, and Susan Hiller's in particular, are capable of achieving as modes of insight and experience.

When describing the artist's method in formal terms, the sheer quantity of 'J. Streets' featured is significant, and not just because we are told that this includes every one to be found in Germany. Within Hiller's oeuvre as a whole, the 305 postcards she collected for *Dedicated to the Unknown Artists* (1972–76), all showing huge waves hitting various spots on the British coast, are a classic precedent – in purely formal terms – for the assembling of a 'critical mass' of pictures of places. The key point here, however (signalled in both cases by the title), is that what appears as 'mere' collecting is actually much more than that. Rather than a feeling of terse coolness in the tradition of Minimalism or conceptual art (think of early Ed Ruscha, or Bernd and Hilla Becher), Hiller's pieces set up a constant oscillation between emptiness and weightiness, a kind of psychoactive restlessness. This restlessness arises from the clashing of a pointedly distanced, technical-serial, conceptual method with something that has a particularly strong semantic charge. In both works, this clash is already present in the title: in the case of the postcards, the dedication to unknown artists links the motif of heavy seas with that of the Romantic artist's tempestuous spirit, and both of these with the motif of Great Britain defined chiefly by its status as an island. The combination of these three motifs, that have long since become clichés, suddenly turns each of the many anonymous commercial photographers who once supplied the images for these postcards into a solitary observer, alone with him/herself, the sea and a camera. Emptiness switches to weightiness, effect turns into affect.

In the title *The J. Street Project*, the abbreviation of 'Jew' or 'Jewish' to 'J.' is already ambivalent. In the context of conceptual art, one might initially think of the openness of the indexical – 'J' as a semiological cipher, like a working title that has become the actual title of the work, open to a multiplicity of different readings. But this thought immediately collides head-on with the unambiguous use of the letter 'J' by the Nazis, who from 1938 stamped it in red ink on the identity cards of all Jews. The potential for openness turns into destruction, 'mere' naming into stigmatization, persecution and extermination. Moreover, the fact that street names like 'Judengasse' are in themselves not just an expression of customs and local colour, some kind of rose-tinted 'shtetl' world of cultural difference before the arrival of the Nazis, but clear evidence of centuries of previous segregation and stigmatization (to varying degrees at different times and places) of the Jewish population as 'alien'.[1] And this in spite of the fact that in parts of the country, as along the Rhine in former Roman settlements, the Jewish population had in fact been there longer than the supposedly native 'genuine Teutons'.

The abbreviation 'J. Street' and the English language in which it is written thus function as a twofold distancing from stigmatizing naming in German – but without leaving this stigmatizing naming itself unnamed. And the linguistic gesture of double distancing itself is an expression not of cool calculation but, on the contrary, of being touched emotionally by the insoluble contradiction that lies, after Auschwitz, in the continuity of names labelling streets in Germany as 'Jewish'. How can they still be called 'Jewish' when the Jewish population in question was expelled and then exterminated? And how, on the other hand, could these streets be renamed and no longer called 'Jewish' without it constituting an attempt to cover up this absence?

It is precisely this ambivalence named by the title *The J. Street Project* – between the historical wealth of Jewish life in Germany and its destruction, between stigmatizing naming and the naming of this naming – which, when we come to look at the work itself, makes us search with the restless eye of a detective for signs of some unexpected presence of Jewish history today at these locations where it formerly took place. But most importantly, it inevitably makes us look at the same time for legible signs of an awareness of the persecution and destruction, or signs of unawareness in the form of repression and denial by those who live there today. This search for signs is aggravated by the fact that Hiller helps us neither with a narrative or plot, nor with commentary by a voice off, and certainly not with her own presence in front of the camera as a figure to identify with. In the film we see a series of sequences featuring static, mostly calmly-edited footage of everyday scenes in German villages and small town pedestrian zones. But this does not give us the potentially comforting feeling that something has been resolved by the artist completing the arduous task of visiting all 303 places scattered across today's

Germany on behalf of all of us. In this sense, the piece is neither an absolution nor a conclusion, but an appeal not to take the traces of history in our surroundings for granted and to take part actively in their interpretation.

Although Hiller chooses a conceptual, technological-serial approach over a conventional narrative documentary style, the film is still composed, organized along subtexts. This begins with the sequence of seasons (starting with winter, followed by autumn, summer and spring), and times of day (an evening shot is followed by a night shot and so on, resulting in a subtle overall sequence of parallels). Another key tool in this compositional linking of images is the soundtrack, which quietly but firmly subverts the purely documentary synchronicity of sound and image (i.e. the matching between a place and what was actually heard there at the moment of filming). There are, for example, several consecutive shots quite obviously not filmed at the same place or time of day that are accompanied by a carillon, as if this ringing joined the scenes to form an imaginary neighbourhood. The melody played by the bells is that of an old revolutionary song from around 1780, banned by the Nazis – '*Die Gedanken sind frei*' ('My thinking is free'). Later, similar use is made of street music (children playing a version of 'Smells Like Teen Spirit') and a musical box tune – '*Das ist die Berliner Luft*', a popular song from around 1900. Musical box melodies act as a topos for childhood memories; the tolling of bells as a topos of cosiness and intact village community – and in both cases, especially in horror films, this kind of cosiness immediately becomes uncanny, signalling repressed trauma and lurking violence (as Freud remarked and Hiller has commented, the *heimlich* and the *unheimlich* are very close). Hiller evokes this convention of musical boxes and bells (reinforced by the fact that they play 'typically German' melodies) as a way of echoing, not without a trace of irony, the above-mentioned feeling of a detective-like search for traces of Germany's past in totally banal everyday scenes from Germany's present. Hiller however does not mean to sabotage the genuineness of attempts to read traces of trauma and violence: in my eyes at least, her use of these stylistic elements instead distances the undertaking from the pathos-laden or even triumphant gesture of the detective solving a case. There is one scene which illustrates this particularly clearly: an old man with a walking stick and a hat is walking along the edge of a country road towards the sign at the entrance to the village of Judenbach when a large truck comes towards him and he pauses to let it pass. The distance between the man and the truck turns out to be very small, so that the turbulence of its passing blows the hat from his head. Taken on its own, this shot is an unspectacular piece of slapstick, but in connection with the subject – visible in the form of the place name sign – a strange tension develops between the comedy of this scene and the question of whether it is suggesting that we might interpret the unexpected gust of wind that whisks away the hat, or the established order, as a tragicomic image symbolizing, for example, the belated failure of attempts at total repression and denial of guilt ('we had no idea') typical of the generation of Germans to which this man belongs.

In one sense, our attempts to charge up these 'light' images with such 'heavy' meanings are constantly failing, without ever coming to rest. Everything appears loaded with significance, but we never achieve final certainty. At one point, we see a man obviously waiting for someone in front of a church. His clothes are remotely reminiscent of Jewish orthodox dress, but it is impossible to know for sure whether or not the person we are seeing is a Jew (probably not). In another scene, we read a slogan sprayed on the wall of a house, calling for an '*NPD-Spinner-freie Stadt*' (nutty-neo-Nazi free town). Of course, this is someone making a laudable attempt to protest against neo-Nazi tendencies in Germany, but it is done presumably unintentionally – using an expression that echoes typical neo-Nazi talk of 'foreigner-free zones', in turn inspired by the Nazi term 'judenfrei' (Jew-free). Whereas the title *The J. Street Project* displays the artist's awareness of the danger of inadvertently repeating that which one is combating, the 'Nazi-free' slogan shows that the rhetoric of segregation has even affected those who combat it.

Very few scenes refer legibly to concrete and easily researchable facts. These include the one featuring 'Jüdenstrasse' in Berlin, which the Nazis renamed 'Kinkelstrasse' after a racial theorist in 1938 and which was only given back its original name in 2002, after decades of discussion (the renaming ceremony was marred by anti-Jewish jeering). The two names are mounted above one another, with 'Kinkelstrasse' struck through in red, and both are framed by the kind of Christmas lights that are typical in shopping areas.

And then there are passages where scenes are sequenced on the basis of specific similarities: cars zooming past; 'one-way street' signs under the 'Jewish' street sign; or scenes in which passers-by have become aware of the presence of a running camera.

Even if one watches the film several times, over the course of its 67 minutes each impression is of course overlaid by the next, resulting in a kind of intuitive overall impression: one remembers some details with great clarity, while others become blurred. By contrast, the reproduction in the publication of the photographs taken at all 303 locations shifts this position: as individual observers, we can navigate back and forth, examine images cursorily or in individual detail, link them directly with the corresponding place names via their numbers, or look more systematically for overall similarities or specific features. One might notice the relatively large number of waste disposal and cleaning-related devices (three street cleaning machines, dustbins at least four times, one woman with a broom), or a certain frequency of idyllic and romantic views of fields and forest paths (at least ten times). Three or four commemorative plaques can be identified, whereas the street signs often collide – sometimes in obscenely thoughtless ways – with commercial signs placed immediately above or next to them, advertising butchers, wine bars, funeral parlours or, for example, 'Gasthof Stern' (The Star Inn) whose star is painted in yellow on the outer wall, or 'zum Bahnhof' (to the railway station) with an arrow pointing the way.

This comparison between the book and the film, then, makes one thing especially clear: the above-mentioned ambivalence of naming (between 'Judenstrasse' and 'J. Street', between stigmatizing naming and the naming of this naming) matches an ambivalence between the contemplative character of looking at all the images put together (especially in the film) and the evidence of the pictures themselves in the sense of potential or actual 'pictures from the scene of the crime' (an aspect that is particularly strong in the book). These two readings – 'soft' everyday scene and 'hard' crime-scene image – can each be understood as dangers of an inappropriate handling of Jewish-German history. The 'soft' contemplative character brought on by the sheer number of places shown – as we look at one picture after another and lose ourselves in the steady succession of scenes of rural and small town everyday life – stands for the danger of being lost in the present, our awareness of history eroded by the sheer abundance of everyday banality. By contrast, the 'bare' evidential character, the unaffected gaze at shabby, mundane street corners and forlorn tracks through the woods, stands for the danger of a kind of 'pleasure in guilt' that revels in the viewer's own horror at the gravity of historical atrocities even in their absence at the empty 'scene of the crime'.

The relationship between these two aspects is the key to *The J. Street Project* – in different ways for the book and the film. Instead of rhetorically invoking or tacitly affirming 'forgetting' or 'pleasure in guilt' as two dangers involved in (German) dealing with history, the two are placed in a relationship of structural tension (in turn contributing to the above-described 'psychoactive restlessness'). Instead of constituting an end in itself to create an effect, this tense relationship points to the unresolved nature of the historical status of these places – it remains unclear whether the continuing existence of names such as 'Judenstrasse' should be read as an expression of remembrance of past crimes or precisely as an expression of their being ignored, as long as no further 'sign' of historical awareness is added (as in the case of a commemorative plaque). Only names like 'Jüdischer Friedhof' (Jewish cemetery) – especially if an intact cemetery is still to be found there – appear capable of maintaining a non-stigmatizing character for themselves based on the status of dignified burial and respect for the dead. Even here, however, an implicit level of respect immediately gives way to disrespect and stigmatization if the name is 'Jüdenfriedhof' (Jews' cemetery) instead of

'Jüdischer Friedhof' (Jewish cemetery), linguistic inflection turning religious attribution into subject of racism.

The compact format of the book is reminiscent of both church hymn books and travel guides, and the cover features not a picture but the long list of the streets – like a litany for the dead, the constant repetition of what's absent. In this light *The J. Street Project* – especially in book form – can also be understood very concretely as a potential guide for future historical study: where are these streets and what is their respective local historical background? Furthermore, Hiller's work enriches the discussion about monuments to the Holocaust, a debate which has yet to progress beyond a confrontation between minimalist-indexical (Peter Eisenman's Holocaust Memorial in Berlin) and symbolic-illustrative approaches (e.g. Alfred Hrdlicka's memorials in Hamburg and Vienna).[2]

Hiller's *The J. Street Project* cannot be assigned to one or other of these positions. It contrasts Minimalist abstraction as a marking of the absent and the unrepresentable with conceptual abstraction as presence: the street names, and thus the stigmatizing naming they represent, are listed and shown as pictures of over 300 places. The subject matter itself is not presented as a theatrical *mise-en-scène*, but held in a precarious tension between conceptually structured contemplation and documentary evidence. This tension is the exact artistic equivalent of the mixed feelings that overwhelm one at the sight of a sign bearing the word 'Judengasse' as everyday life goes on unabated all around.

1 The historian Alfred Haverkamp writes that 'isolated earlier attempts to close off existing Jewish residential areas in towns against the will of their inhabitants, or to resettle them in remote districts, only began to find scattered implementation in the late 15th century. As such, the ghetto was an institution that only became more common later, in the modern age, and which even then was far from ubiquitous. The same is true of the implementation of regulations on the marking of Jews.' Alfred Haverkamp, 'Europas Juden im Mittelalter – Streifzüge', in Europas Juden im Mittelalter (Speyer: Palatinate Historical Museum/Berlin: German Historical Museum, 2005) 34.

2 In the original plan submitted by Eisenman and Serra for a field of concrete stelae for the Holocaust Memorial in Berlin, geometric abstraction was used as a principle to represent something without depicting it – as a physically present marking of an absence and at the same time as a symbolic marking of the impossibility of depiction. This is in line with the view that the Shoah is not suited for illustrative representations of horror, whereas Alfred Hrdlicka's memorials in Hamburg and Vienna are examples of the figurative-mimetic approach based on the idea that mimetic faithfulness to the crime is somehow linked with the highest degree of historical awareness. Cf. Diedrich Diederichsen, 'Memorial to the murdered Jews of Europe', *frieze*, no. 91, 108 ff.

Jörg Heiser, 'Afterword', in Susan Hiller, *The J. Street Project* (2002–5) (Berlin: DAAD/Compton Verney, Warwickshire: Compton Verney Trust, 2005) 618–27.

Secrets in the open sea consists of twenty-nine photographic prints that were found buried under the rubble during the 1993 demolition of Beirut's war-ravaged commercial districts. The prints were different shades of blue and each measured 111 × 173 cm. In 1994, the prints were entrusted to *The Atlas Group* for preservation and analysis. *The Atlas Group* sent six of the prints to laboratories in France and the UK for chemical and digital analysis.

Remarkably, the laboratories recovered small black-and-white latent images from the blue prints. The small images represented group portraits of men and women. *The Atlas Group* was able to identify all the individuals represented in the small black-and-white images, and it turned out that they were all individuals who drowned, died or were found dead in the Mediterranean between 1975 and 1991.

Walid Raad/The Atlas Group, text for *Secrets in the open sea*, 1994/2004

Mark Beasley
Walid Raad/The Atlas Group//2006

Violently displaced from its body, a car engine lies in a pool of leaked oil. In case it should suddenly leap into life again, a military official levels an automatic rifle at the inert lump. Presented as a group of framed inkjet prints, *My Neck Is Thinner than a Hair: Engines* (2000–3) is the first in a series of works [at FACT, Liverpool, December 2005 to January 2006] that examine the spate of car bombs detonated in Lebanon between 1975 and 1991. A wall text informs us that the engine is 'the only part that remains intact after a car bomb explodes', and that 'during the wars photojournalists competed to be the first to find and photograph the engines'.

The Atlas Group has gathered 100 such photographs from the archives of the An-Nahar Research Centre and the Arab Documentation Centre. Forming a tight horizontal grid, the photographs reveal the aftermath of detonation; explosives specialists and military investigators prise apart twisted metal in search of clues while bemused young men close around the scene. A peculiar trophy of a struggle so viciously played out, the car engine – a now lethal delivery mechanism – takes on an almost talismanic importance.

Established by the artist Walid Raad, The Atlas Group is an imaginary foundation whose aim is to research, document, study and produce audio, visual and literary artefacts that shed light on the contemporary history of Lebanon. Described as 'reigniting our curiosity in the truth', the project runs a convoluted line between fact and fiction, replacing unitary power with fragmented assemblage. In part the work exploits the notional understanding of the gallery or institution as the site of venerated liberal truths. How are we meant to view the work? The multiple images of violent display are reminiscent of Gertrude Stein's assertion that 'ugliness repeated becomes beauty'. This leaking oil heart is now a stand-in for a struggle that is in part unknowable.

Raad uses the conventions of archival museum display: sombre grey walls, crisp white text and soft lighting lead us through the galleries. In the next room a network of dark, undulating spherical holes punctuates a low-level circular dais. Described as a scale model of all the detonations in Beirut between 1975 and 1991, the work is attributed to one Nassia Hassan, a senior topographer in the Lebanese Army. Upon being presented to the Lebanese parliament's Committee on Development and Reconstruction, the original model – this is a replica – caused 'the most heated and contentious parliamentary sessions in Lebanon's recent history', resulting in the dismissal of Hassan. As a sculpture, *I Was Overcome with a Momentary Panic at the Thought that They Might Be Right* (2005) formally spins the anthropomorphic Minimalism of Donald Judd with the etherealness of John McCracken; radicalized aesthetics in the form of a diagram-*cum*-sculpture.

Raad's critique of documentary formats continues with *We Can Make Rain but No One Came to Ask* (2005), a 'possible' video collaboration between a leading ammunitions expert and a photojournalist that examines a specific detonation at Furn Ech Chubak, Beirut. The footage appears largely innocuous: street corners blend into each other and unknown figures loom large, as digital architecture twists and slides across the screen. This is video document as digital wallpaper, an endless shifting surface that expresses slight unease. Collectively the works propose a triangulated discussion that examines acts of extreme violence through the fractured lens of photography, sculpture and moving image.

In the second gallery *Hostage: The Bachar Tapes (#17 and #31)* (2001) is introduced with the statement 'Yes our story is tragic, yes it is sordid, but you have to remember that it is first and foremost a story.' Souheil Bachar, we are told, was held captive in Lebanon between 1983 and 1993. In two-minute video sequences – a duration equivalent to periods spent in interrogation – he tells of his days spent in the same cell as five American men. Bachar, a low-level employee at the Kuwaiti Embassy in Beirut, discusses the alienation, in part sexual, he feels when at one stage his aroused passions are suppressed violently by a fellow captive. In *I Only Wish That I Could Weep* (2000) we are privy to the 'donated' surveillance tapes of a seaside boardwalk and potential meeting-place in Beirut made by Lebanese army intelligence officer 'Operator #17'. After observing the passers-by the camera is inexorably drawn to the setting sun and the glimmering horizon line. Rather like King Kong, Operator #17 cannot help but be drawn to the beauty of the dusk, and for this he is dismissed – a satirical suggestion of universal desire.

Is the Atlas Group's work simply an overwrought examination of truth, the first casualty of war? Perhaps, but to a greater extent it represents the liberating imagination of independence from fixed ideologies, sharing something of the 'literary forgery' of Jorge Luis Borges. Raad self-consciously reconstructs his relationship to what came before, presenting a battle between oppositional systems working towards the creation of fictional worlds distinct from each other, competing for the readers' attention.

Raad describes a state of cultural, political and existential fragmentation that challenges the simplistic polarization of complicity and resistance. As Robert Smithson stated in *The Artist and Politics* (1971), 'direct political action becomes a matter of trying to pick poison out of boiling stew'. Raad is in favour of an art that, like 'the mirror in vampire films', suggests displacement – a form of gaze that provides the viewer with a new sense of agency.

Mark Beasley, 'Walid Raad/The Atlas Group', *frieze*, no. 97 (March 2006) 152–3. www.frieze.com

YOU KNOW WHAT I'M SEEING!

IT'S THAT BEER BOTTLE!

IT'S PROMINENT IN A SHOT I TOOK LAST FALL – AND IT HASN'T MOVED!

Joel Sternfeld, quoted by Adam Gopnik, *Walking the High Line*, 2001

DROSSCAPE

Robert Smithson
The Crystal Land//1966

[...] We arrived at the Great Notch Quarry, which is situated 'about three hundred yards southwest of the Great Notch station of the Erie Railroad'. The quarry resembled the moon. A grey factory in the midst of it all looked like architecture designed by Robert Morris. A big sign on one building said THIS IS A HARD HAT AREA. We started climbing over the piles and ran into a 'rock hound', who came on, I thought, like Mr Wizard, and who gave us all kinds of rock-hound-type information in an authoritative manner. We got a rundown on all the quarries that were closed to the public, as well as those that were open.

The walls of the quarry did look dangerous. Cracked, broken, shattered; the walls threatened to come crashing down. Fragmentation, corrosion, decomposition, disintegration, rock creep, debris slides, mud flow, avalanche were everywhere in evidence. The grey sky seemed to swallow up the heaps around us. Fractures and faults spilled forth sediment, crushed conglomerates, eroded debris and sandstone. It was an arid region, bleached and dry. An infinity of surfaces spread in every direction. A chaos of cracks surrounded us.

On the top of a promontory stood a motionless rock drill against the blank which was the sky. High-tension towers transported electric cable over the quarry. Dismantled parts of steam shovels, tread machines and trucks were lined up in random groups. Such objects interrupted the depositions of waste that formed the general condition of the place. What vegetation there was seemed partially demolished. Newly made boulders eclipsed parts of a wire and pipe fence. Railroad tracks passed by the quarry, the ties formed a redundant sequence of modules, while the steel tracks projected the modules into an imperfect vanishing point. [...]

Robert Smithson, extract from 'The Crystal Land', *Harper's Bazaar* (New York, May 1966); reprinted in *The Collected Writings of Robert Smithson*, ed. Jack Flam (Berkeley and Los Angeles: University of California Press, 1996) 9.

Italo Calvino
Invisible Cities//1972

The city of Sophronia is made up of two half-cities. In one there is the great roller coaster with its steep humps, the carousel with its chain spokes, the Ferris wheel of spinning cages, the death-ride with crouching motorcyclists, the big top with the clump of trapezes hanging in the middle. The other half-city is of stone and marble and cement, with the bank, the factories, the palaces, the slaughterhouse, the school, and all the rest. One of the half-cities is permanent, the other is temporary, and when the period of its sojourn is over, they uproot it, dismantle it, and take it off, transplanting it to the vacant lots of another half-city.

And so every year the day comes when the workmen remove the marble pediments, lower the stone walls, the cement pylons, take down the Ministry, the monument, the docks, the petroleum refinery, the hospital, load them on trailers, to follow from stand to stand their annual itinerary. Here remains the half-Sophronia of the shooting-galleries and the carousels, the shout suspended from the cart of the headlong roller coaster, and it begins to count the months, the days it must wait before the caravan returns and a complete life can begin again. [...]

Italo Calvino, extract from *Le Città invisibili* (Turin: Giulio Einaudi, 1972); trans. William Weaver, *Invisible Cities* (New York: Harcourt Brace/London: Secker & Warburg, 1974) 63.

Eric Schwab and Walead Beshty
Stumped//2005

[...] The test construction for the arch is mentioned in passing in Albert Speer's memoirs,[1] but to seek it out you need its street address, which is noted in a recent architectural monograph on Speer's Berlin.[2] It's easily spotted from the Kolonnenbrücke: an innocuous concrete block among the trees, tucked away in an unlikely corner of Schöneberg. It's also easy enough to climb the fence, if you ignore the few faded *Betreten Verboten* signs. You can walk right up to it, poke around behind it, beneath it. But the fact of the matter is, the thing hardly imparts an overwhelming impression: just a big, round cement block, overgrown by foliage and overshadowed by postwar high-rise apartments.

Eager efforts to experience this thing as something more than an abandoned mass of concrete meet with unexpected resistance. If only it offered some trace of Nazi insignia, or some odious corner suggesting atrocious acts – instead of a mute grey lump, not nearly huge enough to overwhelm its surroundings, let alone a curious traveller. If it were ruined, at least it would have ruin-value, the notorious *Ruinwert* that so preoccupied Hitler and Speer in their grandiose building plans: to erect edifices with such great masses of stone that their ruins would outlast even the Thousand-Year Reich. But the great arch was never completed – just this one, unfinished remnant, not the kind of thing one might wish to visit and contemplate as a monument or a memorial, not the kind that have proliferated in Berlin especially since the period when this thing and things like it were being built. In a way, its sheer grey obtrusiveness echoes the rows of innumerable smaller blocks recently installed as a Holocaust monument in the centre of Berlin. Or Berlin's few remaining concrete bunkers, which have at least been refitted as scenic lookout towers, or climbing rocks, or movie sets. Though equally indestructible, this block of cement managed to remain altogether useless and ignored – not even a small sign or plaque explains its presence here.

Rejected by history, ignored by tourism, indigestible by nature – what's left to learn from this silent, stump-shaped lump of concrete? A tree stump, at least, can be made to reveal its own age, its own history – you simply cut it open and count its concentric rings. That tree lived X years, grew Y high, died in year Z – and this was its place in history. But this concrete block? Never finished, never really alive, it never really had its moment in time, its place in history – built to test the possibility of its ever reaching its full size, its sheer bulk instead demonstrated its impossibility, the same impossibility that fated it to remain here: too huge to build, too huge to demolish.

In a passage from W.G. Sebald's *Austerlitz*, the author ruminates on a recent conversation with the book's building-obsessed title figure, in which the latter had speculated that only small-scale buildings – forest cottages, bridgekeepers' huts, scenic pavilions, even tree houses – had the capacity to evoke a sense of peace, whereas in the case of more massive buildings, the larger they grew beyond reasonable human dimensions, the more they seemed to cast a shadow of their own impending destruction, to the point where they could be reasonably understood only as eventual ruins. So Sebald sets off to explore a massive nineteenth-century fortress in the Belgian countryside, expecting to confront the geometric perfection of towering star-shaped fortifications, a ruined emblem of overbearing military rationality. What the author encounters instead is an inscrutable mass of overbaked and wrinkled concrete that, for him, evokes nothing more than a great beached whale, a faceless and formless monstrosity that seems to demand submission even as it defies every effort to comprehend it.[3]

Lurking in Sebald's incomprehension is really a kind of stubbornness, a refusal either to submit to the brutal necessity of such masses of concrete or else to retreat into a way of understanding them – as ruins or relics conquered by time, superseded by history – that tacitly preserves one's own sense of superiority. Such mental manoeuvres only mimic the polarities of scale and mass these edifices impose: we all are free to deplore such brutal measures until the day we're relieved to find refuge in them. Perhaps the same stubbornness is what drove Sebald to insist, in *On the Natural History of Destruction*, that Western civilization had yet to come to grips, even fifty years later, with the devastation inflicted on German cities by Allied bombing in the final years of World War II. Does the victory over unlawful aggression and manifest evil, he wonders, suffice to explain such acts of reciprocal destruction, or does such destruction stand instead as 'irrefutable proof that the catastrophes which develop, so to speak, in our hands and seem to break out suddenly are a kind of experiment, anticipating the point at which we shall fall away from what we have thought for so long to be our autonomous history and sink back [*zurücksinken*] into the history of nature?'[4]

A stillborn monstrosity of human ambition. Conceived to commemorate the climax of an era that aimed to last a millennium but destroyed itself in hardly more than a decade. Now just another beached leviathan, slowly sinking back into the sands of timeless nature. So maybe the only remaining question is, will it disappear altogether before the present historical era, of industry and capitalism and democracy, of cities and civilization and autonomy, itself sinks back into the nature from whence it sprang?

For Sebald, Hitler and Speer's plans to demolish and rebuild great swathes of Berlin were merely a prelude to the actual devastation wrought by Allied bombers – both part of the same experiment in catastrophe. Sebald finds his intuition confirmed in an essay on Speer's memoirs by Elias Canetti, the author of *Crowds and Power*, who obsessively dissects Speer and his boss's increasingly megalomaniacal architectural aspirations as symptoms of the paranoia produced by pure unlimited power. 'Contemplating these plans', Canetti notes with resignation, 'makes one aware of the terrible destruction of Germany's cities. You know how it ends, and now suddenly you're shown what began it, in all its scope.'[5] Indeed, even at the time, it was assumed that Berlin's total reconstruction and the ever-expanding plans for total war were inseparable; Speer and Hitler openly discussed the fact that the bombing of Berlin would alleviate some of the need for extensive demolition, not to mention the displacement of tens of thousands of Berliners. For Canetti, this inhumane indifference to the actual human cost marks the central paradox of Speer's embrace of Hitler's plans: 'building and destruction, which in Hitler existed side-by-side'. For wasn't it the unwavering enthusiasm of these same German masses that Hitler hoped would infuse these buildings with an aura of unsurpassable power – as 'symbols of a mass that will never perish' [*Symbol für eine Masse, die nicht mehr zerfällt*]?[6] What for Canetti remains an unfathomable paradox in the very nature of power, however, for Sebald reflects a far more basic urge: a drive to transcend human life, human history, once and for all. 'Speer's plans', Sebald observed, 'which nowhere incorporate his society's actual social life, serve as the setting for a dead age; they represent the triumph of ideology, frozen into a monumental panorama. The yearning for total order has no need of life.'[7]

In the end, of course, most of Speer's grand plans for Berlin were realized only in miniature as architectural models. Then again, in retrospect it seems clear that these plans and models were never really meant to have a life-sized version. Speer himself recognized that such buildings would be not only bigger than anything yet built but, in effect, beyond all dimension, *über*dimensional. Indeed, as Speer notes sardonically, he had to design the vast People's Hall to contain mass demonstrations of over 150,000, which required such an immense scale that Hitler himself, when he appeared on its grand ceremonial balcony, would literally have disappeared 'to an optical nothing', *zu einem optischen Nichts*.[8] For Sebald, it is this sort of drastic shift in perspective, more than the buildings themselves, that encapsulates Hitler's most secret desire. Paraphrasing Speer's observations, Sebald writes, 'Thus Hitler was so enthused by the Pyramids, those petrified extensions of domination and the irreversibility of death, which obsess the paranoiac emotionally because death – as the administrators of Kafka's castle well knew – represents the most random but also the most seamless of all systems of order.'[9] The quest for perfect order becomes the desire for death only because the paranoiac cannot keep things in the proper perspective. This is a lesson already available in the teachings of Kant: To apprehend the sublimity of the Egyptian Pyramids, he explains, one must regard them from the proper distance; viewed from too close up, their sheer scale and upwards sweep overwhelm the individual, but from too far away they lose their grandeur and appear as simple geometric shapes.[10] Perhaps this rule explains the sense of perspective that eludes both Canetti and Speer: where Canetti's efforts to fathom the essence of Hitler's power are overwhelmed by the sheer, unfathomable excessiveness of it all – the scale of the masses, the scale of delusion, the scale of brutality[11] – Speer's memoirs view recently past events from a contrived distance in which events appear as diminutive as the architectural models he made for Berlin. Unlike those two, who spoke directly from experience, Sebald, writing from the next generation, was perhaps just far enough away to attain the proper lack of distance.

1. Albert Speer, *Erinnerungen* (Berlin: Propyläen, 1969) 169.
2. Hans J. Reichhardt and Wolfgang Schäche, *Von Berlin nach Germania. Über die Zerstörungen der 'Reichshauptstadt' durch Albert Speers Neugestaltungsplanungen* (Berlin: Transit, 1998) 13–19.
3. W.G. Sebald, *Austerlitz* (Frankfurt am Main: Fischer, 2001) 31–2.
4. W.G. Sebald, *Luftkrieg und Literatur. Züricher Vorlesungen* (Frankfurt am Main: Fischer, 2000) 17; Sebald, *On the Natural History of Destruction*, trans. Anthea Bell (New York: Random House, 2003) 67 [translation slightly modified – Eric Schwab].
5. Elias Canetti, 'Hitler, nach Speer' (1971), in *Das Gewissen der Worte* (Frankfurt am Main: Fischer, 1981) 172.
6. Ibid., 174.
7. W.G. Sebald, *Summa Scientiae. System und Systemkritik bei Elias Canetti, in Die Beschreibung des Ungluecks. Zur oesterreichischen Literatur von Stifter bis Handke* (Frankfurt am Main: Fischer, 1994) 95.
8. Speer, *Erinnerungen*, op.cit., 168.
9. Sebald, *Summa Scientiae*, op.cit., 95.
10. Immanuel Kant, *Critique of Judgment*, Section 26.
11. See the final sentence of Canetti's essay (199): 'The shame over this situation, the insight into this disgrace, the essence of this false vision – everything comes together here into an indestructible impression.'

Eric Schwab and Walead Beshty, extract from 'Stumped: What Remains of the Thousand-Year Reich?', *Cabinet*, no. 20 (Winter 2005–6) 75–7.

Patrick Keiller
Imaging//2010

[...] In 1979, I embarked on a postgraduate project in Peter Kardia's Department of Environmental Media at the Royal College of Art, where I began to make films and identified a canon of relevant texts, including Benjamin's 'Surrealism' (1929), in which I read that 'the true creative overcoming of religious illumination ... resides in a profane illumination, a materialistic, anthropological inspiration'; and that

> No one before these visionaries and augurs perceived how destitution – not only social but architectonic, the poverty of interiors, enslaved and enslaving objects – can be suddenly transformed into revolutionary nihilism. Leaving aside Aragon's Passage de l'Opera, Breton and Nadja are the lovers who convert everything we

> have experienced on mournful railway journeys (railways are beginning to age), on Godforsaken Sunday afternoons in the proletarian quarters of the great cities, in the first glance through the rain-blurred window of a new apartment, into revolutionary experience, if not action. They bring the immense forces of 'atmosphere' concealed in these things to the point of explosion. What form do you suppose a life would take that was determined at a decisive moment precisely by the street song last on everyone's lips?

The Surrealist *frisson*, as a phenomenon, is described in literature (most explicitly in Aragon's *Le Paysan de Paris*), but is experienced primarily as a subjective transformation of appearances. It is easy to associate it with the impulse to take a photograph, with *photogénie*, which Christopher Phillips refers to as 'the mysterious transformation that occurs when everyday objects are revealed, as if anew, in a photograph or on the motion picture screen'. While Surrealism, especially after the Second World War, may not have lived up to Benjamin's appreciation of its revolutionary potential – Lefebvre, writing in 1945, was particularly scathing – the Surrealist preoccupation with transfiguration, and hence the sacred, endures for us in the now-commonplace presence of everyday objects in art, and in the subjective transformation, radical or otherwise, of everyday surroundings, the most familiar manifestations of which are the various practices of urban exploration so widely established, especially in London, since the early 1990s.

My image-making developed over several years. In 1977, I began assembling a collection of colour slides documenting 'found' architecture, and discovered a precedent for this in the Surrealists' adoption of particular locations and structures in Paris. The buildings I found were certainly interesting, but the pictures were not always very successful. I had embarked on the project with the intention of extending it with moving-image media, either video or film, but had been discouraged by their poor definition compared to that of photographs, and by the limits of the camera's frame. I spent several months trying to develop a technique of architectural photography, and eventually, on a trip to France, made a series of photographs which became the basis of an installation combining monochrome slides and spoken narration, which was followed by another made with photographs of a high wall behind the prison on Wormwood Scrubs. These two works were fairly well received – they were later included in an exhibition at the Tate Gallery – and I recovered the project's initiative, which led me, a few weeks later, to cycle along Harrow Road.

When I arrived at the place I had seen from the train, I found that it was overlooked by an extraordinary structure, a metal footbridge I had not noticed as the train passed beneath it. About 200 metres long, it carries pedestrians over both the main line and a branch that passes underneath it, at an angle, in a tunnel.

The longer of the bridge's two spans is oriented so that Wembley Stadium is framed between its parapets. The bridge's architecture suggested a renewed attempt at moving pictures: its long, narrow walkway resembled the linearity of a film; its parapets framed the view in a ratio similar to the 4 x 3 of the camera, and its elaborate articulation, with several flights of steps, half-landings and changes of direction, offered a structure for a moving-camera choreography which might include occasional panoramas.

The resulting film had two parts, the second of which was photographed a few weeks after the initial visit to the bridge, by walking a hand-held camera across it during a continuous ten-minute take. By this time, I think I had already decided to write fictional narration to accompany the picture. I discovered another footbridge, a square of walkways above the nearby junction of Harrow Road and the North Circular, with a spiral ramp at each corner, and photographed another ten-minute moving-camera walk, which became the first half of the film. This bridge was demolished in about 1992, when an underpass was built at the junction. The film was called *Stonebridge Park* (1981). Its narrative, such as it was, recalled the context, in the first part, and the immediate aftermath, in the second, of a theft committed by the narrator.

This rudimentary film was neither made nor conceived in a moment, but it originated in the unusual, unexpected experience that produced the photograph from which it evolved. Becoming more experienced in making images, I came to rely less on anything resembling the experiential phenomena of Surrealism, and became increasingly uncertain about their political significance. Exceptional moments of natural light seemed to offer similar conceptual transformations, and produced better pictures; for many who work with photographic media, the weather is not merely analogous with a state of mind. I have sometimes wondered whether I might have addressed these questions better if more of Henri Lefebvre's writing had been translated into English sooner than it was. *La Production de l'éspace* was first published in 1974, but did not appear in English until Blackwell published Donald Nicholson-Smith's translation in 1991. I first encountered the book in 1994, before which I knew of Lefebvre and his relationship with the Situationists only from a brief mention in *Leaving the Twentieth Century* (1974), Christopher Gray's anthology of Situationist writing, an essential text for any would-be-literate punk-rocker in the 1970s. There I had found Gray's translation of part of Raoul Vaneigem's *Traité de savoir-vivre à l'usage des jeunes générations* (1967), known in English as *The Revolution of Everyday Life*, from which I often quoted:

> Although I can always see how beautiful anything could be if only I could change it, in practically every case there is nothing I can really do. Everything is changed

> into something else in my imagination, then the dead weight of things changes it back into what it was in the first place.

(Nicholson-Smith's 1983 translation is closer to the original: 'though not everything affects me with equal force, I am always faced with the same paradox: no sooner do I become aware of the alchemy worked by my imagination upon reality than I see that reality reclaimed and borne away by the uncontrollable river of things'.)

In *The Production of Space*, Lefebvre writes: 'the fact is that the space which contains the realized preconditions of another life is the same one as prohibits what those preconditions make possible' – a thought not unlike that in Vaneigem's paragraph. I wondered if the prohibition that Lefebvre identifies is sometimes suspended within the spaces of a film, and, if so, whether this might explain some of the attraction, and the seemingly utopian quality, of so much film space, and why some people are willing to devote so much time and effort to making films.

In the third volume of his *Critique of Everyday Life* (1981), translated into English in 2005, Lefebvre wrote of

> Intense instants – or, rather, moments – it is as if they are seeking to shatter the everydayness trapped in generalized exchange. On the one hand, they affix the chain of equivalents to lived experience and daily life. On the other, they detach and shatter it. In the 'micro', conflicts between these elements and the chains of equivalence are continually arising. Yet the 'macro', the pressure of the market and exchange, is forever limiting these conflicts and restoring order. At certain periods, people have looked to these moments to transform existence ...

Lefebvre often writes of 'moments'. 'What is Possible', the final chapter of the first volume of the *Critique*, written in 1945, contains this:

> Mystics and metaphysicians used to acknowledge that everything in life revolved around exceptional moments. In their view, life found expression and was concentrated in them. These moments were festivals: festivals of the mind or the heart, public or intimate festivals. In order to attack and mortally wound mysticism, it was necessary to show that festivals had lost their meaning, the power they had in the days when all their magnificence came from life, and when life drew its magnificence from festivals.

And in the opening chapter of *The Production of Space* he identifies another kind of *moment*:

> The fact is that around 1910 a certain space was shattered. It was the space of common sense, of knowledge (*savoir*), of social practice, of political power, a space thitherto enshrined in everyday discourse, just as in abstract thought, as the environment of and channel for communications; the space, too, of classical perspective and geometry, developed from the Renaissance onwards on the basis of the Greek tradition (Euclid, logic) and bodied forth in Western art and philosophy, as in the form of the city and the town ... Euclidean and perspectivist space have disappeared as systems of reference, along with other former 'commonplaces' such as the town, history, paternity, the tonal system in music, traditional morality, and so forth. This was truly a crucial moment.

This paragraph had already appeared in 1990, quoted in David Harvey's *The Condition of Postmodernity*, also published by Blackwell, and Harvey quoted it again in his afterword for Blackwell's edition of *The Production of Space*. Harvey's interest in the passage arises, I assume, from its identification of the beginning of a period that ended with the 'profound shift in the "structure of feeling"' that signalled the onset of postmodernity in the early 1970s, with the break-up of the Bretton Woods fixed-exchange-rate system and the subsequent slide to neoliberalism. In the autumn of 2008, it began to seem possible that this period might be giving way to another.

If such moments of historical transition, however questionable their identification, open possibilities for creativity, for those moments to which, in Lefebvre's words, people have looked to transform existence (1910 was, among other things, the year in which Apollinaire invented the art of going for a walk), it seems strange that Surrealist and Situationist techniques– *flânerie*, the *dérive* and psychogeography – should have become the subject of so much attention, even if they were not quite 'revived', in London during the 1990s. At the time, I suggested that their purpose had been overlooked: psychogeography and the *dérive* were conceived, in a more politically ambitious period, as preliminaries to the production of new, revolutionary spaces; in the 1990s they seemed more likely to be preliminary to the production of literature and other works, and to gentrification, the discovery of previously overlooked value in dilapidated spaces and neighbourhoods.

In an essay on 'contemporary London Gothic', Roger Luckhurst has suggested that the Gothic genre that he and others identified as characteristic of London in the 1990s was a response to 'that curious mix of tyranny and farce that constitutes London governance', particularly the dominance of the City of London, with its mediaeval peculiarities and its untiring pursuit of an ever more unequal, damaged world. Among the writers Luckhurst identified with the contemporary London Gothic, several have invoked the techniques of Situationist urbanism, as if the power of the financial sector is such that subjective reimagination offered the only possibility for change that had become unattainable in other ways.

In 2008, cycling along Harrow Road, I did not encounter any explosion of the 'intense forces of "atmosphere"' that are undoubtedly concealed there; but unexpected memories of earlier discoveries, at a time when it seemed possible that a dysfunctional economic orthodoxy was finally collapsing, suggested that such experiences still have some value.

Patrick Keiller, extract from 'Imaging', in *Restless Cities*, ed. Matthew Beaumont and Gregory Dart (London and New York: Verso, 2010) 146–53.

Rebecca Solnit
The Ruins of Memory//2007

[...] A city – any city, every city – is the eradication, even the ruin, of the landscape from which it rose. In its fall, that original landscape sometimes triumphs. One day, I looked up from an intersection in San Francisco's densely urban Mission District and saw down the street to the south the undomesticated crest of Bernal Heights, with its coyote and wild blackberries, and up the street to the west the ridgeline of Twin Peaks and with a shudder perceived, still present as a phantom, the steep natural landscape that underlay the city, the skin beneath the clothes, the landscape that reappeared amid the miles of ruins of the 1906 earthquake and that someday will reassert itself again. Another day, I walked down Hayes Street west of City Hall and saw suddenly the surprising view of a vista opened up by the belated removal of the freeway overpass damaged by the 1989 earthquake. Some months before, I watched the wrecking ball smash that overpass into chunks of rebar-threaded concrete small enough to truck away. The concrete mined from some place out of sight was being sent back over the horizon. A place like San Francisco could be imagined not as one city stretching out since 1846 but dozens of cities laid over each other's ruins, the way that archaeologists experience the unearthed ruins layered in strata, the ten or twelve cities that lay above Homer's Troy. Dolls, whiskey and medicine bottles, buttons, sometimes ships and skeletons, reappear along with the sand whenever a new foundation is dug in central San Francisco.

To make this city, much of a windswept, fog-shrouded expanse of sand dunes and chaparral-covered hillsides was smoothed over, dunes removed, hilltops flattened, bays and marshes filled in, streams forced underground, endemic species driven into extinction. Even the view of the resultant simplified topography was obscured by the buildings everywhere, though one of San Francisco's charms is its still-surviving steepness: the crests and heights offer views of the distance – not only of the rest of the city, but the sea, bay and hills beyond it. Another is the pure geometry of its grid, often criticized for being an overly two-dimensional response to a wildly three-dimensional terrain, but these straight axes also open up the distance visible at the end of the long shafts of streets. San Francisco is the least claustrophobic of cities. Both big earthquakes of the twentieth century shook the place loose of its bonds – the carpet of architecture in 1906, the ugly shackles of the Embarcadero and Central freeways in 1989.

In natural disasters, the natural landscape reasserts itself and reappears, not only as force but as the contours beneath the cityscape. Cities are always maintained, for natural processes of decay produce ruins as surely as violence and fire, flood and earthquake do; and only maintenance and replacement postpone the inevitable ruin – the entropy of the built and the return of the organic. [...]

Man proposes, earthquake disposes, the maxim might be revised to say, though earthquakes are only one small source of the ruins that are in some ways the inevitable corollary of the very act of building. That nothing lasts forever is perhaps our favourite thing to forget. And forgetting is the ruin of memory, its collapse, decay, shattering and eventual fading away into nothingness. We don't quite recognize how resilient cities are, how they arise over and over again from their own ruins, resurrected, reincarnated, though every Rome and London is such a resurrection, or reinvention. So it seems strange to see the ruins of then become the smooth façades of now, to see not the entropy that leads to ruin but the endeavour that effaces it so thoroughly that its ruinous past is hardly believable. Yet this happens again and again: Frank Gohlke's 1979–80 photographs of the tornado at Wichita Falls, Texas, show a place torn apart by wind and the same place a year later, restored as though nothing had happened (or so that the same thing can happen again?). Ruins are evidence not only that cities can be destroyed but that they survive their own destruction, are resurrected again and again.

Ruins stand as reminders. Memory is always incomplete, always imperfect, always falling into ruin; but the ruins themselves, like other traces, are treasures: our links to what came before, our guide to situating ourselves in a landscape of time. To erase the ruins is to erase the visible public triggers of memory; a city without ruins and traces of age is like a mind without memories. Such erasure is the foundation of the amnesiac landscape that is the United States. Because the United States is in many ways a country without a past, it seems, at first imagining, to be a country without ruins. But it is rich in ruins, though not always as imagined, for it is without a past only in the sense that it does not own its past, or own up to it. It does not remember officially and in its media and mainstream, though many subsets of Americans remember passionately. [...]

Rebecca Solnit, extracts from *Storming the Gates of Paradise* (Berkeley and Los Angeles: University of California Press, 2007) 352–3; 354–5.

Ralph Rugoff
Circling the Centre//2006

[...] The Center for Land Use Interpretation is a nonprofit educational organization that examines how we use, envision and think about different kinds of landscapes in the United States. A few individuals from different backgrounds who nonetheless had come to work and think in similar ways founded the Center in 1994 in Oakland, California. Operating from a rickety office along that city's industrial waterfront, they began presenting exhibits that examined areas where the man-made, the cultural and the natural seemed to merge. They also conducted tours focusing on little-observed features of the surrounding urban area, and installed interpretive plaques commemorating unusual types of land use (such as one marking a site in New Mexico where in 1957 a hydrogen bomb hit the ground after having been accidentally dropped from an aeroplane).

Audiences for these initial programmes were small, but that was of little consequence. What mattered was that the Center was inventing, piece by piece, a new type of institution: a grassroots clearing house that presented documentation of the curious, astonishing and sometimes alarming transformations of the contemporary American landscape. Looking at material that was off the radar of both the mass media and mainstream academia, the Center's programmes addressed not only the way that land is used, but also how it is perceived. To a certain extent, it could be said that its real subject is how we look at, and conceptualize, the world around us (but more on that later).

I first picked up on the Center in 1996 after it had relocated to Los Angeles, opening a small office next to another unique organization, the Museum of Jurassic Technology. The Center's exhibits in its new home continued to look at aspects of how the country's lands are used and perceived, examining an eclectic array of sites ranging from field-test facilities for high-impact technologies to sites of 'geo-transformative' activity undertaken by government agencies. Among other memorable exhibits from those days were a display of aerial photographs of open-pit mines, shot as a hobby by a retired mining engineer, that were disconcertingly beautiful, and a screening programme featuring films of nuclear testing programmes of the world's declared nuclear powers (which was a study of different cultural approaches to propaganda as much as it was about perspectives on land use).

Over the years, the Center's exhibits and publications have been remarkably astute, noteworthy not only for illuminating our understanding of mundane as well as extraordinary landscapes, but also for their even-handed and lucid exposition. Even when describing odd, disturbing or even potentially humorous phenomena, the tenor of these presentations is never dramatic or self-conscious. Texts tend to be straightforward and factually oriented, while the Center's photographs typically resemble the seemingly authorless images compiled in government and industrial archives (though, for the most part, these photographs are produced by the Center's extended family of volunteers). In their tone, at least, these programmes conjure the work of a benevolent social science agency or think tank, or perhaps a forward-looking research division of the US Army Corps of Engineers. (The Center's name likewise suggests some such bureaucratic organization.) And as it has grown over the past decade, this organization has in many very real ways come to resemble a public research institute, developing an impressive array of databases, libraries and archives as well as far-flung 'research training stations' and myriad outreach programmes.

Yet unlike its institutional counterparts, the Center has remained curiously unmoored from any recognizable policy platform. Its programmes – as far as can discern – reveal no overt or even implicit political or social agenda. Indeed, whether documenting nuclear proving grounds or the architecture of show caves (subterranean caverns that have been decorated and turned into tourist attractions), its exhibitions and publications are always disarmingly – at times, almost unnervingly – free of any editorial viewpoint. They are as detached from the positions of environmental politics as from those of the military or commercial industry.

But if this organization is not trying to sell us an ideological bag of goods, what purpose(s) could possibly be motivating its public exploration of how land is used and apportioned in the United States? It is not only the more cynical among us who may regard the Center's osensible neutrality, its flagrant nonpartisanship, as slightly suspicious as well as provocative. Its non-judgemental attitude goes against the grain of our expectations, especially when it is applied to contentious subjects like nuclear weapons testing or strip-mining, which we are accustomed to considering within an explicitly political or moral framework.

This conspicuous absence of editorial slant is paralleled by the expansive – almost indiscriminate – selection criteria used by the Center in choosing subjects for its exhibitions and publications. Besides reportage on such subjects as shipping channels, defence installations and aspects of urban infrastructure, the Center's purview embraces less straightforward phenomena: underwater towns created by dam-produced floods; fictionalized spaces ranging from movie set locations to civilian emergency training sites where life-size props simulate toxic fuel spills and collapsing buildings; and the alternative universe of the Nellis Range, a five-thousand-square-mile area of military-controlled terrain in Nevada, which since 1940 has been a virtual nation unto itself, a kind of time capsule cut off from the rest of American society. Significantly, the Center treats all these diverse subjects in an identical manner, assigning no more weight to an exhibit on anti-terrorist barricades than to one looking at period travel postcards. Within the broadly defined field of 'land use interpretation' they are all comparably noteworthy.

In this way the Center's programmes deliberately bypass the familiar categories and classifications that we rely on in making sense of the world. A very curious effect results from this benignly subversive approach: we may end up looking at one place or activity through a lens we normally reserve for evaluating another. By treating a nuclear test site in the same manner as an outdoor sculpture, for instance, the Center's exhibits gently prompt us to reconsider the sculpture as possible waste while appreciating the aesthetic value of the radioactive hole (think of it as a type of vast earthwork). In engineering this subtle shift, the Center introduces us to a landscape of uncertainty where our ready-made convictions and judgements lose their traction. But it undermines our assumptions in a very generous manner, encouraging us to look at things from more than one perspective and alerting us to other ways of understanding that can renew our interest in the larger landscape.

From another point of view, of course, it can be argued that the Center's apparent lack of editorial bias is itself a kind of editorial stance – though one directed not against any particular issue so much as the fallibility of our knowledge in general. Indeed, a tonic trace of scepticism runs just beneath the surface of many of the Center's activities, including its archival projects that involve ordering mountains of information so they can be productively mined. Yet even while it divides this material into categories and subcategories, indexing it with keywords and cross-references, the Center seems subtly to acknowledge that its own ordering system is inevitably flawed – that arbitrarily to classify things and place them in conceptual cubbyholes involves cutting them off from the continuum of existence.

In contrast to our culture of experts – the pundits, academics and government analysts who regularly appear in the media to tell us what to think – the Center is a haven of amateur agnostics. Its members are specialists who specialize in non-specialization. Their approach is not so much multidisciplinary as nondisciplinary: it traces out an underlying logic that connects disparate fields and perspectives, linking them to the common ground of land use and its interpretation. And on one level, at least, it speaks to a desire to transcend the increasingly differentiated, specialized and disconnected worlds of science, commerce, culture and politics.

To a certain extent, I think of the Center as a type of informational test site or lab where different modes of presenting data are tried out and developed. In the process, its far-ranging programmes have also charted an alternative map of the United States. Filling in blank spots in our collective perceptual field, they call attention to neglected, overlooked and often highly telling aspects of the American landscape. And once exposed to this information, our everyday picture of the world around us – and our sense of our role in it – can never be the same again. Yet the specifics of how our perspective may change is something that each visitor works out on his or her own. The Center is not interested in lobbying us for a particular point of view or trying to mould our opinions. It simply suggests that things might be different than we had previously thought.

In other words, the Center never pretends to have all the answers. Instead, its programmes suggest that answers often come in the form of questions, and as the result of finding the ground beneath the middle of an apparent conflict. That conflict may be one of values. Many of the Center's projects emphasize the contradictory qualities of a given subject: a suburban landscape that is at once banal and melodramatic, an industrial harbour that is simultaneously unsightly and sublime. If the Center has a function – and I am not sure it does, at least not in any conventional sense – it might have something to do with recognizing and celebrating this kind of paradoxical perspective, and with disseminating the idea that truth exists only in conditions of contradiction.

Yet I suspect that the Center, however indirectly, also functions as an agent of intelligent change, possibly even revolutionary change. Its politics are oblique, of course, and it may be that they are most conspicuous in terms of the Center's decentralized organizational model. A largely volunteer outfit with contributors from across the country, independently researching and investigating and producing new materials about land use and its interpretation, the Center has continued to develop in unpredictable directions (I long ago lost track of how many desert research outposts, interpretative stations and regional offices it has opened around the country). Distributing the fruits of this open-source research in myriad forms (including its excellent website and printed newsletter, *The Lay of the Land*), the Center eschews any central voice of authority. It presents no master narrative that demands an exclusive path of action. Its politics, if they can be described in such terms, are indirect and elusive. They evade conventional forms by refusing to embrace recognizable 'positions' – positions that easily become reified postures that can be targeted and dismissed. Embracing a post-protest ethic that moves beyond simple binary oppositions, the Center sets out to reframe the nature of debate itself. Its work confronts contradiction and grey areas, prompting us to question the points of balance in our existing notions about land use and to grapple with the daunting complexities and scenarios of contemporary landscapes. It presents opportunities for opening up new avenues of knowledge rather than reinforcing ready-made conclusions. Needless to say, the question of land use is an area of increasing concern, and I imagine that the future impact of this organization's work will grow exponentially in the years ahead. Of course, what we do with the awareness it provokes is up to each of us in the end, but on its own the Center is already evolving tools that can transform the way we think – not only about politics, but about the very ground beneath us all.

Ralph Rugoff, 'Circling the Center', in *Overlook: Exploring the Internal Fringes of America* (New York Metropolis Books, 2006) 35-41.

Iain Sinclair
Lights Out for the Territory//1997

[...] It was prescient of Rachel Whiteread, after months of careful searches through housing lists, and a collaboration with James Lingwood of Artangel, to arrive at the one site where her project – 'a mute memorial to everyday existence and the pathos of remembering' – would fuse all the loose wires of potential catastrophe. The whole affair seems to have occurred with a dreamlike logic: obstacles were overcome, implications were ignored. Whiteread drove forward with the courage of a sleepwalker. *House*, seen from across the field, was a giant bone plug feeding current into the madness of the city. Feeding and receiving.

Grove Road had the lot: an end of terrace house with three exploitable sides (and a sitting tenant), a hyperactive local politico willing to play the heavy (Bob Hoskins as UK casting, Danny DeVito in the US), anarchist squatters, post-Situationist music business trouble-makers looking for the grand gesture, and peg-eyed psychogeographers prophesying war. This terrace was in the wrong documentary. It was blatantly touting for millennial funds. It stood as an affront to the radiant blankness of the Green Way, an all too human shambles. High art had to be capable of making the transition, erasing the tape. The 'old sweat' intransigence of the last inhabitant, Sydney Gale (as he was known to the broadsheets), or 'Sid the War Hero' (to the tabloids), was the only thing keeping the ruin upright. 193 Grove Road belonged, through right of long occupation, to Mr Gale and his family. The ex-docker had nothing else to feel so bloody-minded about, to exercise his hereditary prerogative for cussedness. Even his surname seemed to allude, punningly, to the night of the Great Storm, the 16th of October 1987: a natural drama hijacked by the Parks Commttee. The storm, with its tangled avenues of uprooted trees, was the perfect front for a strategic refurbishment, the sequestration of Victoria Park Lido – as a car park (with no direct access to the grassland). Mr Gale became the incarnation of the wind, a self-generating hurricane of grievance. He was even ready to busk as a performance artist, to display his hand-painted banner: THIS IS MY HOME, I LIVE HERE. A tautology that was all too soon to be confounded.

Up to this point, before the work on *House* began, Artangel and the LibDem caucus, and even Mr Gale, held to their uneasy alliance. Contracts were drawn up. Mr Gale would be rehoused and Whiteread, no stranger to the area, would move in her team – forensically wrapped and masked – to commence the process of mummification. Whiteread's earlier Turner Prize contender, *Ghost*, had been exhibited at the nearby Chesenhale Gallery, a traditional (ex-industrial) East London art space. The Chisenhale specialized in emptiness, absence: mediated gestures in a culture vacuum. Fetish objects possessing just enough presence to keep out the smell of the veneer factory, the echoing voices of the women who turned out Spitfire propellers. Vacuity is what these transitional structures promote: mind art. 'Mute pathos' is their shtick. They set-dress minimalism, make it feel good: the least disturbed, the most effective.

Ghost, encountered unexpectedly (in company with Patrick Wright, backing away from the trash destined as a sculptural rinse for the Bow Quarter), was a revelation. Literally so: the cube of retrieved and imprisoned light illuminated the windowless gallery. The relationship between sculpture and containing space was dynamic. The piece did not dominate (or deny) the history of the chamber to which it had been brought. A lengthy period of solitary labour in the original Archway room, casting and reversing, had resulted in this mysterious monobloc: this icy and unforgiving depiction of the unconscious. *Ghost* outranked pathos, it was much crueller and brighter than that. The allusions are to Egyptian and Assyrian plunder in the British Museum, to the whiteness of an idealized past, not to the sentimentality of false memory, colonized domestic enclosures. The Archway room was not called upon to surrender the shades and movements of the lives it had witnessed: it was elevated to an archetype, demotic overwhelmed by hieratic. Whiteread's art was profoundly female, not feminist, responsive and shaping – purposefully limited, open to a biological flow of time. Set outside in a sculpture park, a corporate watercourt, the venom of *Ghost* would be dissipated. It would be as ineffective as one of those 'period' rooms you can yawn through in the Geffrye Museum.

House, a few hundred yards to the west of the Chisenhale Gallery, exposed to the spasms of passing traffic, was a much trickier proposition. Whiteread, innocent of irony, remarks (in her video diary) on how surprised she was to discover that the park would not be secure: 'I hadn't realized the gates would be open the whole time.' She will be constantly under observation. The prolonged and silent hermeticism of the Archway room will not be possible. *House* from its conception was under sentence of death. It would never (except for the computer mock-up at the Tate) be brought inside. The entire process of conversion would be as visible as an act of public surgery, a virtuoso amputation. A bride stripped bare by her bachelors. *House* was front-lawn art, a sponsored bastard. The stakes were high enough to alert every demon in the dictionary: vampire aesthetes, strollers and stalkers, all those factions prepared to underwrite any challenge on the torpid energy balance of the Green Corridor. [...]

Iain Sinclair, extract from *Lights Out for the Territory* (London: Granta, 1997) 210–13.

Richard Grayson
Mike Nelson: *24A Orwell Street*//2006

At night [Sydney's] Darlinghurst and Macleay Streets are like something out of a movie; the main drag is alive, alight. There is loud music playing from different bars and people shrieking at each other in the neon spill of the McDonald's next to the Asian grocery into the hot tropical darkness. When navy ships dock in Woolloomooloo Bay at the bottom of the road that leads up to the Cross, the streets fill up with men in white uniforms, walking in gangs with a flotilla of girls and hangers on, drifting up and down, seeing what sort of fun they can have and what trouble they get into, before they are recalled to ship and head off to sea again in the morning. Their progress is watched by hookers standing under the neon lights of the strip clubs and drunken boys from the western suburbs. Each morning it's more the Kris Kristopherson song 'Sunday Morning Coming Down'. Strangely quiet under the high blue sky, just the sounds of small domestic activity, music from radios in distant kitchens, the streets smell of jacaranda blossom and beer and disinfectant and piss. Thirty-somethings in dress-down Hugo Boss and Prada drink good lattes and read newspapers and talk about media deals over breakfast at the café tables that spill onto the pavement. Just down the hill there's a small square with turquoise metal seats where an Aboriginal couple are nodding off, bulging plastic tartan laundry bags at their feet, syringes carefully placed on the wall beside them.

Facing this square is a red-painted shop on Orwell Street. On either side there are backpackers' hostels and red-brick apartment blocks from the 1930s and 1940s. When you stand in the street and look up at the flat shopfront, you can see the words 'Magic' painted in faded yellow on its red front. There are two doors, and on either side of the doors there are windows containing logs and dried and dusty foliage and other objects that are hard to make out through the dirty glass. It looks closed and, well, if not intimidating, unwelcoming. There's no sign but this is definitely 24 Orwell Street where Mike Nelson has made a work for the 2002 Sydney Biennale.

When you finally press the doorbell and are buzzed in from the pavement you see that the space has been fitted out to accommodate small creatures. There's a narrow corridor with traces of aboriginal-style animal paintings on the walls and floor, lined with glass-fronted cases and vitrines. As you make your way through you discover that each one of these cases holds a small environment or landscape, a sketchy diorama: maybe sand and a mummified head, or a painted backdrop of a hill, or a wider, deeper one containing two steeply rearing, conical termite mounds which might be made out of papier-mâché surrounded by collapsed dry leaves and branches. What every single one of these cases, with their different environments and landscapes has in common, is the total absence of any living thing. The reptiles or animals that the vitrines had been designed to accommodate are gone, their only trace a fragment of sloughed, transparent snake skin.

You also got to go behind the scenes, backstage, to the rear of the proscenium arches of the deserted tanks. You pushed open a door into the access corridors with their splintery wooden walls, with broken electric fans and small rough louvred doors that opened into the cases: maybe for cleaning them out, putting in food and water or introducing new captives. Just when you were convinced that you might indeed be behind the scenes of an abandoned reptile house, or some strange private collection, or a shop maybe, dedicated to selling rare exotic species, you came upon a workspace at the rear of the building that was filled with the half-finished structure of a pond. This took you back yet another stage, behind another scene, and allowed the X-ray flicker of seeing the artwork in construction, the fiction in an unfinished state, whilst at the same time inspecting an unfinished feature of the deserted facility.

For Mike Nelson this work was singular. By this I mean that it offered a (nearly) unitary presence and space, rather than it consisting of a number of spaces that slip from one identity and function and into another in a constant segue of narrative and implication, as in *The Coral Reef* (2000) at Matt's Gallery, London, or *The Deliverance and The Patience* (2001, commissioned by Peer) at Venice. Here, in contrast, Nelson had taken over premises that had recently housed a dodgy 'outback adventure' company – that's where the maybe fake aboriginal pictures came from – and in its place he'd constructed a single fiction: a deserted reptile house/viparium/collection. In common with his other works, however, *24a Orwell Street* generated multiple layers of narrative and reference which radiated into the internal histories of the work and out into the surrounding environment. Like Doctor Who's Tardis – or any multidimensional space worth its salt from science fiction – it seemed to contain immense spaces within its boundaries (and within those worlds, other worlds) and at the same time it served subtly to alter the world in which it had materialized.

When you considered this building's corridors and vitrines in terms of these previous works, you became aware that here Nelson had built a sort of model and analogue of those complex fictional environments. The individual dioramas stood in for the deserted bikers' bars and Turkish taxi offices, but here the ghostly suggestion of human presence had been replaced by traces of another species. This shift initially seemed to position the visitor differently in the mechanics of this work: we seem to be no longer direct players in the piece – moving through the corridors and spaces as stand-ins for the previous inhabitants, seemingly just departed. Instead we have stepped back, become viewers, and now observe from the outside through the glass wall, rather than from the inside. However, this illusion of spectatorial distance was momentary. The vitrines that we were peering into were in turn components of the architecture that enclosed us. Spaces, we deduced, that were shared with whatever it was that had escaped from behind the glass. Suddenly the shop becomes overlaid with frames from films like *Aliens* – the wooden corridors, the service shafts and ducting systems through which the protagonists clatter in search of the alien presence, to find that they themselves are prey and are about to meet a sudden brutal death, as jaws lunge through a sheet of cladding in a moment of half-seen close-up.

The hunter hunted, the collector collected, such turns and reversals are at the heart of so many stories that talk of the relationship of the human to the non-human, be this in the 'high' literature of *Moby Dick* or *The Island of Doctor Moreau*, or of *Aliens, 1–3*; it reflects a sort of existential xenophobia as to 'what is not us' and its relationship to 'what is us'. Collecting animals is an act of ordering, a grammar of power expressed in the syntax of those who collect and that which is collected. A collection is a dominion, a sort of imperial hubris. But once you have introduced that which is 'not us' into 'us' by something escaping, or its penetration through exchange or purchase – like the cute furry animal bought from the oriental store at the start of *Gremlins* – all hell then breaks loose, you undermine determined boundaries. Once seepage starts, these syntaxes collapse, to be replaced by ideas of miscegenation and contagion, infiltration and a refusal. A revenge, where structures become unstable; a world upside down, of change, of extinction. At the time that *24a Orwell Street* was being constructed, ideas of 'what is not us' and the definitions of 'us' had been given a particular charge and urgency through the events of 9/11 a few months before, and the sudden arrival in the Western mind and imagination of a new pernicious 'other'.

There is no better place for the introduction of 'that which is not us' into 'that which is us' than a port. These are places of transients, people jumping ship, rats jumping ship, where sailors and the Black Death come ashore, lawless and wild. Nelson has always been attracted to such liminal zones: his works talk of Burroughs' 'Interzone'; places that exist between states and between cultures, where laws become contingent and mutable, ideas viral. Kings Cross, the area of Sydney where *24a Orwell Street* was built, is one of these places. High up on the hill you can look down to the water and see which destroyers have drawn in at the Naval base below. The poet Kenneth Slessor said 'Kings Cross will always be apart from the rest of Sydney, still contemptuous of the rules.' From the 1920s onwards it was the site of an Australian bohemia, where new ideas were incubated and introduced into the stifling social matrix of a British colony trying to erase its convict past. In the 1940s this became the 'Sydney Push': angry young men and a few women meeting in the cafés and bars of the Cross, defining a predominantly left-wing subculture, seeking permanent opposition shaped by the ideas of Vilfredo Pareto and Wilhelm Reich, and regarded as dangerous and 'un-Australian', a phrase still used in everyday political discourse. At the same time the Cross was the centre of crime, bagmen, gambling and drinking dens, the hub of jazz and rock 'n roll and the red light district. During the Vietnam War it was one of the major stops for rest and recreation for American troops. It accommodated their needs, be it through the Tête à Tête Café renaming itself the GI's Hut, or through the establishment of numerous new brothels. This is where the street kids come to, where black Australians gather in the square to drink and sleep in the shade of the El Alamein Fountain, a centre of sleaze where the sex trade flourishes, where heroin has colonized every small side street and alleyway.

Or rather, this is as it was. With the inevitable rise of property prices the area is slowly being transformed into another trendy suburb, young professionals moving in with palm-pilots and balsamic vinegar. In 2002 the various populations shifted uneasily for position in the area. Since then money has further established its dominance. The Cross is being cleaned up.

In Australia such shifts and histories have a particular resonance, the entire movement of colonial history being one of alien introduction and indigenous dispossession. White settlement changed and devastated indigenous cultures, humans were moved off land in favour of sheep (in a land of marsupials), ecologies and animals were eradicated by the introduced species. Disease, spread by chance or through the vectors of blankets previously warmed by the sweat of convicts and jailers with TB and purposely distributed to the local tribes, in a stuttering rehearsal of germ warfare, wiped out language groups, memories and cultures.

At the same time, this settlement was forced, captured and convict. People had been collected and transported away from their environment to small reinforced conurbations that echoed the places and cultures that had produced them, but were now surrounded by an immense and foreign land. Modern Western Australia can almost be seen as the process of these small isolated simulacra joining up to construct a new cover, a new identity. Mainstream Australia still sees much of what lies underneath this as 'other'. As a visitor you soon learn that the indigenous fauna and flora are talked about in terms of the toxic, the dangerous and extraordinary. You are regaled with tales of snake bites, jellyfish, blue ringed octopus – the touch of which will paralyse the respiratory system – funnel web spiders killing joggers doing warm-up sit-ups in the local park, redbacks, crocs in the rivers and sharks in the sea. Even the cute platypus has a poison spur, irrevocably alien, in implacable opposition to the migrant, modern human. Then there is the everyday presence of Aboriginal Australians, who have been made outside and strange by the dominant culture and economy of the land, who move through this new world, regarded by much of Australia as an exoticism, an irrelevancy, a reproach and a danger.

The cramped dusty corridors of *24a Orwell Street* and the empty gaze of the vitrines worked as an uncanny container for, and an amplifier of, these endless inexorable narratives. It suggested an ongoing dialectic of escape and contagion but it refused to make any of these narratives solid or overt, nor was any element didactic, symbolic or illustrative. This powerful work made no judgement or statement. The leaky spaces of the reptile house, the small traces of what it may have once contained, offered no such possibility of definition or closure: rather it speaks instead of an ongoing uncertainty and a constant unease.

Richard Grayson, '*24A Orwell Street*, Sydney, Australia 2002', in *Mike Nelson: Between a Formula and a Code* (Margate: Turner Contemporary/Cologne: Verlag der Buchhandlung Walther König, 2006) 18–21.

Jeremy Millar
Hinterland//2002

The van skates lazily around the roundabout, around us; in its wing mirror, floating against the bare banks and concrete flyovers, a face swollen with swearing. Welcome, it seems to be saying; you're welcome to it.

The island seems a very different place, but then islands often do: self-contained, bounded (I can hardly say insular). We have decided to walk along around its south-eastern corner, the exact area visible from our shore on the mainland, taking some photographs, perhaps, and talking about Adam [Chodzko]'s work. It seems appropriate, given that so much of it seems concerned with the description of place, and the rituals that might make up that description. At the side of the road, as we approach the bridge, lies a mass of blood and fur – a badger, or a boar even? It seems to mark a place where the memory of a journey begins, Adam says, mnemonics being made more vivid by the liberal splashing of blood. I bear this in mind as I peer forward into my wing mirror.

Approaching the roundabout, we notice that the junction to the right leads to the prisons, so we decide to visit there first. A flag hangs halfway down the pole outside the fire station; a burned-out house opposite persists like a dark rumour behind a thicket of bushes and trees. We pass a number of different buildings, and areas for parking, and follow as the road slides straight ahead, and down into a view of the sewage works and marshes below. At the top of a grass bank on the left hand side, its position seemingly arbitrary, a circular road sign proclaims 'OUT OF BOUNDS', though there are no bounds to see except, perhaps, the darkening and dissolving shadow cast by the sign itself. We stop the car and take a photograph.

It is the last frame on my roll and so I begin to replace it, dropping the exposed roll into my pocket. I fiddle with the spools as a security guard walks towards us. We give him our names, where we're from, and no we didn't realize that we were on Home Office property. Was there a sign? Oh, we must have missed it. I imagine Adam's registration number being checked at the gatehouse and telling its own story. 'So, why were you taking photographs of the buildings?' I look at Adam. 'We like prison architecture ... Where d'you think we could get some slides?' he says, hoping this approach will discourage further interest.

The sun lights the unlit signs above the washboard-shuttered shopfronts, but not all of the amusement arcades are closed. A couple of them seem barely awake, grumbling onto the street like bad risers needing their first cigarette. We park the car around the corner, next to a pitch of wasteground; a mass of concrete slabs (walls? ceilings? floors?) jagged at its centre, behind it a crushed can caravan. Two men park just behind us and watch as we get out and walk towards the arcades. A short section of Jean Michel Jarre's 'Oxygene' echoes across the road, three versions actually, phased from one another, each separated by the second or two it would take to switch each machine on. It seems an appropriate soundtrack to this place, its theme tune caught somewhere between an inescapable past and the escapes of the future, and destined to play itself out like this, again and again, day after day.

We walk past the 'Talk of the Town Fun Pub', past the seaside flotsam of aluminium barrels and plastic wash baskets, cushions and carpet washed up against its back wall, and into a small area of residential maisonettes. Flat-roofed and balconied, they have a vaguely Iberian feel to them, as though drawn up by a municipal architect after a particularly traumatic holiday. The council's money had obviously run out before they surfaced the road. A large community hall stands empty to one side of the residencies, occupying a fenced-in section of land directly by the sea. It is extraordinary. Someone has placed colour photocopies in the windows, like a section from an encyclopaedia, showing the bombs that dropped here, or a liner that sailed from here, or even a photograph of Westminster Bridge from the turn of the century

('Look no cars' it points out, helpfully). In the next window, a herd of toy dinosaurs roam around the spider plants. In the yard at the front, someone has planted plastic flowers in the borders.

We continue further down the coast, past the holiday villages and along the shoreline. The road deteriorates badly – at first A and then B, we had now come to the end of the short highway alphabet – and we swerve and swoop down and around the craters in its surface. We slow, then stop further down the road, in a grassy lay-by marked by a bin, plastic rubbish bags and a pink and blue divan. On the other side of the bank, a boat is berthed on a wooden cradle at the top of the beach, reluctant to enter the water it looks out upon. Its windows are boarded over; it has a suburban front door. Adam walks off up the beach, taking photographs, while I hold back, watching the man in one of the beach houses watching Adam through binoculars. I wonder what stories, what fantasies of paranoia or vengeance are being projected through those lenses into the dark space of his mind (probably none worse than those we attribute to him as we walk back past his dark windows minutes later). Further down, the district council sign informs us that 'CLOTHING MUST BE WORN BEYOND THIS POINT'. Some birds take off behind us.

The path is about the width of the drainage ditch beside it, the one mirroring the other. As though prompted by our presence, the water splits suddenly through the cushion of grass on the bank and spills across the earth just before us, as though they might change places, that the water might once more take control (if it had ever relinquished it completely). Round the curve at the end, we reach the beach

– made, it seems, almost entirely of oyster shells, like scaled-up scales – and make our way towards the concrete lookout post. Across the marsh, water and grasses, thick blues and yellows, look like a bad old bruise. Nearby, huge chunks of wood lie amongst more concrete wreckage, and the frayed nerves of steel rope twisted from the ground. The concrete structure is low and angular, its corners cut off, with a slightly more elevated lookout position rising from its roof. Small black holes punctuate the grey-brown walls, a slice having been taken from the corner that looks out over the brown-grey water to our town. It is alien and appropriate and sadly beautiful. I walk around the structure and approach the empty corner that marks its entrance, Adam watching me. The walls lead one way and then another, now trapping light from its interior as it was once designed to trap incoming shells. I wonder what I might find in there, who might be found in there, who might have found themselves in there. How safe are these outposts of security, and is sanctuary always to be found within its thick sound-swallowing walls?

Inside is not so bad; no piss-streaked walls, no porn, no condoms, no needles. A couple of beer cans and 'THUG' sprayed onto one of the walls. Relief, and perhaps a little disappointment.

The tide seems to be coming in much faster now. The beach has set into waves of its own along which we walk, sliding down its weed-flecked crests. The sound of shell washing against shell, delicate and all around us. We stay there for some time, unable to leave, held like the water as it enters the drift of reeds, slowing, thickening, transformed.

Below the path, to the south, the bends of streams add a fearfully grinning mouth to eyes excavated from the marshland. Perhaps the faces are deliberate, the portrayal of malevolent spirits living within this strange in-between world. Perhaps they are part of some local ritual. 'The faces on Jammy Dodgers are exactly based on these', Adam says, with a certain irrefutable authority.

The bird watchers' hide has been visible for some time, a point on the landscape to which we are drawn, and around which the landscape is drawn, like the lookout earlier on. I think of a poem – Wallace Stevens' 'Anecdote of the Jar' – which had been read out during a symposium on Robert Smithson at which Adam and myself had both spoken. The poem begins:

> I placed a jar in Tenessee,
> And round it was, upon a hill.
> It made the slovenly wilderness
> Surround that hill.

The jar becomes a point of focus for the surrounding landscape, a point of closure, perhaps, a point of entry in a vast open space. Adam comments on some pieces of litter lying at the side of the path. Perhaps this is less laziness, or a lack of care, than a simple desire to mark the landscape, to determine one's own presence within it. I think of Lawrence Weiner setting off a firework to mark a boundary, a sign no different in some ways from the one the Home Office had erected and which we had used to mark our first stop and first photograph. A choice both deliberate and yet somewhat arbitrary, which is probably just another way of saying 'history'.

Perhaps it is the thought of fireworks, perhaps it is this watery place, but we begin to talk about Peter Greenaway's film *Drowning by Numbers*. The boy, Smut, sets off a firework to celebrate each violent death he comes across in the countryside, a marking of something which is at once ordinary and extraordinary; which death is, of course, perhaps even more so than life. It is a game, of sorts, a ritual, by which the world and its uncertainties are held within some sort of framework, and if the framework can be known and to some extent predicted, then the world can be also. He is not the only one: the film begins with a girl skipping, and with each revolution of her rope another star is named and added to her collection, up to the number 100 – 'A hundred is enough. Once you've counted a hundred, all the other hundreds are the same.' Yet even knowing the stars so well, she cannot foresee, as she had been warned, that skipping in the road may lead to her being run down.

'Sheep are especially sensitive to the exact moment of the turn of the tide. In this game, nine tethered sheep react, pull on the stakes, jolt the chairs and rattle the tea-cups. Bets are taken on the combined sensitivity of any three lines of sheep – read vertically, horizontally or diagonally. Since there are normally three tide-turns every twenty-four hours, it is normal practice to take the best of three results. Reliable clocks, calendars and timetables are used to determine the accuracy of the sheep's forecast. In the game of sheep and tides, a referee should be appointed to determine fair play, distinguishing correct reactions from other interferences. On account of their special relationship to sheep, shepherds are disqualified.'

I ask Adam about the relationship between ritual and place. 'These kinds of movements within the landscape' – we were talking about the games within *Drowning by Numbers*, in particular the vast complexity of Hangman's Cricket – 'are about a heightening of focus and perception: about the relationship between people and place becoming closer, but also they're about a getting "out of it", losing oneself into the collective and into the landscape. In the performing of self-conscious gestures within an environment we somehow inscribe ourselves onto our consciousness of the place. Which is why they should be constructed and reinvented within every community.'

He talks some more about an idea for a 'folk event' for our town – something involving all the alleyways – towards which I look back across the water. I think about what he is saying and the way that the words themselves seem to be performing the very thing that they are describing. Would it be possible to invent a new tradition in a town that already had its own festival, its own rituals?

'The important thing is that many of these folk events are dynamic and contemporary and adapt and change all the time; as the folklorists would have us believe. For example, the Burry Man' – I check that here Adam is referring to the man covered in burrs who walks through a town centre, and who appears in *Plan for a Spell* – 'the Burry Man changes according to the whim of the few people involved every year, as does the burr costume, as does the precise date it takes place on. However, you can guarantee that, whenever it is or whatever he is wearing, they'll always visit the canteen of the local Hewlett Packard factory.'

We approach the hide through a strip in the reeds. The door is closed, and we can't see if anyone is in there. We walk towards the weather-silvered wood, up the steps, and open the door onto emptiness. Outside Adam notices that the front of the hide, which we have just approached, has been sprayed in lead shot. What games have been played here?

Some houses, farm buildings and a church. One of the houses is derelict, a tree growing out through one of its walls. I look through the empty window frame into an empty room. The wallpaper is the colour of mould, its paisley pattern almost following the shapes of the stains upon it, swarming around them, curling around each bloom, around each curved tear. A rabbit tears through the undergrowth; a kettle hangs from a branch. We enter the church and look at the collection of gifts available from the table: colouring books, pencils, chutneys. There is no electricity, simply unlit gas lamps and candles.

We reach the pub much later than we thought and are nervous that they may no longer be serving either drink or especially food (this was the point on the map to which we were walking, even if it wasn't the point of the walk). A pint of Guinness and pheasant casserole. The pub used to mark the point where a ferry crossed to the mainland, a straight line – not far – when the estuary mud slid below the water. But no more. Now new reasons must be made for coming this far, and as we walk out – rather happier than we walked in – we notice the numbered booths sheltered down into the bank, from which gunmen shoot at clay discs hurled into the air. Isn't this a kind of drawing also, a marking out in space? Red plastic cartridges emerge from the ground like spring bulbs.

I walk out to the shore along the remains of the jetty, and look out over the flats. The mud is heavy, old. I wonder how I might mark it, if I could, and can think only of the Dennis Oppenheim print I have back home where the words 'MUD FLATS' are written in massive letters upon the surface of such a landscape, as though the information printed upon the map were transformed into actuality, making it literal rather than symbolic. I look over the water, along the line which the ferry used to travel, and try to imagine its wake, like the flattening of grass along a well-trodden path. Pylons mark the far shore like musical bars. I'm reminded of that old TV programme *The Changes*, which scared, scarred me, as a child, in which the pylons were known as the 'bad wires' and a terrible sound forced all that heard it to smash all technological devices. The ribs of boats stick out of the brown mud. I allow myself a photograph.

We walk back to the car along a different route, along lanes and hedgerows, pheasants bursting from cover, the elastic-band whirr carrying them halfway across a field and hidden once more. There seem to be new ditches, and some new roadways, cutting across or swerving from the lines on our map. A row of mobile homes lie flattened on a piece of flat ground; a plastic barrel, now moved, leaves a yellow target on the grass at the edge of a field. Through a farmyard, and next to a holiday village, a stone marker stands a few feet high, slanted on its top a piece of square slate which has been engraved:

> THE FIRST POWERED FLIGHT IN THIS COUNTRY BY A BRITON J.T.C. MOORE-BRABAZON TOOK PLACE NEAR THIS SPOT ON 2ND MAY 1909

Perhaps it was the relative flatness of the land here, near the water's edge, which encouraged him to rise above it into one more dimension (another being time, history), to mark a trajectory across space, to draw a line with his shadow across the landscape.

We drive back to our town: from B to A (and then M to A, actually), numbers 2231 to 249 to 2 to 299. And we pass a lorry which has been steadily losing its load of hay over the past few miles, and through which we have driven, like many others. I wonder whether I should signal to the driver but then maybe he knows what he is doing after all, performing a ritual, drawing a line, turning concrete to hay. Here, you're welcome to it.

Jeremy Millar, 'Hinterland', in *Adam Chodzko: Plans and Spells* (London: Film and Video Umbrella, 2002) 44–51.

Jonathan Crary
Vera Lutter: Spectres of Negation//2004

At a time when many artists are working with large-scale photographic images and installations, it's tempting to engage the images of Vera Lutter in the context of these contemporary trends. Lutter is clearly playing an important role in this broader cultural revaluation of the cognitive and aesthetic status of the photographic medium. Her work, like that of a number of other internationally known artists, is inseparable from this historical moment when globalization has radically transformed the way images circulate and take on meaning, and when new imaging technologies have rendered obsolete many of the most enduring assumptions about photography and its relation to any presumed 'reality'. However, Lutter is also pursuing lines of thought and creative pathways that simply have no parallels anywhere, and it is the remarkable singularity of her practice and of her images that this essay addresses.

By now it's well known that Lutter works with the principle of the camera obscura to generate her work. I say 'principle' because there is no durable model of what, in fact, a camera obscura is. It is anything that works from the understanding that when light passes through a small aperture into an enclosed darkened interior, an inverse image of the outside environment will be visible to some degree on a wall or surface opposite the opening. The photographic camera, as it was developed in the nineteenth century, is the most familiar application of the camera obscura. However, for several centuries before photography, the camera obscura was used in other ways, sometimes for drawing, sometimes just for the demonstration of how focused light rays could produce an image. A camera obscura could be a small box-like object; it could be a large room-size space, as it has often been for Lutter. Some historians suspect that the concept of the camera was first discovered by accident in the ancient Mediterranean, where a combination of bright sunlight and tightly shuttered rooms may have occasionally, and without human intervention, produced the phenomenon of inverted images. For many centuries such optical occurrences were incorporated into forms of magical or wondrous display, but it wasn't until the late renaissance that scientific understanding led to the fabrication of the first functional camera obscuras. By the 1600s, philosophers had arrived at one of the most influential conceptualizations of the camera: the analogy between the camera and the human eye. The analogy was extended by thinkers such as René Descartes, John Locke and G.W. Leibniz to assert that the human mind, not just the eye, was modelled like a camera obscura. Basically, for several hundred years the Western imagination believed that the mind and the eye functioned like a camera obscura, and as such were able to perceive the world directly and truthfully. Much of our attachment to photographic imagery is still bound up in the residual power of this older faith in the possibility of a true representation of the world.

But the culture of modernity, as it took shape in the nineteenth century, developed an abiding suspicion of anything purporting to be a direct or unmediated version of the real. In the work of two of the most consequential modern thinkers, Marx and Freud, the camera obscura was demoted from its status as a model of truth to a metaphor of distortion and falsehood. Marx used it to diagram the operation of ideological mystification, in which imaginary representations of social relations were passed off as reality; Freud believed it was analogous to the way in which the unconscious mind controlled or censored which contents of the mind entered into the space (or room) of conscious awareness. Lutter's relation to the camera, though, stands over and above both the classical celebration of its objectivity and the modern critique of its duplicity, since she draws deeply on a wide register of its historical resonances and meanings.

One of her most consequential choices has been to use the camera obscura to produce negative images. In other words, she is deploying the camera obscura for its photographic possibilities but she has chosen to present what is effectively the direct luminous trace of that photographic procedure instead of going through secondary processes to achieve a positive image. Her images record the immediate inscription of light on photo-sensitive materials within the camera's interior. In that sense they have more of a claim to truthfulness than more conventional pictures produced through subsequent processes and manipulations. For Lutter, the 'truthfulness' of the camera is in the very operations of inversion and reversal that Marx, Freud and others saw as falsifications. Her use of the camera recalls the philosopher Hegel's account of the 'inverted world' where black is white and white is black, but for Hegel, inversion and 'the power of the negative' were only stages in a larger process, inexorably leading to greater knowledge and social unity. Lutter's sense of the negative, both in the actual formal aspect of her images and on a conceptual level, is closer to the thought of Theodor Adorno. For Adorno, the negative, which emphasizes difference and non-identity, was a means of resisting the rationality on which forms of social control depended.

The effects of Lutter's images depend on the extraordinary conjunction of her particular choice of motifs with the negative format. The world she holds up to us may have familiar elements in it, but it remains a sealed realm of Lutter's creation. It is an uncanny aggregate of places in which we as spectators can never intuit any prospect of feeling 'at home'. As many recent critics have insisted, the uncanny is no longer best understood in the individual psychoanalytic terms given it by Freud, but instead as a broader characterization of central features of modern urban existence. It is a sense of estrangement that is forced on us by contemporary reality itself. For Lutter, the distancing from the familiar takes place first on the level of the sign – that is, the visual syntax of black-and-white photography, perhaps the most familiar of all naturalistic codes. We intellectually understand this reversal as a mechanical fact, but emotionally it continues to disturb us by evoking a world with some familiar contours but which remains foreign and unknowable. There is an indeterminate opacity to her images that disrupts any attempt to navigate them intellectually or to imagine human activity taking place in them. This frustration of any cognitive mastery is the antithesis of the rational and illuminating goals associated with the camera obscura in the 1700s.

By limiting our access to familiar or habitual visual cues, a negative image deprives us of the ability to invest it with other familiar sensory associations, such as sound. Thus, Lutter's world seems not only nocturnal but implacably silent, even when the objects represented (jet engines or immense industrial structures) are, in principle, highly auditory objects. It is a visual figuration of an effect of silence comparable to what de Chirico achieved by very different means in his 1911–1914 paintings. Aesthetic uses of the negative image came first in film, rather than still photography. An early influential example was in F.W. Murnau's 1922 *Nosferatu*: An innocent traveller is on his way by coach through the mountains to a haunted castle when the film switches abruptly from a positive to a negative black and white image, turning dark pine trees into a forest of white. It is an effect calculated less to evoke the supernatural than to relocate the place of the fantastic to the arena of technological invention and control. Since Murnau, hundreds of other filmmakers and photographers have made related uses of the same technique, including Jean-Luc Godard in *Alphaville* (1965), which conjures up an urban-techno night world with certain affinities to Lutter's work.

Part of the uncanniness of Lutter's images is their evocation of absence. There is a pervasive sense that something is missing which ought to be present, but it is not possible fully to articulate what it might be. Estrangement overlaps with an effect of deprivation, situating us in a viewpoint that could be termed melancholic. For important cultural critics like Walter Benjamin, melancholy was something distinct from a state of individual sadness; rather, melancholy was a particular sensitivity to the dislocating experiences of modernity. It was a privileged position from which the disappearance of stable meanings from the world could be most acutely apprehended. Melancholy, in this sense, is a piercing insight into the impossibility of a state of immediacy, of recovering the origins of things, or of finding order, permanence and coherence in the world of appearances. In Lutter's work, there is a related sense of deprivation – a sense that something substantive is either withheld from us or no longer accessible. Sometimes her images recall the work of German author W.G. Sebald, whose photograph-filled texts often record the unsettling dissonance between individual experience and the built world of technological culture. The unsparing narration in his book *Austerlitz* (2001) of passing through airports, train stations and other inhospitable urban milieux seems akin to Lutter's rendering of city spaces, jet runways and power plants. In spite of the imposing physical presence of such sites, they effectively function as vacant points in more abstract networks of circulation and flow, whether of objects, bodies or streams of energy. As spaces they are the antithesis of anything affectively like a dwelling or a home, and they constitute a world in which the desire for a return to a home or community of origin fitfully persists, but in which any route back (or forward) is blocked by the catastrophes of modern history. A related sense of the image as a modern form of ruined memory pervades the work of both Sebald and Lutter.

Photography has become so naturalized and familiar over the last century and a half that we have forgotten that at the time of its invention, many people responded with uneasiness to its disconcerting capacity to create uncanny likenesses of people and things. Since then, the ubiquitous phenomenon of exact likenesses within our era of digital and now biotechnical reproducibility rarely awakens our lost or repressed surprise at the double as a kind of hallucinatory phantasm. One of the impressive achievements of Lutter's work is to recover something of the spectral power of the photograph and its effects of doubling. Since the nineteenth century, the word spectral has come paradoxically both to connote that which appears to the eye and to suggest its unreal or ghostly character. Beginning with the writings of William Blake, Karl Marx, Max Stirner and others, the 'spectral' became a powerful way of describing what was assumed to be the fraudulent and delusional quality of life in modern society. Even the very recent political analyses of Antonio Negri and Michael Hardt assert that we are all now living under 'the spectral reign of global capitalism'. Such accounts carry with them the implication that another 'unmasked' order of experience might be possible within a transformed social world – a world in which there presumably would be a more directly experienced 'reality', where things would in fact be what they appeared to be. Whatever Lutter's thoughts about global capitalism might be, her work suggests that spectral effects are a more enduring feature of human experience, rather than something that could be overcome or eradicated. Her images intimate that 'spectrality' is what we all live with, that it is an inevitable condition of our functioning in our world at present. The longer we contemplate her work, the closer we come to the apprehension that her negative images are not reversible, that they are not part of a dialectic movement of positive and negative, of dark and light. Once seen, her photographs never offer up the possibility of transposition to a more familiar set of surfaces. Rather, we find ourselves inhabiting her world on its own terms, amid its own rigorous code of black and white. It is a place of suspended temporalities where the threshold between revelation and fear, between beauty and desolation, is kept stunningly imprecise.

Jonathan Crary, 'Vera Lutter: Spectres of Negation', in *Vera Lutter: Battersea* (London: Gagosian Gallery, 2004) 8–15.

Magali Arriola
A Victim and a Viewer: Some Thoughts on Anticipated Ruins//2005

The idea of visiting a place such as Prypiat, the ghost town that lies in the vicinity of the nuclear plant of Chernobyl, seems curiously compelling. Like so many urban complexes that grew following the industrialization that shaped the twentieth century, Prypiat was built to house the workers of the power plant. But, unlike most other modern towns of this sort that have been abandoned as their economies changed, Prypiat exists as testament to an abrupt end. It not only suffered a sudden devastation after just sixteen years of existence, but it has remained untouched since that day in 1986 when the nuclear reactor exploded and its settlers were evacuated. Travellers and the guards who watch over it say that people's reasons for visiting Prypiat range from a fascination aroused by deserted places and decaying industrial cities to the curiosity that the site of the catastrophe itself inspires, since, for many, it stands as a perfect preservation of the shell of daily life under the Soviet regime. Some say that the fear which occasionally drives tourists away is inspired by the emptiness and silence of a city where time seems to have stopped, rather than by the high levels of radiation that still emanate from its ground.

Why do so many people share the urge to verify the completion of a future brought to a premature end, the will to become a late eyewitness to history? From where comes this necessity to confirm that the 'actually existing' scenario matches the images of devastation provided by the media? Is it because this is the real thing, not a simulacrum? Unlike the ruins of an idealized small town in Kansas – such as the one depicted in the early 1980s TV movie *The Day After* – wiped out by a nuclear bomb in a blaze of special effects, it is a nondescript dump in the Ukraine, the very real and irreversible remains of an extinct civilization. Perhaps this is the key: for many visitors the ruin of Prypiat is silent evidence of the first time a modern civilization known to them has disappeared. From that perspective, images from Prypiat inevitably bring to mind the work of Ilya Kabakov. By engaging individual and collective memory. Kabakov's work not only operates as a reminder of the transience of our civilizing impulses – be they utopian, messianic or profane – but the sense of immediacy implicit in the sustained abandonment found in his 'total installations' also points to the fact that the spectator must be 'simultaneously a victim and a viewer'.[1]

So, again, what is it that encourages us to perceive debris as waste in one place and as ruins, or even monuments, in another? A work such as *School No. 6* (1993) installed by Kabakov in the old military barracks at Marfa, Texas, may provide us with a clue. When describing the concept behind this work, Kabakov says:

> For many years the village school was in this place ... If only something had not started to occur beyond the walls of the old school. The working village where it was located and the children of which ran there with such pleasure every morning, gradually started to decay and die. Perhaps there was no point in working in it any longer: the factory around which the village had been built decayed, grew old, or perhaps life itself, isolated from other places, was becoming excessive and hard, or perhaps there are other reasons ... Today there is emptiness and oblivion there, where yesterday there was life and voices resounded.[2]

Even if the artist refers to the slow and painful deterioration of the place, the school – despite lying in a state of sudden abandonment – is the only place in the old military fort acquired by Donald Judd that still contains, paradoxically, any trace of life. From that perspective a question remains: how important is it to detect the precise moment when an event is recorded and thus celebrated as justification of the outcome of history? Let us imagine, for the sake of the argument, the collapse of the communist regime in the face of the capitalist empire as some sort of retroactive prophecy. Might it not be better to try to bridge the voyeuristic gap that separates us from the places that, having run ahead of their destiny, turn into anticipated ruins?

In the modern era the picturesque ruin works to establish an historic and aesthetic distance that promotes a contemplative nostalgia for a 'better' past, while simultaneously legitimizing a present that looks forward to a visionary future. This idea of the ruin found its culmination in the notion of 'ruin value', proclaimed by Albert Speer while planning the redesign of the Zepellin Field in Nuremberg in 1934. By replacing reinforced concrete with traditional masonry techniques, the dreary sight of rusting rubble would be avoided while the decaying process of a building would be hastened. This, in the future, would allow the architecture of the present to stand as a remembrance of heroic and historical times. As the twentieth century progressed, this idea of anticipated ruins at times acquired a prophetic weight. W.G. Sebald suggested something similar when he referred to the dark fascination triggered by huge constructions born of arrogance and ambition: a 'kind of wonder which in itself is a form of dawning horror, for somehow we know by instinct that outsize buildings cast the shadow of their own destruction before them, and are designed from the first with an eye to their later existence as ruins'.[3]

While there was confidence in the linear and progressive construction of history, traditional ruins promised redemption, in as much as they secured an understanding of continuity. Having experienced the disruptions and disasters that resulted from the myths of social progress and mass utopia that shaped the history of the twentieth century, it now seems that there is no possibility of redemption, only a longing for an interrupted future of gloomy reassurance that one has survived its ruin.

> In traditional landscapes the productions of man, his constructions in particular, surrendered themselves progressively to nature in the form of the ruin ... There is nothing of the sort in the contemporary city where objects, if they don't disappear all in the one go, as if by magic, are instead relegated to obsolescence, a bit like the living dead who endlessly haunt the landscape preventing it from ever becoming peaceful again.[4]

In a sort of reversal, contemporary ruins seem slowly to accumulate signs of the multiple transformations that the urban landscape has undergone. (Re)visiting these secular spaces not only opens up the possibility of resignifying the sedimentation and stratification of remnants and waste, but also for the recovery of the residual narratives that inhabit them in order to engage their present life and function.

Henri Lefebvre established a clear distinction between what he called the 'representation of space' and 'spaces of representation'.[5] While the first was the work of architects and urbanists – buildings and plazas whose symbolic value as power structures were sustained by ideological networks – the second generated different codes of representation, related to the clandestine and subterranean nature of everyday life. By calling for the conversion of planned urban space into the product of its users, Lefebvre was looking to generate a form of resistance against the regulation and instrumentation of the public sphere. This resistance is also associated with the various artistic manifestations that were looking to modify our perception of the dominant ideological constructs that architecture and urban planning represent. The infiltration of live organisms or parasitic formations into structures that were once conceived as incarnations of a social utopia turns these spaces into conflicted and contested arenas that simultaneously contain traces of their aspirations as they carry the marks of their failure. In other words, if we take for granted that a certain functionalism at the very basis of the construction of modern cities goes hand-in-hand with its own obsolescence, the use of public space proposes its simultaneous decadence.

Robert Smithson was one of the first artists to detect 'that area between events ... [those] that exist in the blank and void regions or settings where we never look and the monumental vacancies that define, without trying, the memory traces of an abandoned set of futures'.[6] By collapsing notions of past and future in what he called 'an objective present', Smithson pointed out that the modern was dated, while discrediting any historical continuity as cultural construction. However, even though this brought him to sense the importance of the entropic condition in the premature decay of suburban spaces, he never quite crossed the threshold of its fractures and chinks. When Allan Kaprow asked him if he thought that there existed 'an alternative on the fringes of life and art, in that marginal or penumbral zone which you've spoken so eloquently of, at the edges of cities, along vast highways with their outcroppings of supermarkets and shopping centres, endless lumberyards, discount houses ...', Smithson replied: 'I am so remote from that world that it seems uncanny to me when I go out there; so not being directly involved in the life there, it fascinates me because I am sure of a distance from it, I am fabricating as much distance as possible.'[7]

Smithson's later fascination with the wreckage he found at Hotel Palenque is certainly due to the fact that it seemed to offer a concentrated version of some of the categories of monuments that he identified on his first trips to the suburbs of New Jersey. Not only might he have recognized the 'dead-spots ... empty sites as dry swimming pools, parking lots, degraded land masses' and the 'ruins-in-reverse ... buildings [that) don't fall into ruins after they are built but rather rise into ruins before they are built', but he also detected in its structure 'all the convolution and terror, in a sense, that you would find in a typical Mayan temple'.[8] By establishing an analogy between the sedimentation of the construction stages of the hotel's modern structure and the ruins in the archaeological site, Smithson suggested that the 'dysfunctional' architect of the Hotel Palenque and its state of abandonment were the result of natural and eternal laws that dominated the region.[9] But such scenarios, suspended between their construction and decay, correspond to a recurrently interrupted functionality rather than to a dysfunctional design. After all these years one can ask why its visitors find that 'Hotel Palenque is still standing and retains its original name. It has been continuously transformed, a second floor has been added and a new building and a pool have been constructed. It still remains unfinished.'[10]

When the political and economic settings of a context break through and permeate the construction of social space, they tend to create a gap. Through it, the processes of negotiating expected uses and alternative possibilities can be explored. Today some artists are recovering those 'spaces of representation' that have lost visibility under the haze of the contemporary urban landscape. This might help to redress what Jennifer L. Roberts envisioned as 'a "fundamental memory" of indifference' in Smithson's thinking.[11]

In that sense, by illuminating for a few hours an unfinished building damaged by Mexico City's 1985 earthquake in *Edificio Iluminado. Calle Arcos de Belén No.2. Mexico, D.F. Agosto de 2003* (2003), Santiago Sierra monumentalized an abandoned structure that had quietly fused with the urban fabric. With the most minimal of gestures, he provided his viewers a transient reminder of a shared historical episode whose long-term consequences haven't been entirely acknowledged. A floating population of homeless people and street vendors often inhabits such ghostly structures. Sierra points to this quotidian appropriation of the spaces, highlighting the symbolic and tacit negotiations that activate the porous boundaries which pretend to contain urban fluctuations. In a similar way, Venezuelan artist Alexander Apóstol has repeatedly worked with the simultaneous development and crisis that has accompanied the modernization of the city of Caracas, reflecting the promises and failures still rooted in the urban imaginary of its inhabitants. In one of his videos, *El Helicoide* (2003), Apóstol focuses on the monumental structure of El Helicoide, an emblematic building astride a hilltop dominating the city, and intended to be the biggest shopping mall in Latin America. The project was abandoned a few weeks prior to its opening in 1957, in the wake of a civil and military coup. For some time the unfinished building gave shelter to various populations evacuated as a result of natural disasters, demolitions and collapses. More recently, the Hugo Chávez administration took over the defining dome as the provisional location for the new headquarters of the political police. Apóstol washes these sedimented layers of symbolic meaning from the building's photographic image by dousing it in the flow of a fountain. Far from nostalgic, the work reveals the tension that results when the ever-precarious expectations of a better future enter into conflict with the sometimes hazardous outcome of its subsequent failures.

Giorgio Agamben has suggested that, after the dislocation of the old binary parameters on which the articulation of cities as disciplinary spaces were based (centre/periphery, inside/outside, inclusion/exclusion), we have entered into an indeterminate zone where the temporary suspension of any legal order has become a permanent state. Under a generalized 'state of exception', entire layers of population move through zones of exclusion and/or abandonment 'in which power confronts nothing other than pure biological life without any mediation'.[12] These naked, disposable lives represent a consummation of a process of elimination of all whom have been previously excluded, rather than a failure in the modern democratic goal of political and economic integration.[13] These superfluous, disruptive people normally inhabit the scattered ruins of contemporary cities, those spaces whose existence, when not deliberately ignored, tends to be the object of a scatological celebration. This not only points to a questioning of the 'representation of their spaces' in Lefebvre's words, but also to some sort of rehabilitation of their 'spaces of representation'.

Artist and writer Walead Beshty has documented the decaying environments that once pretended to integrate the urban and suburban populations of the United States into a democratic-capitalist project. His photographs of half-inhabited/ half-abandoned buildings refer us to the contamination of those icons of modern architecture, a failure that is rooted in their original conception as isolated microcosms and security zones. By depicting this architecture as a permeable and perishable container, Beshty suggests that its process of deterioration is inherent in its own planning since it is activated by the users' disrespect of its spaces. This can be seen in photographs such as *The Excursionist Views* (2001–5), which registers the decay of now-desolated master-planned communities from the 1960s and 1970s.[14] It can also be seen in Beshty's series *Dead Malls* (2002–4), which show abandoned spaces occasionally infiltrated by solitary elders, their presence similar to the evacuated inhabitants of the restricted zone around Chernobyl who return to their abandoned and contaminated homes knowing that they don't have much to lose.

The sight of architectural ruins tends to inspire fear and excitement in those who observe, from a distance, the quiet displacement of the half-hidden narratives that inhabit those spaces – be they the subterranean and informal economies of the poor or the homeless, the desolated phantasmagorias in which the consumer is abandoned to his or her own fate, or the emanations that filter from failures and fractures of the networks of control and surveillance. It seems necessary to carry out some sort of exorcism that would restore a space of visibility to those stories, and purge the spectacular pathos that tends to relocate the limits of tolerance and conformity, not only of those who experience them directly, but also of their passive spectators. Perhaps only a newly found balance between the contemplative nostalgia of ruins and the morbid enthusiasm provoked by their sustained state of decay could prevent man-made catastrophes from taking root in our cultural imaginary as natural disasters. Baudrillard suggests that we run the danger of bearing witness to history too late to effect change; that we will find ourselves standing in an empty lot, just as seems to be the case with Prypiat.[15] If we wish to avoid discarding an uncompleted future that seems to have brought on its own destruction, we must approach the contemporary ruin as a tool that allows us to read our present condition in the stratification of cities and in the topography of landscapes. This may be the only way to prevent the sterilization of history that occurs when a place such as the Thyssen steel factory in Duisburg is converted into a cultural park, an Intercontinental Berchtesgarden hotel is erected where Hitler's Alpine retreat once stood, or the remains of the World Trade Center are removed in a rush in order to build a sanitized, monumental memorial for its invisible victims. As the Mexican artist collective H Comité de Reivindicación Humana (H Committee of Human Vindication – where the H may or n not stand for Honourable) said when they proposed Air Crash Memorial for the city of New York long before the collapse of the twin towers, 'monuments unequivocally indicate that Man learns from his own history, and that – contrary to popular belief – he enjoys repeating it'.[16]

HCRH's proposal might be seen as a mere coincidence, but could also be considered a sombre prophecy. If we look at predictions and prophecies as a system of surveillance of history whose function is to administer fear and uncertainty, we begin to understand how a place like Prypiat can embody the ruin of modernity's interrupted future, and at the same time become a monument to the disintegration of the USSR. The pretence to have an anticipated knowledge of history and its workings is just an exercise of ideological juggling that, through the creation of retroactive myths for an already proposed audience, generates expectations that end up fulfilling those myths. Rather than discovering unsuspected events, these histories and moral fables tend just to repeat themselves. Maybe only through a reactivation of the memory of a circumstantial past can the official chronicles of history be opposed and, thus, new possibilities for the future imagined.

1 Ilya Kabakov, *On the 'Total' Installation* (Ostfildern-Ruit: Cantz, 1995) 245.

2 Ilya Kabakov, *School No. 6* (1993), http://www.chinati.org/english2/collectino/kabakov.htm

3 W.G. Sebald, *Austerlitz* (New York: Modern Library, 2001) 19.

4 Antoine Picon, 'Anxious Landscaps', *Grey Room*, no. 1 (Fall 2000) 76–7.

5 Henri Lefebvre, *La Production de l'espace* (Paris: Anthropos, 1986).

6 Robert Smithson, 'What is a Museum? A dialogue between Allan Kaprow and Robert Smithson', in Jack Flam, ed., *Robert Smithson: The Collected Writings* (Berkeley and Los Angeles: University of California Press, 1996) 44; and (second quotation) Robert Smithson, 'A Tour of the Monuments of Passaic, New Jersey', in ibid., 77.

7 Ibid., 45.

8 These quotations are taken from the following sources (in order): Robert Smithson cited by Ann Reynolds, in Ann Reynolds, *Robert Smithson: Learning from New Jersey and Elsewhere*, (Cambridge,

Massachusetts: The MIT Press, 2003) 102; Robert Smithson, 'A Tour of the Monuments of Passaic, New Jersey', op. cit., and Robert Smithson, *Hotel Palenque*, slide show with voiceover, 1969.

9 For an analysis of the extension of nineteenth-century expeditionary culture and the colonialist gaze in Smithson's work in Yucatan, see Jennifer L. Roberts, *Mirror-Travels: Robert Smithson and History* (New Haven and London: Yale University Press, 2004) 87–113.

10 As reported by artist and curator Pablo León de la Barra after his trip to Hotel Palenque in April 2000.

11 Jennifer L. Roberts, op. cit., 113.

12 Giorgio Agamben, *Means without End: Notes on Politics* (Minneapolis: University of Minnesota Press, 2000) 41.

13 'In this sense, our age is nothing but the implacable and methodical attempt to overcome the division dividing people, to eliminate radically the people that is excluded. This attempt brings together, according to different modalities and horizons, Right and Left, capitalist countries and socialist countries, which are united in the project – which is in the last analysis futile but which has been partially realized in all industrialized countries – of producing a single and undivided people.' Giorgio Agamben, *Homo Sacer: Sovereign Power and Bare Life* (Stanford: Stanford University Press, 1998) 179.

14 The title and the work are an oblique reference to Jacob Riis' magic lantern shows that portrayed nineteenth-century New York's slums through a phantasmagorical realism, with the intention of generating social consciousness.

15 Jean Baudrillard, 'The Anorexic Ruins', *Looking Back at the End of the World* (New York: Semiotext(e), 1989).

16 HCRH, *New York Awake* (1998).

Magali Arriola, 'A Victim and a Viewer: Some Thoughts on Anticipated Ruins', *Afterall* (Autumn/Winter 2005) 109–15.

Tom McDonough
The Archivist of Urban Waste: Zoe Leonard, Photographer as Rag Picker//2010

[...] Zoe Leonard began *Analogue* by walking through her neighbourhood and similar working-class commercial districts in Manhattan and Brooklyn. Favouring the morning when the sidewalks were empty of pedestrians, she photographed those derelict or down-at-heel storefronts that caught her eye. Her peripatetic gaze is a distant echo of one of the founding paradigms of modernist artistic production: that which compared the artist to the chiffonnier, the rag-picker who scavenged the daily cast-offs of the great city:

> Here is a man entrusted to gather up the remains of a day in the life of the capital. All that the metropolis has rejected, all that it has got rid of, all that it has scorned, all that it has broken, he catalogues, he collects. He examines the archives of debauchery, the *capharnaum* [a dump, a pigsty] of trash. He makes a selection, an intelligent choice; he gathers, like a miser a treasure, the refuse that, when ground again between the jaws of the goddess Industry, will become objects of utility or of delight.[1]

That was Charles Baudelaire writing in his 1851 essay 'On Wine and Hashish', at the very dawn of those forms of consumer capitalism that today flourish so abundantly. Perhaps the most radical aspect of this profile of an 'archivist' of urban waste was its implicit redefinition of art-making under the transformed conditions of modern urban life and the incipient regime of the commodity, which would now of necessity become a labour of scavenging, of making meaningful what happened to be left at one's disposal.[2] Baudelaire sensed this to be the case already in his lifetime, and eulogized the rag-picker in his poetry; the two shared a secret complicity, as the discarded clothing the latter collected was sold to be remade into paper, the very physical support for the poet's work; but more importantly, Baudelaire positioned his writing in an analogous relationship to the city, salvaging bits of urban detritus in his poems. '*Lumpensammler oder Poet – der Abhub gebt beide an*', Walter Benjamin remarked in regard to this Baudelairean analogy: 'rag-picker or poet – refuse concerns both'.[3] We might say something similar of *Analogue* and its maker, that *Abhub* – refuse, garbage, the discarded and scorned – is at the centre of their concerns.

These connections are perhaps most clearly articulated in a series of photographs that began in 2001 when Leonard was exploring the streets of Williamsburg in Brooklyn. Walking through a district of warehouses, small-scale industry and wholesalers found just north of the Brooklyn-Queens Expressway, she found large bales of used clothing stacked up on the sidewalk, of which she made a number of colour and black-and-white images, such as the photograph of Leonard Street, in *Williamsburg, Brooklyn* (2001), with its sculptural array of bundles shot at an angle against the red-brick wall of the building behind. Three years later, Leonard was able to trace the itinerary of these used clothes, which – like the majority of garments donated to charitable organizations in the US – were destined for markets in the developing world. In 2004 she visited Uganda and photographed the stalls and displays of local vendors, the end point of a long trajectory that began in donation bins in New York, to the kind of wholesaler she encountered on Leonard Street in Brooklyn, through worldwide buyers, and on to the streets of cities like Kampala.

What is unwanted trash in the US returns as coveted goods in the Global South, in an early twenty-first century update of Baudelaire's chiffonnier. For this trajectory is indeed very contemporary: only since the early 1990s, and the imposition by the US and the IMF of trade liberalization on the formerly protected economies of much of the developing world, has this trade in used clothing flourished. What Leonard captures in her Kampala photographs is in a sense the opposite of what she had been documenting in New York – not a residual economy being eradicated by global capital, but an emergent formation linked precisely to those transnational flows of money and commodities.[4]

This is not to claim that the politics of this global trade appears as Leonard's 'subject' in these photos, much less that she is offering a critique of this dynamic; the rise of an international trade in used clothes constitutes the horizon of possibility for these images, but their resolute focus on the point-of-sale in conjunction with the earlier images of bales in New York perhaps suggests her interest lies in what Arjun Appadurai has called 'the social life of things', or in a 'biographical approach to things' (a particular approach that has long existed within Leonard's oeuvre, from the *Trophies* and *Wax Anatomical Models* to *Strange Fruit* and *1961*, works spanning the late 1980s through the later 1990s).[5] In this sequence of *Analogue* she takes a processual view of her subject, tracing something like the life history of this commodity; we grasp the passage from clothing-as-use, to its withdrawal from usage, to its re-inscription within a commodity circuit, and a presumed second life in Africa. *Mitumba* and *salaula* (Swahili words for 'used clothing') become the latter-day echo of New York's *schmatte zamlers* – as the used-clothing dealers were known in this predominantly Jewish neighbourhood – and Paris' chiffoniers. And once again a self-reflexivity – an analogy between clothes and photographs – can be apprehended here: the circulation of these used garments stands in some relation to the circulation of her images. (And wasn't there something fated in the coincidence of encountering the used-clothing processor on a street name, Leonard, that is also hers?) 'Images' is the wrong word in any case, since she insists on the materiality of the photograph and its support, in distinction to the contemporary turn towards digitized mobility and the dematerialization of the image in projection: 'I [...] love how tactile a photograph is; [its] physical presence is very beautiful to me.'[6] Hence her predilection for the postcard – whose collection and display has occupied her almost exclusively in the years since completing *Analogue* – in which the photograph becomes a physical means of exchange and communication through space, a kind of token passed from hand to hand. It is perhaps relevant to add here that, in addition to its presentation as a large-scale installation and as a smaller portfolio of prints, *Analogue* exists as an artist's book, whose buckram cover recalls the standard library binding of older volumes and hence emphasizes its passage among multiple readers.

Appadurai, in tracing the social life of things, was interested not only in their movement along well-trodden paths of commodity exchange but also in the possibilities for more eccentric diversions or subversions. Take the collector, for example, who removes or protects objects from the commodity context, who 'enclaves' them in a special zone outside the regulated flow of things. But that gesture, as he notes, is fundamentally ambivalent, since 'such diversion is not only an instrument of decommoditization of the object, but also of the (potential) intensification of commoditization by the enhancement of value attendant upon its diversion'.[7] The rag-picker as an analogue of the artist contains something of the same duality, on one hand embodying devotion to what has been rejected, cast off from the circulation of the capitalist economy – since 'it is precisely when they no longer circulate, as well-behaved commodities should, that things begin to give signs of a more subversive potential' – while on the other hand occluding what Theodor Adorno called, in a famous riposte to Benjamin's characterization, 'the capitalism function of the rag-picker – namely, to subject even rubbish to exchange-value'.[8] If poverty is not exactly made beautiful in *Analogue*, the dereliction of the urban landscape is brought within the precincts of the museum, where it coexists uneasily with its surroundings.

One more word is in order, however, before we leave this account of the artist-as-chiffonnier. For the analogy has been, throughout its history, a resolutely masculine one, closely bound up with that literature of modernity that has characterized the modern city as a male preserve and relegated women to the domestic sphere.[9] Indeed, such an explanation of *Analogue* risks separating it entirely from Leonard's longstanding queer and feminist practice, but there are compelling links between this project and the larger concerns of her work that allow us to see it, too, as somehow continuous with her gender politics. Most notably, the elegiac quality of *Analogue* – the mourning for a lost city – binds it to other works of mourning tied to the AIDS crisis: this is clearest in the photographs depicting abandoned storefronts where just the ghost of old signage remains, such as the image for Grand Street in Brooklyn (2001) or Manhattan Avenue in Greenpoint, Brooklyn (2006), which recall the dried husks of *Strange Fruit* (1992–97), a body of work begun in the wake of David Wojnarowicz's death. Something similar may be detected in the prevalence of analogues for the human body or, to be more precise, for absent couples – pairs of empty chairs in the image of Rivington Street or of Avenue A, or two pairs of shoes in the photograph of Praga Market in Warsaw (all 1999). But we could say that there is something generally queer about the archive constituted by *Analogue*, that its conjunction of conceptual documentation and personal idiosyncrasy derives precisely from an awareness that lesbian and gay history has made clear that an archive 'must preserve and produce not just knowledge but feeling', that in fact the archive is a site of 'profoundly affective power'.[10] *Analogue*, like her explicitly queer documents such as *The Fae Richards Photo Archive* (1993–96), mobilizes memory and affect to compensate for institutional neglect, now on the urban scale itself.

If this series looks back to a longer history of recording the lived effects of capitalism on modern urban agglomerations, and constitutes one of the most challenging and remarkable photographic documents of the present, we may nevertheless discern some of its ideological limits in the quoted description with which we began. There is much force in the statement 'my own neighbourhood is filled with the signs of a local economy being replaced by a global one, small businesses being replaced by large corporations, multinationals taking over', but perhaps also as much misrecognition; it was not only multinationals that were pushing out her mom-and-pop businesses, but more typically, as we have seen, other small, entrepreneurial shops now serving an entirely different social class. Leonard's stark dichotomy of small business/large corporation implies what we might call an ecological view of the urban economy, with local stores that created a responsive, equilibrated ecosystem being eradicated by the invasive species of multinational brands, the 'honest' commerce of the former undone by the wastefulness of the latter. These views were already taking shape upon her return from a trip to India in late 1992, where she 'was impressed with how each scrap of paper [...] was used to its maximum, to the wry end of its possible useful life', and further elaborated during her long sojourn in backwoods Alaska.[11]

The link is made clear in an interview in which Leonard elaborates a series of questions implied in the photographs, and in her approach toward her subjects: 'How am I connected to people who make my clothes, to people who buy and sell my clothes and food? Who benefits from the connection? Who suffers from the connection?'[12] But the contemporary urban landscape is no distortion, and the dynamic transformation of the city recorded in *Analogue* is no alien excess imposed on a more natural arrangement. 'People who denounce incitements to wastefulness as absurd or dangerous in a society of economic abundance do not understand the purpose of waste', noted Guy Debord some four decades ago.[13] Waste, ruin, destruction are constitutive of present order, not mere surplus negativity, and capitalism thrives on crisis, not equilibrium. *Analogue* brilliantly captures the surface of this world, the regrettable symptoms of an irrational economy, but it cannot name the cause itself. And in that, it truly marks the ideological limits of a certain practice of photography as well.

1 [footnote 7 in source] Charles Baudelaire, 'On Wine and Hashish' (1851), *Artificial Paradises*, trans. Stacy Diamond (New York: Citadel Press, 1996) 7. Translation modified by the author.

2 [8] These terms are derived from Ewa Lajer-Burcharth's outstanding discussion of this Baudelaire essay, found in her 'Modernity and the Condition of Disguise: Manet's "Absinthe Drinker"', *Art Journal*, vol. 44, no. 1 (Spring 1985) 21–2.

3 [9] Walter Benjamin, *Charles Baudelaire: A Lyric Poet in the Era of High Capitalism*, trans. Harry Zohn (London: New Left Books, 1973) 80. Translation modified by the author.

4 [10] The best account of this trade is found in Karen Tranberg Hasen, *Salaula: The World of Secondhand Clothing and Zambia* (Chicago and London: University of Chicago Press, 2000 [...] [see also] George Packer, 'How Susie Bayer's T-Shirt Ended Up on Yusuf Mama's Back', *New York Times Magazine* (31 March 2002) [...]; Naomi Klein, *The Shock Doctrine* (New York: Picador, 2007).

5 [11] See Arjun Appadurai, 'Introduction: Commodities and the Politics of Value', in idem., ed., *The Social Life of Things: Commodities in Cultural Perspective* (Cambridge: Cambridge University Press, 1986) 3.

6 [12] Zoe Leonard, 'Zoe Leonard Interviewed by Anna Blume', in Kathrin Rhomberg, ed., *Zoe Leonard* (Vienna: Secession, 1997) 12.

7 [13] Arjun Appadurai, introduction, op. cit., 28.

8 [14] See Irving Wohlfarth, 'Et Cetera? The Historian as Chiffonnier', in Beatrice Hanssen, ed., *Walter Benjamin and the Arcades Project* (London and New York: Continuum, 2006) 15. For the Adorno quote, see Adorno and Benjamin, *The Complete Correspondence, 1928–1940*, trans. Nicholas Walker (Cambridge, Massachusetts: Harvard University Press, 1999) 284.

9 [15] The classic analysis remains Janet Wolff, 'The Invisible Flâneuse: Women and the Literature of Modernity', *Theory, Culture & Society*, vol. 2, no. 3 (1985) 37–46.

10 [16] Anna Cvetkovich, 'In the Archives of Lesbian Feelings: Documentary and Popular Culture', *Camera Obscura*, no. 49 (2002) 109–10.

11 [17] Zoe Leonard, quoted in 'Zoe Leonard Interviewed by Anna Blume', op. cit., 17.

12 [18] Zoe Leonard, quoted in Drusilla Beyfus, 'Zoe Leonard', *Daily Telegraph* (11 February 2010).

13 [19] Guy Debord, *The Society of the Spectacle* (1967) (New York: Zone Books, 1994) 140.

Tom McDonough, extract from 'The Archivist of Urban Waste: Zoe Leonard, Photographer as Rag-Picker', *Afterall*, no. 25 (Autumn/Winter 2010) 24–9.

— ORLY, SUNDAY. PARENTS USED TO TAKE THEIR CHILDREN THERE TO WATCH THE DEPARTING PLANES.

— ON THIS PARTICULAR SUNDAY, THE CHILD WHOSE STORY WE ARE TELLING WAS BOUND TO REMEMBER THE FROZEN SUN, THE SETTING AT THE END OF THE JETTY,

— AND A WOMAN'S FACE.

NOTHING SORTS OUT MEMORIES FROM ORDINARY MOMENTS. LATER ON THEY DO CLAIM REMEMBRANCE WHEN THEY SHOW THEIR SCARS. THAT FACE HE HAD SEEN WAS TO BE THE ONLY PEACETIME IMAGE TO SURVIVE THE WAR. HAD HE REALLY SEEN IT? OR HAD HE INVENTED THAT TENDER MOMENT TO PROP UP THE MADNESS TO COME?

— THE SUDDEN ROAR, THE WOMAN'S GESTURE,

— THE CRUMPLING BODY, AND THE CRIES OF THE CROWD ON THE JETTY BLURRED BY FEAR.

— LATER, HE KNEW HE HAD SEEN A MAN DIE.

— AND SOMETIME AFTER CAME THE DESTRUCTION OF PARIS.

— MANY DIED. SOME BELIEVED THEMSELVES TO BE VICTORS. OTHERS WERE TAKEN PRISONER.

— THE SURVIVORS SETTLED BENEATH CHAILLOT, IN AN UNDERGROUND NETWORK OF GALLERIES.

— ABOVE GROUND, PARIS, AS MOST OF THE WORLD, WAS UNINHABITABLE, RIDDLED WITH RADIOACTIVITY.

— THE VICTIMS STOOD GUARD OVER AN EMPIRE OF RATS.

Chris Marker, *La Jetée: ciné-roman*, 1964/1992

Tacita Dean
Fernsehturm//2001

The Fernsehturm has become the beacon on my Berlin horizon. I look out for it wherever I am, in all weather, with its head so often lost in the low cloud or standing high above the city brilliantly catching the sun. I think it is beautiful; it excited me, yet so many people don't like it. Most Berliners from the former West have never been up it, yet large groups from the former East still book long in advance to have dinner in its revolving restaurant. The Fernsehturm has retained its political edge despite its consumption by the tourist world.

I went up it in 1986 on a college trip to Berlin. I remember the smell, the cloying cakes and the utilitarian atmosphere of this café above the clouds. But I loved it. I was told recently that in those days it took an hour to do a single rotation, and that that was exactly how long you were allowed to stay there for: one look at the full 360 degrees of the Berlin horizon and then out, never allowing for a second glance. There were not many public places to eat in the former GDR so a seat in the Fernsehturm restaurant was highly sought after. Consequently, it was one of the better jobs to work for the tower, so the staff were inevitably 'approved by the Party'. It now takes half an hour to do the full rotation. So with the progress of reunification, they have doubled the speed. And now you can stay as long as you like. But the staff, who are for the most part the same staff, still seem to work with the old system. Your order is taken and delivered with impeccable speed and efficiency. They move around the restaurant floor as if choreographed for the corps de ballet, never pausing to show disorientation or doubt as their world continually shifts and moves away from them.

Like the perpetual rotation of the spacecraft in Stanley Kubrick's *2001: A Space Odyssey*, a conceit to maintain gravity on board a ship, the Fernsehturm restaurant continues to turn almost imperceptibly like the movement of the planets in Space. It was visionary in its concept and a symbol of the future, and yet it is out of date. The Fernsehturm embodies the perfect anachronism. The revolving sphere in Space still remains our best image of the future, and yet it is firmly locked in the past, in a period of division and dissatisfaction on Earth that led to the belief that Space was an attainable and better place. As you sit up there at your table, opposite the person whom you are with, and with your back to the turn of the restaurant, you are no longer static in the present but moving with the rotation of the Earth backwards into the future.

Tacita Dean, 'Fernsehturm' (2001), from *Selected Writings* (Göttingen: Steidl/Paris: ARC, 2003) n.p.

Martin Herbert
The Dead Town//2005

In 2004, when I accompanied a British artist to the city of Norilsk in Northern Siberia, we were only the twentieth and twenty-first non-citizens of the Russian Federation to visit that year and it was late October, deep into off-season in a place that has no on-season. Norilsk's borders are all but closed. Between 1932 and 1953 when the area, above the Arctic Circle and accordingly inhospitable (a temperature of -76°C has been registered here), was known as Norillag and was one of the largest and most notorious of the Soviet gulag camps, this was a hard place to leave; now, for most, it is a hard place to enter. For us, however, entry was fairly easy, mainly because the artist had visited previously when its burghers were slightly less defensive (there being an unknowable substratum of reasoning that determines whether Norilsk raises or lowers its portcullis vis-à-vis the Western world) and had made contact with the head of the rescue service there, an enthusiastic hunter who stocks up for winter by embedding a half-dozen freshly shot reindeer in the ice outside his house. Nevertheless, we both arrived with several thousand dollars of bribery money secreted around our persons, bottles of bribery scotch clinking in bags, and, in my case, a solar plexus seesawing with fear of the unknown.

Our rickety internal flight from Moscow having touched down, in darkness, several thousand miles into Siberia's colossal negativity of tundra, my nerves were not soothed by the sight of Norilsk itself. A grid of wide, featureless avenues slashed by nostril-searing Arctic winds, with those edifices above three stories built on pilings because permafrost makes sinking foundations impossible, Norilsk feels like a kind of ruin preserved in a deep freeze, unaltered since Stalin's death in 1953. The adjective that the few travel writers who have wanted and been allowed to visit invariably resort to in describing the place is 'grim'. Once there was work here (although one could not call it 'employment', and it didn't exist in conceptual contrast to leisure) building the narrow-gauge railroad from the port to the city: a labour in which tens of thousands died. Frozen bodies were used as ballast for the tracks, and their skeletons emerge every year during the brief thaw. Now, Norilsk's only real industry is its nickel mine, also built by slave labour and one of the largest and most profitable in the world. As disturbing as the city is to visit, however, something lurks on its outskirts whose appellation suggests it might be worse still. When the locals refer to a place as 'the dead town', human curiosity beats apprehension hands down. Shortly later, we're on an ice-slicked highway, zigzagging towards it.

There is only one road here, connecting the city, the airport and the port town of Dudinka. Along the roadway, the bare black pines that push exhaustedly up out of the tundra are dwarfish and bent, poisoned by the rotten air. The snow is blackened for miles outside the city: Norilsk, with its refineries endlessly pumping smoke into the wind like the national flag of hell, has been described as the most polluted city in the world, and there is no small irony in the fact that the nickel pulled out of its hot depths is one of the main elements in eco-friendly catalytic converters. The only habitation for endless miles of virgin whiteness, it figures as an eerie, spreading orange glow on the horizon and has one reaching inescapably for cancer metaphors. But people live here and, by Russian standards, they have money, because those who work at the mine are compensated for a life expectancy ten years less than the national average. And at one point developers decided to build a cluster of apartment buildings approximately equidistant from the airport and Norilsk – about 40 kilometres from the city. Who was it going to serve? People who worked at the airport? The airport is minuscule. This architectural black hole is shrouded in rumour and misinformation: at one point we're given to understand it has something to do with the army, who've deserted it, but this is later refuted. If it's connected to the airport, it dates from after the mid 1970s, when the latter was built. Here – as so often in Russia – information runs out. This, whatever it was, is the Dead Town, where, possibly, someone once lived.

It comprises a huddle of horizontal, nine- and five-story concrete shells the colour of weak tea or of poured concrete, checkered with stains, facing each other down: high Soviet modernism with its lights out, empty rectangular sockets where the windows and doors should be and, hilariously, balconies for sunning oneself. (The fact that it is -28°C and I'm wearing the wrong kind of boots adds to the effect.) Out back, there is a dump of some sort, containing architectural wreckage – which helps make the buildings themselves look like paragons of uprightness, albeit on a radically recalibrated scale. At first, the artist wants to make some work about the Dead Town. What quickly becomes clear, though, is that this is a place that resists the will to transform it into 'art' – because nothing needs doing to it. It cannot be slanted, it is what it is: pure morbid atmosphere. It's a place that, because of the confluence of location and design, inevitably conjures up images of a seventy-year (1917–1989) experiment in human coercion: unhappy ghosts peopling a social project now left to rot.

But it is not, we come to realize, perpetually uninhabited by living beings, for these ruins are a potential shelter from the blistering cold. Reindeer tracks lead up to the entrances nearest the road; we elect not to follow them. But no doubt this particular building's interior is like those of the others, systematically ransacked. There are no doors, no light bulbs. Floorboards are missing, revealing intricate icy lattices of rusted pipework. I don't trust the stairs, but my companion goes up.

Underneath the pilings outside, I find forensic remains of human habitation: drained vodka bottles, crushed and oxidized food cans containing miniature drifts of snow, a waterlogged powder-blue mattress. And a torso. A frozen limbless cylinder, the ribs furred with brown flesh. In the wrong boots, I kick it over, stagger out from under the building, and find the artist, who takes a swift look before convincing me that it must be reindeer – the remains of a wintry feast. Amazingly, it seems the Dead Town contains something still deader than itself.

After a while, late afternoon sunlight starts to pink the façades, which gain a faint, illusory glamour. Even without that gilding, there's something fiercely attractive about this kind of architecture, because it's so perfectly comprehensible in its dehumanization, its idealist sparseness. As a wreck, shrouded in secrecy, that nobody can be bothered to tear down – because real estate is not exactly at a premium here – the Dead Town can't help but be metonymic. Yet nothing is ever that simple. For the people of Norilsk, totalitarianism is not entirely vanished. It built the mine they work in and the buildings they live in. The city was founded on death and continues to produce death, via the pollution which usually determines that few outsiders are allowed to get a view of what goes on here. But the locals are not miserable: those people we met have foreign holidays and gadgetry to compensate for their truncated life spans. Mostly they don't want to leave Norilsk, although they inhabit buildings that, from the outside at least, look only marginally more habitable than the Dead Town. (Inside, you could be in any middle-class European home, except that the heating is cranked up brutally high.)

The Soviet system is only half-gone here, and what has filled up the other half is also far from innocent. For example, there is one good place to eat in Norilsk. It is called Kabinet (Russian for 'office'); it'd be a fine restaurant wherever you put it, and it's where we go to defrost after leaving the Dead Town. The plush and woody décor is sumptuous. The chef seems comfortable with international cuisine, although he or she'll serve you the local fare (reindeer, pickled mushrooms, dill) if you ask. The waitresses are stunning and patrol the floors according to a rigorous and mathematically refined system of shift-work. The prices are, for the typical mineworker, prohibitively steep. Kabinet is open all day, and there are very rarely more than three people in it; often the people who are in it drive big black cars and shake hands elaborately. Everyone here can put a name to this business, and knows not to. I picture Kabinet, in fifty years' time, as an entropic wreck to compare with the Dead Town. Then optimism fades and we ask Anastasia to bring us, *puzhalsta*, one more round of liquid amnesia.

Martin Herbert, 'The Dead Town', *Cabinet*, no. 20 (Winter 2005–6).

Lytle Shaw
The Utopian Past//2007

> All past events are more remote from our senses than the stars of the remotest galaxies, whose own light at least still reaches the telescopes.
> – George Kubler[1]

In 1963 *Playboy* magazine invited a group of eminent science fiction writers to participate in a round table conversation on the subject of their special speculative expertise: futurity. Among the larger topics woven into stunning and largely inaccurate predictions were the development of space stations, encounters with aliens, space travel, longevity, as well as the future of sex, religion, the cold war and daily life from 1984 to roughly the year 2000. As in Gerard Byrne's previous video works – *Why it's time for Imperial, again* and *New Sexual Lifestyles* – this one, titled *1984 and Beyond*, also involves a dramatization of what was initially a purely textual artefact – a '(re-) enactment' in which a range of information unavailable (or only partly provided) in our experience of the *Playboy* interview (the setting, the writers' physical appearances, body languages, tones of voice, clothes and occasional bursts of laughter) is now not so much recovered archivally as invented.[2] If this invention seems in one sense a realization, an honouring of the interview's ambitions through a move into real time and real space, it is also an awkward literalization. 'The literal meaning,' as Paul de Man argues, 'asks for the concept ... whose existence is denied by the figurative meaning'.[3] Literalism derails the figurative by insisting – as if naïvely – on the grammar from which it must emerge. Part of the allure of the *Playboy* article (part of its figurative meaning, we might say) is the implication that a kind of epochal event has unfolded in their offices – the leading science fiction writers, the leading producers of narrative fictions that stretch our imaginative relations to time and space – engage in live speculation about futurity. And yet the closer one looks at the fragmentary record, the letter, of this 'live' event, the stranger its own time and space become. This strangeness inheres, however, not simply in promises whose falseness must be exposed, but in models of thought and social interaction whose foreignness might be explored.

It matters, now, for instance, that all of these figures (Pohl Anderson, Isaac Asimov, James Blish, Ray Bradbury, Algis Budrys, Arthur C. Clarke, Robert Heinlein, Frederick Pohl, Rod Sterling, Theodore Sturgeon, William Tenn and A.E.Van Vogt) come into view within the elegant (if narrow) sartorial horizon of the early 1960s Professional, even the subset, the Intellectual – thin suits with narrow ties, some with private eye overcoats, tight turtlenecks and fitted cardigans; that the leisurely and speculative ambiance of this gathering of experts is furthered, in that historical idiom, by the continual smoking of pipes and cigarettes; and that these conversations take place in a series of iconic modernist settings including Hugh Maaskant's Provinciehuis in Den Bosch and Gerrit Rietveld's Sonsbeek Pavilion (rebuilt in the Kröller-Müller Museum, where it now houses Barbara Hepworth sculptures).[4] In these settings, the writers' discussion of futurity seems closely paired with both the architecture's and the sculpture's polemical promise of new lifestyles emerging in relation to new man-made infrastructures and objects – an analogy also common in sixties films.[5]

We have been taught for some time now to distrust modernism's frequent claims, be they architectural, literary or filmic, to embody futurity.[6] And it is easy, in a drive-by reading, to see *1984 and Beyond* as structured around the ironic failure of many of the writers' predictions: space stations on the moon by the 1970s; the US becoming more socialistic than the Soviet Union by 1980; the near disappearance of dull, routine jobs and advent of annual three months' paid vacations by 2000.[7] More, the article itself (like the others Byrne has turned into videos) marks a moment when an emergent cultural fascination has reached the stage where it can be administered to mass audiences through the pages of a wide-distribution magazine. But beyond these easy ironies are more powerful effects achieved by the selection and transformation of this specific moment of the printed past into the filmic present: first, in a sense thematically, we are made aware of our distance not just from a moment of naïve exuberance about futurity, but also from a widespread, speculative, open-ended debate about the kinds of future worlds that might be constructed – that is, about the social domain as shapeable, not simply imposed.[8]

This larger thematic concern becomes indistinguishable, however, from the novel social form this debate takes in *1984 and Beyond*.[9] As each writer proposes a hypothetical future, his subsequent commentators sketch its presuppositions as a springboard toward the more thoroughly alien (or simply different) futures they propose. Perhaps the most astonishing example of this process is the discussion of extraterrestrial life, which begins with Clarke re-examining the *Playboy* interviewer's assumption that the chances of encountering life within our Solar System are slim: 'Are [the giant planets like Jupiter and Saturn] really cold, as a matter of fact? It's much more probable that, owing to strong gravitational pressure, there is some level in their atmosphere where it is hot enough for water to exist, and for the complex chemical reactions which animate life.' This leads Tenn to propose that after 'sociologists, psychologists, anthropologists' have been called in and failed to explain how alien the aliens are, Washington will call the science fiction writers, who might in turn complicate

Washington's implicit model of political alterity by insisting on degrees of sexual alterity: 'Well, whether they are collectivists or individualists may not be nearly as important as whether they are asexual, bisexual, trisexual or products of precision manufacture.' From here, Heinlein returns to Asimov's point about life's chemical basis, asserting that far more conditions than we realize might in fact sustain life. Sturgeon and Anderson then develop this problem into a series of further aphorisms – moving from 'Nothing is always absolutely so' to 'Nature tries everything that the laws of physics permit – which in turn includes just about everything we can imagine.' For a series of professional imaginers, this is rather a vast claim. But rather than pause here for its impact to register Pohl inverts the problem yet again: 'I think perhaps the laws of physics may subsume things we can't imagine.' Here, the dialogic movement of thought produced by the group must necessarily come to a brief halt: Byrne's transformation of print into filmic 'drama' gives each of these gaps a specific amplitude and duration – claiming a three-dimensional reality, that is, not only for the strings of statements, but also for their uneven reception, their effects.

Throughout, world historical paradigms are bodied forth in the air and then casually punctured between pipe puffs – the world itself (let alone the nation) often becoming a 'naïve' unit of measure in moves toward galactic and intergalactic thinking. And yet these vertiginously morphing worlds and galaxies – spinning by in succession as a result of scale-jumps, reversals of figure and ground, and inversions of social expectations – take on collectively not so much a dire sense of chaos or evacuated agency as a kind of peppy ambient quality. This is certainly the result of individual optimistic statements in which man's resourcefulness and burgeoning technological prowess are figured as overcoming even the most difficult future situations. But it is also the result of Byrne's directorial attention to the group formation itself,[10] the clear pleasure these professional predictors are shown to take in positing, developing and radically revising hypothetical scenarios among their most esteemed colleagues.[11] In this context, the actors' mild and almost unplaceable accents (they are all Dutch) might be read not just as an avant-garde estrangement effect (it is that too), but as evoking the use of agreed-upon and not necessarily native languages (Latin, French, English) for the professional work of an international discipline, like futurist studies.

But before we move too far into the future of this past, let us further consider its pastness: the tone of these science fiction writers' conversation comes to us as a relic of a historical moment in the United States and Europe – just prior to 'escalation' in Vietnam – in which technological optimism not only held sway (despite debate), but was beginning to be parcelled bureaucratically among a range of professional discourses so that the public might savour futurity's various aspects as presented by its respective experts: outer space (Austin Clarke), architecture (all of the then living modernists), energy use/alternative architecture (Buckminster Fuller), sound (John Cage), cybernetics (Norbert Weiner), and so on. Futurity studies was in an early enough phase, however, that the science fiction writer was not yet an antiquated polymath.[12] Indeed his voracious imagination for interdisciplinary futurities positioned him as a kind of ideal cultural figure – hence this *Playboy* article. Moreover, many of the writers included in the *Playboy* interview were in fact credentialled in one or more futuristic disciplines and could thus contribute professional monographs to those fields (and of course participate in government or corporate think tanks) while also reaching the public more broadly through science fiction novels: Asimov in astronomy, chemistry and mathematics (among other fields); Clarke in space and sea exploration; Heinlein in plastics and space travel.

And yet, despite the attempt to credential writers in futurity studies, the proliferation of futuristic discourses – with their inescapably speculative, literary qualities – in fact helped to call into question the authoritative disciplinary divisions, the discrete regimes of expertise, on which such a project of credentialling was ostensibly based. The more one read the novels of Heinlein, Clarke and Asimov, for instance, the more fictional their own (and others') versions of 'science' sounded. However much these science fiction writers saw themselves as hard scientists, still the blurring of literary and empirical boundaries their work produced now seems legible as part of a much broader debate (usually referred to as the linguistic turn in the humanities) about the authority of science in relation to other disciplines and, more specifically, about the inescapable linguistic and rhetorical dimensions of even the most 'objective' empirical practices.[13] Asking scientists (whether or not they are also science-fiction writers) to discuss the future is a situation that necessarily exacerbates this dilemma, since science must now focus its powerful empirical lens on the non-existent specimens of futurity.

Though we perhaps think of science fiction, too, as a domain for developing dystopian scenarios as modes of critique, it is significant that though most of the writers included had written dystopian novels, for the interview their predictions tended to share faith in technology and generally optimistic versions of futurity. Is this to be attributed to *Playboy*'s steering or editing the round table towards what was presumably a more saleable outcome? Or did the writers feel this compulsion themselves? Either way it's interesting to note the interview's contrast with some of the more paradoxically dystopian writing that was at roughly the same moment coming out of official government think tanks – like Herman Kahn's *On Thermonuclear War* (1960), which, though equally optimistic about technology, now sees its task as managing and developing concrete policy recommendations for a Byzantine series of grisly post-nuclear strike scenarios.

Born in 1944, nuclear arms were in the late 1950s and early 1960s entering their awkward and reckless teen years. It was during this period that their chaperones, or at least the professional advisors to their chaperones, began to undertake a more 'realistic' approach to what seemed the likelihood of their careening into use. Kahn's is the classic formulation of this attitude, a bureaucratized apocalypse; his endless scenarios are approached with new attention to a more refined and professionalized vocabulary of various destruction levels. Kahn has abandoned 'not particularly illuminating' terms like 'intolerable', 'catastrophic', and 'total destruction' – which presuppose overkill 'factors of five or ten' – for more immersive, nuanced models, closer to specialists' recent calculations, in which a quarter to half of the population has been eliminated in a nuclear strike and the others have set to work rebuilding a viable economic and military edifice. 'It is therefore important', Kahn concludes, 'to get a "feel" for what the levels of damage might really be under various circumstances.'[14]

With its scare quotes building a bunker for our literal bodies (while allowing our nonetheless embodied imaginations to wander around in the wreckage), this last sentence is not merely a specimen of cold war politics. Robert Smithson had such a 'feel' in mind when he claimed in 1966, of the art in which he was most interested, that 'the New Monuments bring to mind the Ice Age rather than the Golden Age.'[15] The point for Smithson and others, though, was not just the literal picturing of disaster (past or future), but the attempt to open sculpture both to the time of its own making (process) and, especially for Smithson, to an infinite range of temporal displacements.[16] 'His standard crystallographic boxes', Smithson writes about Donald Judd, 'come in a variety of surfaces from Sarturnian orchid-plus to wrinkle-textured blues and greens – alchemy from the year 2000'. Smithson would himself of course cloud such technological optimism, claiming that the temporality of his sculptures displaced one backwards into geological dystopias rather than forward into technological utopias. And yet perhaps the most significant context for Smithson's gesture of negation was his moment's optimism about futurity. Though obviously fascinated by the temporal speculations of the *Playboy* writers, Byrne, like Smithson, destabilizes any progressive claim about futurity. This happens especially in the photographs Byrne presents with *1984 and Beyond*, which suggest a pocket of alternate temporality (circa the interview date, 1963) located within contemporary quotidian life – most in unidentified rural and suburban areas, others in interiors, a few in New York City: black and white images of the Hemispheres Dome from the 1964 New York World's Fair, antiquated bagel stands, drive-ins, bowling lanes, picket fences. Despite over 40 years of 'progress', the characteristic look of the early 1960s can rather easily be found within the inconsistently (re)built world. Much as Ian Hamilton Finlay can go out into his garden and 'find' Claudes,

Rosas, Poussins, Altdorfers and Ruisdaels, so Byrne shows contemporary life to contain vast reservoirs of early 1960s visuality, recalcitrant or overlooked spaces that now become temporal displacements simply by adhering to their own long-vanished presents.[17] By framing the video installation of *1984 and Beyond* in relation to these photographs, and thus freezing the moment of the interview, Byrne does not, however, bring us closer to the 1960s – closer to an attractive and vanished ambiance. Rather, as islands of temporal stasis, his photographs corrode the rhetoric of the interview, suggesting that the interviewers, who debated only the kind of future that would overhaul everything in sight, were unable to conceive of a future physically laden with residual pasts.

In selecting the moment 1963 Byrne is also rendering infinitely static precisely the moment when new modes of temporality decisively enter art. This entrance has to do not only with exploring how time might be unhinged from the grand narratives of progress, development or teleology, as Smithson suggested. Time was also a new kind of social frame for more immediate corporeal struggles. 1960s art famously (and infamously, depending on who was commenting) began to insist on the role of viewers' bodies as the necessary ground for experiences of sculptures, environments, happenings and a whole range of temporally based physiological processes that operated on the body in various ways (Op art is perhaps the most prominent example).[18] Underneath this familiar shift towards embodied, real-time viewers, however, is a larger question about just what these viewers might do with their hard won participation – how the rhetoric of self-awareness, interactivity and freedom emergent in 1960s art might relate to a range of claimable and even realizable aesthetic-becoming-social possibilities. This, I think, is the real-time dilemma that viewers walk into in Byrne's *In Repertory*, comprised of various stage sets for *Oklahoma!*, *Mother Courage* and *Waiting for Godot*.

It is not a question, any longer, of fighting the good postmodern fight of theatricality against the Friedians.[19] In practice at least, theatricality won.[20] *In Repertory* engages this historic triumph in a novel way. Though first an insult hurled at the minimalists by Fried, the term theatricality later became a banner under which a range of interdisciplinary, real-time art practices could rally. What happens, however, if one imagines it literally as a desired condition for sculpture? Does it produce, as Robert Morris asserted the minimalist object did, a 'more extended situation' in which 'physical participation becomes necessary?'[21] In the documentary videos that comprise the second phase of *In Repertory* we see viewers wandering tentatively over the sets, uncertain whether to touch surfaces, uncertain whether to laugh or scowl, uncertain more generally about whether it is the frame and props that are on display, or their own movements in relation to these.[22]

Byrne's somewhat perverse reading of minimalism is even more explicit in *Nominally an installation*, a performance, or an event, a piece comprised of the public installation of a wooden dummy version of an untitled 1987–88 Donald Judd artwork by two workers. Byrne's gesture here is wilfully to collapse the distinction between the installer and the viewer as a way to tap into another, even more awkward form of 'theatricality' perhaps latent in the social domain of minimalism.[23] Unlike *In Repertory*, there is here for the labourers no uncertainty about how to act in relation to the object; the emerging sculpture seems to control and dictate everything, including the moments of (otherwise potentially disruptive) contact with it. What Byrne stages theatrically, then, is the script that Judd, cruellest of playwrights, has carefully written for his installers, who appear accordingly not as liberated improvisers in public space, but as quiet functionaries completing their assigned tasks. That the results of both of these pieces are bleak and passive is not, I think, a matter of Byrne trying to distance himself from the ambitions of time-based 1960s art.[24]

One possible exit from the theatrical dilemma posed in these two pieces is a kind of inverse project that gets its title, *A country road. A tree. Evening*, from Samuel Beckett's description of the setting for *Waiting for Godot*. Here, Byrne photographs actual trees (along real roads in the early evening) in the areas in Ireland and France in which Beckett lived before writing the play. The self-consciously absurd proposal of locating the actual model for the *Godot* tree seems to give way to a process of converting nondescript natural scenery (through lighting and framing) into theatrical backdrops. The particularity of the tree always operates in a subversively specific relationship to the generality of Beckett's literary description. As in *In Repertory*, this literalness embarrasses us. But if the literal stage sets framed within arts institutions are weighted down and rendered static by their awkward status in relation to their viewers, the infinite stage sets appropriated in Byrne's photograph seem to give rise to a freedom associated precisely with his contingent act of framing them. Under the winking pretence of uncovering a historical origin, Byrne instead shows that origin as subject to near infinite fabrication.

This returns us to *1984 and Beyond*. Byrne speaks of the timeframe governing his magazine re-enactments (from 1963 to 1981) as 'living memory'. This period is certainly 'alive' in the sense that much of what was articulated during the New Social Movements (even as they were disseminated in popular magazines) remain utterly unrealized, a collection of promises to be extracted from the future. What is not living, however, in our relation to this past is an inevitable connection – a collective conscious memory that presses its concerns to become ours. This is less a tragedy that could be avoided than an inescapable condition of historical inquiry.[25] Rather than tapping into a living memory, Byrne seems to have reanimated a dead one.

Such pasts lie everywhere inert, now merely physical residues (as Byrne's photographs for *1984 and Beyond* remind us). It is only the act of selection that builds continuity between one of them and a present, a link that then gets retroactively imagined as always having been there. Claiming such a link to the 1963 *Playboy* interview of *1984 and Beyond* is of course a bizarrely mediated operation. What poses as a connection, or even a more neutral repetition, is also the same kind of self-consciously literal reading practice Byrne explores elsewhere by minimalizing theatre and theatricalizing Minimalism.

Every bit as literal, *1984 and Beyond* is, however, different. Here, the 'realization' of the script leads to a strange excess rather than a lack, a superfluity of imagined futures instead of a waning of freedoms in the present. Certainly the dramatic restaging – the according of event status to a thin, print-ready occurrence – does make for a new kind of abstraction out of 'realistic' video footage. Certainly this process wins back an element of narrative, or story, from the media that had come to own and administer it. But neither of these terms – abstraction or story – will quite frame what's most compelling about *1984 and Beyond*.[26] Could we see it instead as a careful archival selection and moving dramatization of previously forgotten, but increasingly relevant, social desires? Partially. However attractive and relevant, these desires – for a kind of open-ended, improvisatory (though informed) dialogue about a shapeable future – are remade across a vast historical gap that separates us from a moment in American culture when utopian speculation was emergent not residual. This moment has thus not simply been recovered and represented. It has, instead, been brought into the present only through Byrne's characteristically excessive literalism.

In approaching his objects, Byrne insists that we not jump immediately to their rhetorical registers, their favoured sense of themselves: the 'public' quality of the minimalist object that activates 'physical participation' in viewers; the boundless temporal and spatial possibilities of the science-fictional worlds. Literalization allows us to remain focused, instead, on more ambiguous actualities: docile subjects interacting with institutional environments; worlds comprised entirely of (not by) science fiction writers. But while the practice of literalization also implies a level of uncontestable actuality to which one can appeal (like Paul de Man's grammar), Byrne's emphatically present stage sets, Judd sculptures and magazine scripts give rise to performances that, in pretending to be the literal truth or actualization of the objects, can always be but rhetorical readings (or counter readings) of them. And yet this partiality under the sign of the literal also has its salutary effect. In the more temporal context of *1984 and Beyond*, it becomes a figure for how pasts are always remotivated and instrumentalized in the present – how, for instance, mute round tables in obsolescent magazines, seen as excessive utopian scripts, can wind up showing us the irredeemably 'outmoded' as the yet-to-be-realized.

1 George Kubler, *The Shape of Time* (New Haven: Yale University Press, 1962) 79.

2 The term '(re-)enactment' is George Baker's. He develops it in his essay 'The Storyteller: Notes on the Work of Gerard Byrne' in *Gerard Byrne: Books, Magazines and Newspapers* (Steiner verlag, 2003) 66. Baker argues that these works seek to 'release a 'new' form of narrative, a set of truly postmodern stories ... [by attempting] to extract narrative and the story from the very entities [the modern mass media and the rise of 'information' as a communicational mode) that have eradicated the story in the first place.' By 'autonomizing further these already automized structures ... [Byrne produces] second-degree abstractions' (68). I see the key term, however, not as narrative but as dialogue, which operates along a spectrum – *Why it's time for Imperial, again*, being the most instrumental, *1984 and Beyond* the least. That is, while we're securely distant from the outmodedness both of the 'product' and of the staged social encounter (whose would-be spontaneity would sell it) in *Why it's time for Imperial, again*, we are progressively less so with *New Sexual Lifestyles* and *1984 and Beyond*.

3 Paul de Man, 'Semiology and Rhetoric,' in *Allegories of Reading* (New Haven: Yale University Press, 1979) 9.

4 For an account of how Maaskant's high modernist building was received in the changed climate of the late 1960s and early 1970s, see Michelle Provoost, 'Mr Maaskant Meets the Long-Haired Critics' in *Mart Stam's Trousers: Stories from behind the Scenes of Dutch Moral Modernism*, ed. Crimson with Michael Speaks and Gerard Hadders (Rotterdam: 010, 1999).

5 For an excellent account of the vertiginously interwoven relationship between American politics, especially fantasies of authority associated with the president, and the American movies of the 1960s, see J. Hoberman's *The Dream Life: Movies, Media and the Mythology of the Sixties* (New York: The New Press, 2003).

6 Le Corbusier is particularly susceptible to this critique; we see it variously mounted, among other places, in Reyner Banham's *Theory and Design in the First Machine Age* (London: Architectural Press, 1960), Colin Rowe's *The Mathematics of the Ideal Villa and Other Essays* (Cambridge, Massachusetts: The MIT Press, 1977), and Kenneth Frampton's *Modem Architecture: A Critical History* (New York: Oxford University Press, 1980).

7 In *Dreamworld and Catastrophe: The Passing of Mass Utopia in the East and West* (Cambridge, Massachusetts: The MIT Press, 2000) Susan Buck-Morss compellingly rereads the early Soviet Union's debates about self-representation in art through the problem of temporality. She suggests, for instance, that what has traditionally been understood as Lenin's hostility to the radical formalism of the avant-garde might better be seen as a new attempt to ensure that avant-garde art's (historically disruptive) temporality' could no longer attempt to disrupt the continuum of history as defined and led by the party.' (60).

8 Current 'public' discussions about futurity seem, by contrast, to debate only about rates of what are taken as inevitable processes – global warming, population increase, the increasing speed of microprocessors.

9 'Utopian form,' which is for Fredric Jameson intimately tied to the genre of science fiction, and not simply to the beliefs of science fiction writers, 'is itself a representational meditation on radical difference, radical otherness, and on the systemic nature of the social totality, to the point where one cannot imagine any fundamental change in our social existence which has not first thrown off utopian visions like so many sparks from a comet' (*Archaeologies of the Future* [London and New York: Verso, 2005] xii). My interest here, however, is not how these writers' works relate to Jameson's model, but rather how we see something like a real-time version of utopian form emerge in the staged, reinterpreted encounter among these thinkers of futurity.

10 For an excellent account of shifting concepts of group formation in the New Left of the 1960s, see James Miller's 'Democracy is in the Streets', *From Port Huron to the Siege of Chicago* (New York: Simon and Schuster, 1987).

11 This is not to suggest that no tension or competition exists; William Tenn's character in the first interview, for instance, is shown as struggling awkwardly to get a word in and then hold the floor. But his status is perhaps an exception that proves the general amiability.

12 For instance, Clarke's 1960 *Profiles of the Future*, explicitly mentioned in the interview, seems to have been one of the main precedents for the *Playboy* article.

13 Among the many critical writings on the topic of the linguistic turn, I find especially useful Jonathan Culler's 'The Pursuit of Signs' (in *The Pursuit of Signs: Semiotics, Literature, Deconstruction* [Ithaca: Cornell University Press, 1981]) and his *Structuralist Poetics: Structuralism, Linguistics and the Study of Literature* (Ithaca: Cornell University Press, 1975).

14 *On Thermonuclear War* (Princeton: Princeton University Press, 1960) ix.

15 *Robert Smithson: The Collected Writings*, ed. Jack Flam (Berkeley and Los Angeles: University of California Press, 1996) 11.

16 I elaborate on Smithson's models of temporality in 'Smithson, Writer' in *Spiral Jetty: True Fictions, False Realities*, ed. Lynne Cook and Karen Kelly (New York: DIA Foundation/Berkeley and Los Angeles: University of California Press, 2005).

17 Finlay does this in *Nature Over Again After Poussin*, a 1977 installation at the Tate and a 1980 book. By selecting those features of the landscape that had become the signature compositional devices of the landscape painters – from Rosa's blighted stumps to Claude's central vistas – Finlay suggests that these painters do not so much represent landscape as weave a small cross-section of landscape features into signature compositions whose ready quotability proves his point.

18 For a good account of Op artist Bridget Riley specifically, and time in 1960s art generally, see Pamela M. Lee's *Chronophobia: On Time in the Art of the 1960s* (Cambridge, Massachusetts: The MIT Press, 2004)

19 See Michael Fried's 'Art and Objecthood' (1967), reprinted in the book of the same title (Chicago: University of Chicago Press, 1998). Steinberg, Rosalind Krauss and Robert Smithson were among Fried's first perceptive critics.

20 A surprising number of critics, however, never to tire of trotting out the spectre of absorptive 'modernism' to authorize and site their favourite art's transgressions against it.

21 This is from Morris' two part 1966 essay 'Notes on Sculpture,' (reprinted in *Minimal Art: A Critical Anthology*, ed. Gregory Battcock [New York: Dutton, 1968] 23).

22 Exercise for two actors and one listener presents a less bleakly bounded real time dramatic situation.

23 Though Fried did not make the distinction it was actually Robert Morris, not Judd, who in 'Notes on Sculpture' developed what was taken as the theatrical claim of the minimalist object refocusing attention away from its object status toward its environment: 'The quality of publicness is attached in proportion as the size increases in relation to oneself' (Battcock, 230).

24 There is obviously nothing inevitable or final about Byrne's playful proposal that sets by Brecht, Rogers & Hammerstein and Beckett might somehow picture sculpture's fantasy desires. We are free, of course, to imagine more experimental sets just as we're free to uncouple the ambitions of the term theatricality from any literal stage set. The term was, after all, a pejorative hurled at Judd, Morris, Tony Smith and the others, not a self-selected designation.

25 I will not try to engage the large critical trajectory in historiography that develops this line, sometimes unfortunately termed 'relativism,' except to point out that after Nietzsche's well-known *On the Uses and Disadvantages of History for Life* (1874) the works of Carl Becker and Charles Beard develop anti-foundational arguments that actually precede the work of the better-known *Annales* and post-*Annales* historians in France. Becker's historic work can be found especially in the posthumous collection *Detachment and the Writing of History* (Ithaca: Cornell University Press, 1958). Though Beard's methodological writing is found largely within his larger studies, one concentration is *The Economic Basis of Politics* (New York: Knopf, 1922) On Becker and Beard see also Peter Novick, *That Noble Dream: The 'Objectivity Question' and the American Historical Profession* (Cambridge: Cambridge University Press, 1988).

26 These are George Baker's terms in the article described in footnote 2.

Lytle Shaw, 'The Utopian Past', in *The Present Tense through the Ages: On the Recent Work of Gerard Byrne* (Cologne: Verlag der Buchhandlung Walther König, 2007) 121–8.

J.J. Charlesworth
Signs of Life//2008

There has been work going on. Standing on the access balcony of the small block of habitation units on Harper Road, one can look across the grass and the tarmac path towards the large habitation unit called Symington House. Symington House is a tower block, and it is under scaffold. It was completed in 1958, and now, in 2008, it is undergoing renovation. The scaffolding structure partly obscures the façade of the building, its white-painted concrete and windows obstructed by the scaffold's spindly greyish lines and wooden decking, installed at each floor level. But a clear view of the building is hindered by the sheets of blue plastic netting hung from level to level to prevent debris falling to the ground. This blue sheeting hangs like a veil, a screen of cold colour that turns the light-welcoming windows of Symington House into dark, blank squares, dimly glinting, impenetrable.

There is no work going on now. The access decks of the scaffold are not empty, however. There are objects on these decks, but these are not the tools or equipment that would be used for the business of renovation. These are domestic objects; a child's bicycle, a bedside chest of drawers, an ironing board, some exercise equipment. They punctuate the decks at irregular intervals, in little clusters outside one or other of the apartments in the block. They are moments of surplus activity, excesses emanating from the body of the building, currently wrapped in its lattice of grey scaffold and its skin of perforated blue plastic ...

This view of Symington House can be seen from the derelict low-rise housing block, at 151–189 Harper Road, which contains Roger Hiorns' project *Seizure*. This block, Symington House and the complex of council housing further north – the Lawson Estate – were built by London County Council in the 1950s and early 1960s. A half-century later, while Symington House undergoes renovation, 151–189 Harper Road is scheduled for demolition. A set of spaces once designed for human habitation is now empty; built in the heyday of the modernist movement, these spaces faintly echo Le Corbusier's declaration that 'a house is a machine for living in'. Yet as the Harper Road block sits abandoned, after five decades of being lived in, the echo becomes a question: what kind of life can be lived in this place?

Seizure, like many of Hiorns' previous sculptural works, uses the chemical process of crystal formation. Hiorns has regularly used the fast-growing blue crystals that are formed in copper sulphate solution to coat the surface of an object. The objects that have been subject to this process are sometimes organic and natural – as with the desiccated thistles that adorn *Discipline* (2002) – or they are machine-like and industrial, as in the various motor engines of *The Birth of the Architect* (2003), or *All-Night Chemist* (2004). But another recurring object has been the architectural form of the cathedral. Model cathedrals encrusted in blue crystals appear in *The Birth of the Architect* and other recent works, but go back to one of Hiorns' earliest works, *Copper sulphate Chartres, copper sulphate Notre-Dame*, made in 1996.

Throughout these works, we are presented with works of human architecture and technology overgrown and overwhelmed by the growth of blue crystals. Hiorns' use of a model of an object in his sculptures is an exception limited to the cathedrals, which offer themselves as fictions or fantasies of an idea yet to be realized; that of a real architecture overgrown and overwhelmed by the growth of these crystals. It is this idea that is now realized with *Seizure*. And with this shift from the scale of the model to the scale of architecture, and the shift from the imaginary to the real, the growth of blue crystals takes on a troubling new meaning, which questions the very significance of human life and human history, at a time when what it means to be human, and the direction of human society itself seems less certain than ever before.

With *Seizure*, Hiorns expands on a central theme of his work, that of the thing that makes itself, an object that *self-produces* rather than is produced by the agency of the artist. Along with the various crystallized objects, Hiorns has previously made sculptures that produce columns of fine soap bubbles, seemingly endlessly and out of nothing. In parallel to these strictly chemical or physical processes, Hiorns has also made works that suggest various forms of biological production, often turning on metaphors of sexual and asexual reproduction as well as excretion. Birth is explicit in the *The Birth of the Architect*, with its cathedral connected through umbilical cables to a car engine, for example. In some recent projects Hiorns has used semen to coat super-bright light bulbs and light sources. In various steel sculptures such as *L'heure bleue* and *Vauxhall* (both 2003), perfume is sprayed on the narrow standing steel panels, at about mid height, suggesting a pissed-on stain, and in *Untitled* (2006), two old window frames, encased in Perspex, are smeared with what is purported to be excrement.

What is common in all of these works is the attention to forms of human biological production, as much as non-human, physical and chemical processes. Birth, excretion, urination and ejaculation are the various physical substances which indicate those processes that contribute to the reproduction of human life. In Hiorns' work, however, these occur in ambiguous combination with technology and architecture; while emanating from what we know to be human, these substances take on an identity partly independent of their origin. Rather than operating as indexes of human presence, they become material symbols of the process of production and reproduction, separated from the original reference point. This is perhaps why these substances take on the character of something either sacred or alchemical, but in either case something occult, whose properties go beyond the norms of raw matter.

What binds these distinct aspects of Hiorns' work is a preoccupation with the nature of the human and the inhuman, and how we distinguish between them as the different kinds of process that matter can undergo. The form of the crystal and the process of crystallization are exemplary in this respect – it is about as far from the human as matter can be. Entirely lifeless, based on nothing but the dynamics of inorganic chemistry, the crystal nevertheless is said to 'grow'. It invades and coats a surface with absolute indifference, like mould or rust. And yet, unlike either of these – organic or inorganic processes – it is not necessarily an inherently entropic process. While a mould might exploit the decay of the dead tree that it grows on, or while rust signifies the alteration of iron as it is exposed to air and water in a process of oxidization, the process of crystallization is one of resolution; it is what happens when the internal chemical instability of the copper sulphate solution resolves itself through the formation of the crystal. Perhaps it is also significant that in the process of crystallization, transformation is achieved through an internal process rather than external application. In a biological process such as the growth of a mould, the transformation of one sort of matter into another requires some external input of energy or outside substance. Similarly, with an inorganic process such as rusting, the process occurs only through a combination of external elements – the presence of oxygen and water. By contrast, crystallization is an ordering of molecules within the crystal solution itself.

Crystallization, then, is the purest expression of a self-contained, self-producing process of matter which goes from internal instability to stability, indifferent to materials and energies outside of it. In the iconography of Hiorns' work, it is the clearest expression of the auto-generative theme that runs throughout. In the context of Harper Road, and of the crystallization which has overcome an entire space of habitation, it is also the most absolute contrast to the processes of life and of living that this space bears witness to. But what does the contrast tell us about the space that the crystals have taken over?

In his 1923 book of essays *Towards an Architecture*, Le Corbusier writes: 'You employ stone, wood and concrete, and with these materials you build houses and palaces: that is construction. Ingenuity is at work. But suddenly you touch my heart, you do me good. I am happy and I say: "This is beautiful." That is Architecture. Art enters in ...'

It is difficult to imagine whether the little flats on Harper Road did their residents good, or made them happy; harder still to think that art had a part to play in the creation of these austere, reduced, limited spaces; a bedroom which doubles up as a living room, a tiny bathroom and a small kitchen. Le Corbusier's dictum that a house should be understood as 'a machine for living in' had, by the end of the twentieth century, become a degraded parody of itself. Where rationality and utility should have been watchwords for human progress and happiness, they instead became the justification for merely machine-like living. Harper Road, Symington House and the Lawson Estate, like countless other council housing developments across London, were built to replace London's bombed-out and decrepit slums in the austere years of the immediate postwar. Yet while the urgency of rehousing ordinary people in decent accommodation no doubt influences the basic and limited design of much of these developments, there is nevertheless something mean-spirited and ungenerous about these little spaces, that runs counter to the early optimism of the modernist architectural movement. No wonder that today, much of the modernist period of urban planning and architecture is denounced for its inhuman character and dehumanizing effects. The cell-like quality of bad modernist housing projects has been much criticized since then. If this house is a 'machine for living in', then the lives that could be lived in such a place must necessarily have been diminished by it.

It's easy today to complain about the false promise of modernism. Today these buildings stand as monuments not to an ideal of human emancipation, but rather to a dystopic view of megalomaniac town planners and the dictatorial fantasy that human beings could be remodelled by reshaping the spaces they lived in. Some of these buildings are preserved, some are demolished. But it is of little importance if some survive, because the ideal of the modernist era – the vision of humanity expanded and enabled by the advent of the 'machine age' – has largely vanished. We look back to the clean lines and utopian designs of the modernist period quizzically, as if it were out of sync with our own present; and yet, ironically, contemporary society continues to build its living spaces in similar stacks of standardized little boxes.

Our cultural attitude to the passing of the utopian ideals of twentieth-century modernism seems to touch on *Seizure* only indirectly. But between the crystallized flat of 159 Harper Road, its empty neighbours and the slowly renovating, still inhabited block of Symington House, one might attempt to make a set of connections that speak of the place of human life in the structures it builds for itself, of the human energy that the act of building itself represents, of the process of time passing, and our sense of history and the present.

Looking back at Symington House under its skin of scaffold and perforated screening, one notices again the accumulation of domestic things put outside of the flats onto the temporary wooden decks. It is as if the inhabitants have expelled objects they don't need in their immediate day-to-day, onto this handy extra bit of space that has become temporarily available. It seems unremarkable, but it is the creative, ad hoc response of people faced with not enough space for living. Confined to the rigid little boxes of their apartments, people are colonizing spaces that have become temporarily available. It is a sort of growth on the building, a human activity which exceeds the building's limitations.

While the vast modernist house-building projects of the 1950s and 1960s may be out of favour, they still marked a great reconstruction and expansion of human living space. Today, the number of houses built each year has fallen to its lowest level since the war, and we do not build enough to replace what we have, or what would be necessary for future growth.

But how do such realities connect to this strange environment that Hiorns has made happen, in this abandoned apartment in South London? The dense, dark cobalt blue of *Seizure*, its implacable and complete smothering of the straight lines of the original flat, seems to express a blank indifference to the troubles that afflict human building and human dwelling. If *Seizure* had continued its growth, one might imagine how the angles of the space would progressively disappear, as the crystals continued to grow inwards, towards each other. Ingrowing, like a crystal geode, this former space of human habitation – with its worn lino and peeling paint, with all the marks left by a living person – would be filled up, would disappear, transformed into pure crystal growth, with all signs of former human life obliterated. And with its cave-like floor, undulating with compacted crystals, *Seizure* suggests a return of the geological and inorganic world of prehistory. Rather than the complex and unstable relationship between human beings and their own built world, *Seizure* offers a lifeless form which, with its poisonous and lacerating surfaces, cannot even offer the primitive human shelter of a cave.

Auto-generative, inward-looking and ingrowing, independent of human intervention and human touch, *Seizure* continues Hiorns' fascination with the metaphorical potential of the inorganic, and of the strange life of inhuman processes. 'Seizure' might indicate the recovery of something that is rightfully owned, or a moment of paralysis or sudden arrest in the processes of a living organism. Here, in this flat that has become not a cave but a crystal geode, it is as if the living space of modern humanity is being reclaimed by the inorganic. While a more conventionally Romantic ecological narrative might imagine the reclamation of human space by organic nature – ruins overgrown by plants and trees – *Seizure* expels even organic nature in favour of the inorganic, choosing simple molecular growth over that more complex and curious molecule, DNA.

Seizure's perversely inhuman spectacle doesn't present us with the scene of a modern world, derelict or abandoned, or a futuristic fantasy of the ruins of a bygone civilisation. Instead it negates this human world and its human-scaled architecture, filling interior space with hard, inert matter, reclaiming it from those who have given it up. *Seizure*'s paradoxical existence lies in the fact that, like any crystal geode, it has to be cut open to reveal its internal order and complexity, its hidden opulence and dazzling colour. In other words, the very act of seeing its internal form assumes a human presence; yet in this scenario, it is the human witness to the crystallized space which has become alien. No longer a derelict space of modern human habitation, *Seizure* positions the human spectator itself as a trespasser. *Seizure*'s internal order is a physical phenomenon before it is a visual one – by entering it one brings to it one's own human sense of visual, aesthetic value as if it were an intruder. However much we think of it as an artistic spectacle, *Seizure* remains indifferent. All it does is grow, in darkness.

Alien and strange though it seems from the usual shape of everyday existence, *Seizure* nevertheless mirrors a broader anxiety in contemporary society. If the modernist political and aesthetic visions of the twentieth century anticipated human liberation through technological and productive expansion, and the indefinite growth of human society in both quality and quantity, at the beginning of the twenty-first century that ideal of growth and expansion is profoundly undermined and called into question. In all aspects of life, the virtues of human growth and social expansion are challenged and rejected. Apparently, there are too many of us, producing too much and consuming too much, and spreading too far. Tall buildings are celebrated not for their reach and ambition but tolerated because they keep us from spreading. In terms of the built environment, of course, such paranoia about human expansion exerts a powerful and real restraint on change and development. Inertia and entropy are characteristic of the experience of urban space in Britain. If little is built, things are equally slow to be destroyed; the block on Harper Road has been slated for demolition since 2005. Inertia, doubt and restraint are the defining themes of contemporary Western culture, in stark contrast to the optimistic and expansive visions of the previous century. These are partly driven by the political exhaustion that followed the end of the cold war and the putative end of 'grand narratives'. But today, we seem ever more uncertain about our right to exist on the planet, given that our explicitly modern presence appears to be the source of all the planet's troubles. Such strongly misanthropic and alienated perspectives, which envision a world where humanity itself is the problem, are not hospitable to the expansive, human-centred optimism that underpinned the modernity of the last century. In this poisonously downbeat cultural atmosphere, it is not hard to grasp how *Seizure* resonates, even as it remains indifferent. *Seizure*'s entropic, mineral and inhospitable formation, independent of human will, echoes all our worst moments of doubt about what a world without humans would mean. The machine for living in has stopped. There are no signs of life. Art enters in.

J.J. Charlesworth, 'Signs of Life', in *Roger Hiorns: Seizure* (London: Artangel, 2008) 54–60.

Brian Dillon
An Archaeology of the Air//2009

Precinct

The paintings and drawings of Julie Mehretu are keenly and complexly informed by the history and the culture of ruination. Her work has long drawn on both the deep history of Romantic ruin aesthetics and the more politically pressing contemporary reality of urban planning and public architecture. Certain styles of building insist in her earlier canvases, exposing the intimacy of conception, design and effect between the city and the battlefield, the street and the frontier, the sports stadium and the fortress. (The stadium, wrote Joseph Roth in Berlin in 1925, is a place of 'tumult, terror, chaos amongst the placid Brownian floating and drifting of dust particles.'[1]) The political and aesthetic substructure shows through the palimpsest of drawn structures, gestural marks and glyphic artefacts: we recognize, variously, the faint lineaments of the arcades that fascinated Benjamin, Vladimir Tatlin's *Monument to the Third International* (1920), and the profiles of recent celebrated boom-time buildings in Beijing or Dubai.

At first glance, Mehretu's latest paintings simply continue her researches into the built, unbuilt and unbuildable environment. Once more, the streetscape is stratified and stretched across vast tracts of space and (by implication) time; the fortress remains a key motif in her arsenal of real and imaginary edifices; notorious instances of architectural destruction proliferate, whether the results of natural disaster or military action. But there is a sense too that her intricate representations of ruin have been rendered less easily recognizable, that they have lost even the minimal integrity they might once have possessed and become suddenly more dispersed, particulate, spectral. This is not merely a question of subject matter – of scenes and structures that refer more explicitly to historical examples of ruin, whereas earlier paintings were perhaps stalled at the level of architectural dream or hubris – but of the gestural and narrative texture of the paintings themselves. If these are history paintings, as Mehretu's work has been described, they are so to the extent that they explode the very notion of a discrete historical instant.

Embrasure

Mehretu's detonation of the idea of a self-enclosed historical moment has, in part, a very concrete origin in the destruction wrought, for example, on the infrastructure of Baghdad during the Iraq war, images of which form a confusing matrix over which Mehretu's marks hover like dust clouds in her painting

Believer's Palace (2008–9). Such instances of destruction are easily translated into media depictions of individual or cultural loss as much as military victory, but as Mehretu knows, they occlude the real logic of contemporary urban warfare, the effect of which is rather to open the city up to new networks or conduits for infiltration and dispersal. The effect of her scratted rendering of the ruined Believer's Palace is not so much to invite us to contemplate ths specific act of obliteration as to imagine the overall pattern of such attacks, the transformation of the city by a novel, if appalling, form of urban planning. In his book *Hollow Land*, the architectural theorist Eyal Weizman expresses succinctly the logic of such military unbuilding of the city: it has the effect of erecting borders within the fabric of the city itself but also of dissolving those borders when necessary: 'Against the geography of stable, static places, and the balance across linear and fixed sovereign borders, frontiers are deep, shifting, fragmented and elastic territories. Temporary lines of engagement, marked by makeshift boundaries, are not limited to the edges of political space but exist throughout its depth. Distinctions between the 'inside' and the 'outside' cannot clearly be marked.'[2] In contemporary urban warfare, the city is constantly redrawn and reimagined like one of Mehretu's energetically ramifying paintings.

To a large extent, this explosion of the boundary is already fatally inherent in the design of the traditional fortress or the fortified city. In the opening section of his last novel, *Austerlitz*, W.G. Sebald reflects on the increasing complexity of the defences erected over centuries by the European powers: 'Towards the end of the seventeenth century the star-shaped dodecagon behind trenches had finally crystallized, out of the various available systems, as the preferred ground-plan: a kind of ideal typical pattern derived from the Golden Section.'[3] Fortifications bristled with new and more advanced architectural appendages, until, writes Sebald, they became so complex and self-involved that they could safely be ignored by an invading army. They enclosed nothing, in other words, but the seeds of their own eventual ruin.

Littoral

In *Bunker Archaeology*, Paul Virilio's remarkable study of the defensive Atlantic Wall built by the occupying German forces in France during Word War II, the urban theorist writes of the transformation of the French coast into the fractured littoral of a 'liquid continent'. Surveying the hulking concrete ruins some years after the end of the war, he was struck at first by their status as hated relics of the occupation, then by the resemblance of these tenacious, proto-Brutalist buildings to the monuments of a dead civilization. As he walked the line of the doomed defences, however, it became clear to Virilio that the Atlantic Wall had ushered in a new and less material logic of military defence; the lines of sight that the structures traced along the coast composed an invisible network, the concrete mass becoming 'a summary of its surroundings'.[4]

It is to this dematerialization of the fortress – an evanescence achieved even as the individual structure approaches its most dense and unassailable form – that Mehretu refers when she depicts the ruins of the German defences as a thickly overlaid field of computer-aided line drawings in *Atlantic Wall* (2008–9). Where Virilio's photographs, taken of the buildings by the author in the 1950s, foreground their mass, their weathered and shell-pocked surfaces, the implacable gaze that each emplacement directs toward the coast, Mehretu opens the fortress up so that it becomes a mesh of forces and alignments, a mere sketch of a fortress, an airy approximation of concrete actuality.

Unreal City

Transplanted to Berlin, Mehretu's practice – her sedulous engagement with the traditional typology of ruination, her reanimation of the modern ruin across an unruly expanse of line, mark and accretion – might be said to court an overt and literal reference to the historical depredation on that city. Indeed, her archival investigations point initially to a familiar repertoire of such images: the Soviet flag atop the ravaged façade of the Reichstag in 1945, a lone tree adding a jarring note of the picturesque to a desolate and levelled street, the half-cleared rubble of the Humboldthain railway station. The carefully amassed source images for Mehretu's recent works reveal a city which Sebald, in *On the Natural History of Destruction*, conceives as having fallen out of history: 'Is the destruction not, rather irrefutable proof that the catastrophes which develop, so to speak, in our hands and seem to break out suddenly are a kind of experiment, anticipating the point at which we shall drop out of what we have thought for so long to be our autonomous history and back into the history of nature?'[5]

To paint such a catastrophe, or to paint across or above such images, however abstracted, would be to risk both a historical literalism and an ahistorical universalism. Mehretu's response is, rather, an oblique one: in *Berliner Plätze* (2008–9), Berlin appears as a chaos of nineteenth-century buildings, bisected and mirrored by an indeterminate horizon, city wavering and watery, almost fantastical. In fact, what Mehretu conjures is a paradoxically modern Berlin, a city whose very modernity was destined to become almost overnight an image of a vanished past, recoverable now only in the form of antiquarianism or kitsch. Her painting restores to the pre-war city something of the strangeness and potential of which Joseph Roth wrote in 1930: 'Berlin is a young and unhappy city-in-waiting ... a distressing agglomeration of squares, streets, blocks of tenements, churches and palaces.'[6]

Dust

Mehretu has long been aware in her paintings of the extent to which the accretion of images and motifs is its own form of erasure. The cloudlike swarming of architectural drawings – be they of iconic modernist structures such as Tatlin's tower, nineteenth-century façades gutted by the San Francisco earthquake of 1906, or glazed monuments to late capitalism – has the effect of blurring distinctions between forms and effacing the outlines of familiar historical narratives. Typically in her work, the underlying lattice of architectural or cartographic forms has then been further confused by the drama of line, symbol and brushstroke that exercise but almost occlude the images beneath. In these latest paintings, however, a new form of disappearance is evident; the artist has begun to erase selected areas of drawing and marks alike, producing an effect that is only on the surface that of an allegorical obliteration or seething dust cloud.

It would be more accurate to say that the moments of articulate erasure in the paintings amount to a kind of restoration: of openness, contingency and potential at the level both of the painted mark or character and the underlying architectural motif. If there is an archaeology of the recent past in Mehretu's work, it is the archaeology of an atmosphere charged with the dust of demolition and rebuilding. There is a new greyness and indeterminacy in these paintings that it would be trite to conclude is merely melancholy or phantomic: Mehretu's grey is rather the colour of possibility, of the inchoate and unrealized. In this sense, the ruin points no longer towards the recent past but towards a potential future.

Blueprint

This optimism is, on the face of it, a paradoxical thing to affirm of paintings that are so obviously (if obscurely, in terms of their texture) indebted to the imagery of destruction and decay. But if it has always been clear that Mehretu's deployment of the ruin was never a matter of an uninflected melancholy or nostalgia, the paintings seem now more than ever to contain, in their increasingly atomized and aerated surfaces, the seeds of an as-yet-unfulfilled (and perhaps unrecoverable) future. The lines of flight, pursuit and escape that she traced across her earlier paintings are still there but are now accompanied by a more diffuse and expansive painted substance: the grey of a future image that is not yet resolved.

The future, of course, has been grey before; the grey of modernist concrete, steel and smoked glass. In his book *Militant Modernism*, the architectural critic Owen Hatherley writes – apropos of the postwar high-rise social housing of his native Britain – that 'Brutalism, with its rough-hewn rawness, always was a vision of future ruins. This should not console those who always hated it, however. The ruined is dead, safe, and can be regarded with relieved disdain.

Brutalism is not so much ruined as dormant, derelict ... and as such ready to be recharged and reactivated.'[7]

In their agitation of the ruins of the last century and a half of modernism, Mehretu's most recent works do not exactly enact this return to the utopianism of a time gone by. The paintings are too obviously marked by the violence of the modern and, in their gestural expansiveness, too ravishingly at war with the idea of merely representing the history of modern ruin. Rather, they seem at once to mourn the passing of a material and visionary reality and to set it in motion once more, insistently telling the story of a certain grey hope.

1 Joseph Roth, 'The Twelfth Berlin Six-Day Races,' in *What I Saw: Reports from Berlin 1920–33*, trans. Michael Hofmann (London: Granta, 2003) 164.
2 Eyal Weizman, *Hollow Land: Israel's Architecture of Occupation* (London and New York: Verso, 2007) 4.
3 W.G. Sebald, *Austerlitz*, trans. Anthea Bell (London: Hamish Hamilton, 2001) 18–19.
4 Paul Virilio, *Bunker Archaeology*, trans. George Collins (New York: Princeton Architectural Press, 1994; reprinted 2009) 14.
5 W.G. Sebald, *On the Natural History of Destruction*, trans. Anthea Bell (London: Hamish Hamilton, 2003) 67.
6 Roth, 'Stone Berlin' in *What I Saw*, op. cit., 125.
7 Owen Hatherley, *Militant modernism* (Winchester: Zero Books, 2009) 42.

Brian Dillon, extract from 'An Archaeology of the Air', in *Julie Mehretu: Grey Area* (Berlin: Deutsche Guggenheim, 2009) 45–50.

Brian Dillon
Modernologies//2010

A spectre haunts contemporary art – the spectre of modernism. For some years now, artists and institutions have been invoking the disparate shades of the modern in terms that vary from the melancholic to the hortatory, from what sometimes seems a relapse into ruin aesthetics to the urgent call for a newly expanded, even universal, avant-garde. As an instance of the former we might adduce the ubiquity of work that treats of the architectural remains of modernism and the Eastern bloc; as an example of the latter, the renewed question of what comes 'after' (surely a question-begging preposition) postmodernism. Those tendencies are often hard to tell apart, but in sum the urge seems to be to revisit the aesthetics and politics of the modern with a view as much (avowedly at least) to reanimating its radical possibilities as to mourning the dwindling forms, and forms of life, that it has left behind.

The risks inherent in such an ambition are obvious, and in recent artistic and curatorial practice it has sometimes been hard to tell utopianism from archaeology, or nostalgia from catastrophism. In her contribution to the catalogue for 'Modernologies' [Museu d'Art Contemporani de Barcelona, 2009], curator Sabine Breitwieser surveys the historical landmarks that have tended (perhaps too readily) to orient much commentary on the putative return to the problematics of the modern. There is first of all the end, or ends, of architectural and urbanist modernism, here pegged (following Charles Jencks' notorious formulation) to the demolition of the Pruitt-Igoe housing complex in Saint Louis that began on 16 March 1972 – a punctual ending now routinely mirrored or elaborated by easy reference to the destruction of the World Trade Center. Then there are the ostensible infrastructural and political ends of communism and colonialism, also subsequently and respectively complicated by the advent of a certain *Ostalgie* – to which many Western artists have not been immune – and the unending hubris of a globalizing neocolonialism.

Breitwieser is well aware of the paradoxical nature of these narratives of the collapse of modernism. The familiar historical coordinates that she cites make clear the treacherousness of any discourse on historical ends, and a proper suspicion of announcements of our historical distance from the recent past surely carries over too into treatments of a vanished artistic or literary modernism. In her introduction to the 'Modernologies' catalogue, Breitwieser quotes an instructive passage from Raymond Williams' 1987 lecture 'When Was Modernism?' Williams writes, 'The innovations of what is called modernism have become the new but fixed forms of our present moment. If we are to break out of the non-historical fixity of postmodernism, then we must search out and counterpose an alternative tradition taken from the neglected works left in the wide margin of the century ... to a modern future in which community may be imagined again.' The contradictions in that exhortation are telling: On the one hand, we are 'in' the static dehistoricized instant of postmodernism, and must perform the (almost caricaturedly modernist) act of breaking with its impasse. On the other, we can effect that breach only by acknowledging that modernism itself advanced at different speeds, in overlapping moments, and was decidedly unpunctual.

It was around this perplex of competing modernist impulses – rather than, say, a mere archaeology of styles or declared resurgence of a central universalizing imperative – that 'Modernologies' sought to organize more than one hundred works by some thirty artists and collectives, most of them resident in Europe, however expansive the geopolitical histories by which they were exercised. I say 'modernist' because, in truth, the wider topic of modernity flagged in the exhibition's subtitle seemed comparatively occluded in most cases. Or rather, it seemed that at those moments when it was a process of modernization that was at issue – the works that engaged certain colonial histories were the most obvious examples – it was precisely in terms of a cultural modernism that the stakes of the situation were most fully expressed, modernism providing (as Fredric Jameson famously put it) an accelerated response to, or critique of, the predicament of modernity. This was a crucial caveat to the critical and recuperative ambitions of the exhibition, because one inadequate response to Williams' demand for 'an alternative tradition' would be simply to exhume the hidden or marginal practices as yet unrecognized in official histories of modernism. At its most successful, 'Modernologies' instead revealed the complex imbrications of official, 'minor' and (post-) colonial modernisms alike with the machinery of modernity.

Especially apropos in this regard was Ângela Ferreira's installation *Maison Tropicale* (2007), which in scale models, drawings and photographs reworked elements from the design and history of a specifically colonial modernism and its neocolonial aftermath. Only a handful of prototypes of Jean Prouvé's Maison Tropicale – a prefabricated dwelling of steel and aluminium, designed in the late 1940s – were built and flown to Niamey in Niger and Brazzaville in the Republic of the Congo. Since stripped from their sites and sold on the art market as retro-futurist instances of modular living, the structures stand not only as examples of the peremptory imposition (and withdrawal) of modernism but also as lessons in the West's recycling of its own defunct utopianism. Ferreira has photographed the sites where the houses once stood – in one case, the reinforced-concrete pillars of the Maison are still extant, like limbs torn from their sockets, while the juxtaposition of images of construction and ruin recalls nothing so much as Robert Smithson's Passaic, New Jersey: a half-imaginary place stranded between utopia and catastrophe. Ferreira's wooden scale models of the houses, flat-packed for delivery, suggest she is both enthralled by Prouvé's vision of a late- or post-colonial future and quite aware of the ironies of the shift from political paternalism to market opportunism.

A similar historical narrative – though in this case unfolding largely according to the interior stresses of a nascent nation-state – ghosts Katja Eydel's photographic installation *Model ve Sembol: The Invention of Turkey* (2005–6), a record of Turkish national holidays and the architectural backdrops against which their associated celebrations take place. Following the institution of the Republic of Turkey in 1923, modernization soon came to include, at Mustafa Kemal Ataturk's insistence, the construction of a modern capital in Ankara. Contemporary Ankara is filled (as is the country's former capital, Istanbul) with relics of a mid century secular modernism that vies today with the architecture of global capital and tourism. To live among such buildings is to be constantly reminded of the intimacy of modernism and the political construction of nationhood. The force of Eydel's photographs lies precisely in their juxtaposition of monumentally overdetermined buildings with the rituals of daily life.

Several of the artists in the show seemed dedicated to the reanimation of aspects of Western European modernism that had fallen into unmeaning desuetude or had lost their original political charge and become mere reminders of a vanished aesthetic. One of the virtues of 'Modernologies' was that it traced the exploration of ageing modernism back to work that was made uneasily close to the era of architectural modernism itself – work such as Stephen Willats' *Compartmentalized Cliff* (1977), a diagrammed representation of the controlled but potentially liberated lives of the inhabitants of a Paris tower block. Martha Rosler's 1993 video *How Do We Know What Home Looks Like?*, made as part of a collaborative project at Le Corbusier's Unité d'Habitation at Firminy in France, is also not yet of a moment when the dilapidated building could be seen as the embodiment of a recuperable (rather than simply decayed) utopia. Nor had the contemporary sense of nostalgia for the future anterior of modernism yet consolidated itself in 1987, when Dan Graham and Robin Hurst made the six photomontage panels of *Private 'Public' Space: The Corporate Atrium Garden* (subsequently repurposed as *Corporate Arcadias* in *Artforum* at the end of that year). Graham and Hurst present a history of artificial environments that – somewhat in the manner of Peter Sloterdijk's writings on architecture and atmospherics – links nineteenth-century arcades to science fiction via the vitrined precincts of Manhattan office buildings.

More recent work risked a kind of antiquarianism when seen alongside this slightly older critical heritage. (Christian Philipp Müller's new installation-*cum*-archive of 'Forgotten Future', his 1992 show at the Kunstverein München, also suggested that the current critical-nostalgic approach to modernism has been in the air for some time.) Three works, however, stood out for their enigmatic but charged resuscitation of aspects of modernist architecture. In Dorit Margreiter's *zentrum* (2006) – a black-and-white video transferred to 16 mm film – a long-dead neon sign attached to a GDR-era housing complex in Leipzig, Germany, is briefly brought back to life (of a sort) when its tubes are wrapped in reflective tape and spotlights are trained on the building at night. Domènec's installation *Existenzminimum (Existential Minimum)* (2002), consisted of a leaflet, video and sculptural hut or bunker modelled on Mies van der Rohe's 1926 memorial (later destroyed by the Nazis) to Rosa Luxemburg and Karl Liebknecht. Conflating two signal instances of pre-war modernism – Mies' monument and the 'minimum dwelling' proposed at the Congrès International d'Architecture Moderne in 1929

– the work imagines a utopian crawl space in which those histories might be dreamed again. And in Runa Islam's film *Empty the Pond to Get the Fish* (2008), the Austrian pavilion built for the 1958 Brussels World's Fair by Karl Schwanzer, a structure since relocated to Vienna to house the Museum of the 20th Century, is inscribed by Islam's swooping camera with the text of her title, taken from a sentence in Robert Bresson's 1975 book *Notes on Cinematography*. In all three cases, what might be taken as purely formal obliquity is in fact a revelation of the possibilities of the space in question.

'Modernologies' was by no means solely concerned with work that engaged the aesthetics and politics of architectural modernism. A recurring theme was the presentation of information and the display of the artwork itself, notably broached in Alice Creischer and Andreas Siekmann's *Atlas (Updating the Arntz and Neurath Atlas)* (2003) – in which Neurath and Arntz's pictorial renderings of statistics are updated to include the global cultivation of soybeans and the prodigious expansion of Dubai. The most intriguing, if not immediately engaging, work in this respect was Falke Pisano's series of videos, sculptures, posters and found books, in which modernist abstract sculpture was not merely the subject of text, conversation and a dense lecture (on video) by the artist but was notionally translated into other forms and genres. In Pisano's video installation *A Sculpture Turning into a Conversation* (2006), a narrator reads, over enigmatic footage of the work in question, a text in which the transformation in the title is effected. One had the sense, as in the best of the work in 'Modernologies', that when confronted with the spectre of modernism we might usefully mistake it for something quite alive.

Brian Dillon, review of 'Modernologies: Contemporary Artists Researching Modernity and Modernism', MACBA, Barcelona, 2009, *Artforum* (January 2010) 192–3. © Artforum, 2010.

Nina Power
Waiting for the Future//2010

Filmmakers, writers and theorists, The Otolith Group mine the past in order to understand what's yet to come.

There are more futures than we realize, and more failures too. The past is littered with the debris of these futures, while our present incorporates the unstable collective memory of hopes that have long since been abandoned. Formed in 2002, the London-based Otolith Group (which comprises Kodwo Eshun and Anjalika Sagar) doggedly investigates these temporal slips and utopian dreams of 'the temporality of past potential futurity', as they put it.[1] Their use of documentary footage, of archives both familiar and alien, provides a melancholy window onto worlds not created and paths not followed. At the same time, by reasserting the potential of under-used forms, the group reveals the latent promise of various media: letters, television, science fiction, philosophy. Writers as much as filmmakers, theorists as much as producers, The Otolith Group seeks to unearth hidden histories of the future in the name of the present. Their archival and critical work, such as *The Ghost of Songs: The Film Art of the Black Audio Film Collective, 1982–1998* (2007) must be understood as being as central to their project as any of their films, for it is in the recognition of their own indebtedness to the past that the group proves so able to understand the future, however absent it may turn out to be.

An otolith is the part of the inner ear that senses tilt. *Otolith I* (2003), the group's first film (which includes camera work by Richard Couzins), imagines a world in which sustained periods of microgravity on space stations have led to a permanent impairment in the human ability to cope with terrestrial gravity. Humanity has been literally dispossessed of its own worldliness; everything is unbalanced, weightless. *Otolith I* reimagines the Soviet space programme through the fictional accounts of a Dr Usha Adebaran-Sagar, a voice from the future who reports from the International Space Station in 2103. However, at the same time, it also channels the past as Anasuya Gyan-Chand, grandmother of the narrator, remembers the impact and importance of the Soviet space programme on Indian socialism and feminism. Footage of a smiling Valentina Tereshkova, the first woman in space, is intercut with contemporary scenes of anti-war protests in London. The future, the past and the present interweave with a delicate sense of proportion; each narrator from each period expresses their hope (or lack of it) in a tenor appropriate to the genre each represents. The science-fictional reportage of Kris Kelvin, the cosmonaut in Stanislaw Lem's 1961 novel *Solaris*, is invoked in

MICROGRAVITY HAS EVOLVED NEW

HUMAN

SPECIES. WE ARE BETTER

SUITED TO SPACE THAN GRAVIC

HUMANS

COULD EVER BE; BUT ARE UNABLE

TO SURVIVE CONDITIONS ON

EARTH

EARTH IS OUT OF BOUNDS

FOR US NOW; IT REMAINS A

PLANET

ACCESSIBLE THROUGH MEDIA

The Otolith Group, dialogue from *Otolith I*, 2003

Dr Adebaran-Sagar's message: 'Microgravity has evolved new human species. We are better suited to space than gravic humans could ever be; but are unable to survive conditions on Earth. Earth is out of bounds for us now; it remains a planet accessible through media.' The correspondence between Gyan-Chand and her granddaughter, between the past and the future, veers between the personal and the geopolitical: 'Airports look terminal now, customs officers wear sterile masks and military tanks patrol Heathrow. Did the Russian men look away when you caught their eye?' If there is a feeling of wistfulness that permeates the film, particularly in the narration relating to images of the 2003 anti-war protests ('a protest for the right to protest, as if that might stop the war happening'), it is in the tradition of Chris Marker's melancholy science fiction, or, what amounts to the same thing, in his political critique of the present.

Indeed, Otolith is the natural inheritor of Marker's vision, explicitly declaring its debt in particular to his 1983 film *Sans Soleil* (Sunless). (*Otolith I* contains a series of Markeresque formulations: 'There is no memory without image and no image without memory. Image is the matter of memory.') In 2007, this affinity resulted in *Inner Time of Television*, a historical intervention in the name of both Otolith and Marker. The group was invited to participate in the 1st Athens Biennial, but chose instead, with Marker's blessing, to screen the latter's 13-part television series about Greece, *The Owl's Legacy* (1989). Before the series, originally commissioned by Arte, was released, wealthy backers became outraged by critic George Steiner's statement – in an episode about nostalgia – that contemporary Greece and Ancient Greece had nothing in common. Despite including a disclaimer, Marker's series, after having been shown in France and Britain in 1989–90, was never screened in Greece itself, the backers having bought out the rest of the rights. In a piece written to accompany this first screening, The Otolith Group point out the censorship of the series was not only a failing on the Greek side but that 'what is clear is that a television series such as *The Owl's Legacy* could never be broadcast on British television today [...]. [With Marker's series] television became the collective intelligence it could but was never quite permitted to be'.[2] Television's 'collective intelligence', the idea that it could be a repository of ideas, is still unfulfilled – the diffusion of information relegates the medium itself to a mere carrier, a useful vehicle, rather than a critical form in its own right.

The Otolith Group returned, in *Otolith II* (2007), to questions of temporality and utopia, although here the aesthetic is rougher, an effective combination of the trembling images of Marker and the anti-aesthetic of Allan Sekula, with handheld video footage edited alongside documentary footage of Le Corbusier's planned city, Chandigarh. The tone is sharper; the group appear to be attempting to map the complicated processes of capitalism through the juxtaposition of images and histories. Dr Adebaran-Sagar returns to tell us that it is 'the age of human capital, and age of sacrifice [...] Capital, as far as we know, was never alive. How did it reproduce itself? How did it replicate?' Art historian T.J. Demos has compared The Otolith Group's tracking of global capital through documentary and science fiction to Steve McQueen's film *Gravesend* (2007) and Hito Steyerl's video *November* (2004); as Demos argues, both of these works 'are distinguished by the intertwining of the real and the imaginary, which mobilizes a form of address – aesthetic, affective, visual – beyond the strictly information-based correctives of familiar documentary modes of contestation.'[3] This intertwining is expressed beautifully in a sequence in *Otolith II* when the film crew seemingly stumbles upon a gangster film being shot in Mumbai. Mock-ups of British telephone boxes are assembled and disassembled on the waterfront as take after take unfolds, as the Director attempts to get the positions of the actor just right. (The narrator jokes: 'I've come all this way, halfway around the world, only to be met by four red phone boxes.') It's a beautiful scene, strange and humorous; it segues perfectly into a larger reflection on the changes in labour that have taken place in Mumbai and elsewhere, and the way in which immaterial and material works rub alongside one another amidst the ever-consuming process of the spectacle of everyday life.

At one point, the narrator asks: 'Why do Indian artists produce such little science fiction?' A superficial answer would be that there is little need for such fictions in a culture so filled with fantastical Gods and alien deities. But The Otolith Group refuses such reductive answers. While much of their work focuses on India, they can't easily be slotted into the category of 'postcolonial artists'. As Sagar puts it, the group are more interested in 'opening up the question of the postcolonial to a series of complex interlinkages which are implied but which need to be unfolded project by project so that what emerges is a complex and baroque aesthetic of constellations.'[4] This project is pursued far more effectively at the level of form than of content. As Sagar continues: 'The broad question of the postcolonial is connected to the history and the aesthetics of the essay-film – from Dziga Vertov to Esther Shub to Jean Vigo to Joris Ivens to [Alain] Resnais to [Jean-Luc] Godard to [Harun] Farocki to Black Audio Film Collective to Eyal Sivan to Hito Steyerl. The essay-film already contains a sustained reflection upon the colonial condition. There is a persistent anti-colonial politics running throughout the form of the essayistic.'[5]

In a suggestion that formed the basis of the third Otolith film, Dr Adebaran-Sagar observes in *Otolith II* that Satyajit Ray might have radically changed the history of science fiction had the screenplay of his film *The Alien* (1967) been made by Columbia Pictures, as originally planned. Ray's alien would have changed the history of science fiction in more than one sense: far from wanting to destroy humanity, his alien merely wants to befriend it, one young boy in particular: 'Haba is dreaming and the Alien becomes part of his dream. We see Haba and the Alien happy, playing hide and seek in a strange black and white world of geometrical forms.' The friendly alien that never was points to a different history of the cold war, a ghostly possibility that remains even after the War itself is over, or has shifted modality.

Dr Adebaran-Sagar's reflections from 2060 (or thereabouts), by contrast, are somewhat bleaker than this happy alien story: 'Between 2050 and 2060, Earth's population reached its maximum growth of 10 to 10.5 billion. Ninety-five percent of this occurred in the cities of the South [...] There was little data available on the mega slums. They were impossible to control.' The voice from the future contains a warning and a reflection on cities as 'psychological field labs for testing new ways of being human'. The modernist project, as reflected in Chandigarh, sought to intervene directly in the question of what it meant to test new ways to be human. The narrator notes that in his book, *The Establishment Statute of the Land* (1959) Le Corbusier argued that 'the Law of the Sun is of the greatest importance. In Chandigarh, the Sun must be controlled.'[6] This bid for a victory over the sun reveals itself to be a new kind of science fiction: the camera flits from models of the planned city to images of the city as it currently stands, divided into sectors and guarded by gunmen.

In the third part of the trilogy, *Otolith III* (2009), the group returns to investigate *The Alien*, creating – as the original film was never finished – a kind of 'premake' ('20 pages in a drawer. An idea. A possibility. Nothing more'). *Otolith III* imagines searching for its protagonists – the boy, the journalist, the engineer and the director – and includes shots of crowded streets, while an unseen narrator imagines random individuals potentially filling the roles of each character. At one point, the boy declares: 'We are unfinished characters with interrupted biographies', the repeated refrain 'we live in a space of friends and a time of enemies' adding an air of temporal menace to the proceedings.

But it is perhaps with *Nervus Rerum* (the title is taken from Cicero and translates as 'the nerve of things'), the 2008 film shot in the Palestinian Jenin refugee camp on the West Bank, that The Otolith Group's vision achieves its greatest success. The film begins with the camera moving slowly up a backstreet in Gaza. Children look on silently as an eerie soundtrack deepens their gaze. Abandoned cookers line the sides of the road; graffiti are everywhere, a palimpsest of politics. Two men stand talking next to a pick-up truck filled with empty plastic bottles. 'We are death', declares Sagar. 'We are dead when we think we are living.' The words are taken from Fernando Pessoa's *The Book of Disquiet* (first published in English in 1991) and Jean Genet's book about Palestine, *Prisoner of Love* (1986); they both distance us and draw us closer to the slow, quiet images of the settlement. The camera circles the streets and back alleys, more children emerging from doorways. Suddenly, we're inside a modest room; a woman in a headscarf stands by the window with her back to the camera. As the camera turns, we see that the woman is elderly, her hands spread out before her. In stark contrast to the domesticity of the scene, the voice speaks of the death of all creation, a menace haunting everyday existence. In another room, a young man too stands at the window, smoking and gazing out. Back on the streets we see political posters and small shops.

An abstract set of reflections on self-sacrifice and parachuting accompany the slow descent of a cable car; a graveyard, another young man touching the names that cover one of the stones. Back to the streets, and more children, this time shouting at the camera with playful engagement. One of them is handed a toy gun by an older boy and the younger child points it at the camera with steely intent, walking ever closer to the lens. 'Trying to think the revolution is like waking up'; images of Yasser Arafat on television. An elderly woman points to an image of a young man in a family photo; because this is Palestine, we assume he has died violently. 'The image created is quite detached from the man concerned', says the voice. 'Who wouldn't like to be a world hero?' The slow, brooding soundtrack is joined by the harsh notes of a man in the street, blowing too hard into a recorder. The penultimate scene shows two men playing cards, while a story about two men playing cards is read over the footage: the images don't quite match the descriptions in the voice-over, which has an intriguingly jarring effect. This is the success of *Nervus Rerum* and The Otolith Group as a whole: when image and voice fail to coincide; when the 'big story' of Palestine becomes a whole series of smaller tales; when representation fails because it has to.

1 Email interview with the author, January 2010.

2 The Otolith Group, *Inner Time of Television* (1st Athens Biennial, 2007) 13.

3 T.J. Demos, 'Moving Images of Globalization', *Grey Room*, no. 37 (Fall 2009) 10.

4 Email interview with the author, January 2010.

5 Ibid.

6 Le Corbusier, *The Establishment Statute of the Land*, quoted in Bipin Kumar Malik, *City Planning and Realities: A Case Study of Chandigarh* (Chandigarh College of Architecture, 2004) 26.

Nina Power, 'Waiting for the Future', *frieze*, no. 129 (March 2010) 90–93. www.frieze.com

Biographical Notes

Magali Arriola is Chief Curator of the Museo Tamayo in Mexico City. As an independent curator, she organized exhibitions such as the 8th Bienal of Panamá (2008) and 'Prophets of Deceit', CCA Wattis Institute for Contemporary Arts, San Francisco (2006). As an art critic she has contributed to numerous journals including *Art Nexus, Curare* and *Parachute*.

J.G. Ballard (1930–2009) was a British novelist and writer of science fiction. His books include *The Crystal World* (1966), *Crash* (1973), *Concrete Island* (1974), *High Rise* (1975), *The Unlimited Dream Company* (1979) and *Empire of the Sun* (1984).

Georges Bataille (1897–1962) was a French writer and thinker, and 'dissident' associate of surrealism. He initiated the journals *Documents* (1929–30) and *Acéphale* (1936–39) and co-founded the Collège de Sociologie (1937–39). His books include *Inner Experience* (1943/1954), *On Nietzsche* (1945), *The Accursed Share* (1949) and *Literature and Evil* (1957).

Jean Baudrillard (1929–2007) was a French cultural and social theorist and philosopher. His books include *The System of Objects* (1968), *For a Critique of the Political Economy of the Sign* (1972), *Simulations* (1981), *Cool Memories* (1987) and *The Conspiracy of Art* (2005).

Mark Beasley is a British artist, writer and curator at Performa, New York. He has contributed articles and essays to numerous exhibition catalogues, radio plays and journals, including *Dot Dot Dot, Artforum* and *frieze*.

Walter Benjamin (1892–1940) has since the late 1970s been among the most influential cultural critics of the Frankfurt School on the field of visual studies. Translations of his work include *Selected Writings* (4 vols, 1999–2002) and *The Arcades Project* (1999).

Svetlana Boym is the Curt Hugo Reisinger Professor of Slavic and Comparative Literatures at Harvard University. Her books include *Common Place: Mythologies of Everyday Life in Russia* (1995), *The Future of Nostalgia* (2001) and *Architecture of the Off-Modern* (2008).

Giuliana Bruno is Professor of Visual and Environmental Studies in the department of Architecture at Harvard University Graduate School of Design. Her books include *Streetwalking on a Ruined Map* (1995), *Atlas of Emotion: Journeys in Art, Architecture and Film* (2002) and *Public Intimacy: Architecture and the Visual Arts* (2007).

Italo Calvino (1923–85) was an Italian novelist, essayist and critic. His works include *Our Ancestors* (1952–59) *Cosmicomics* (1965), *Invisible Cities* (1972), *If on a Winter's Night a Traveller* (1979) and the posthumously published autobiographical meditations of *The Road to San Giovanni* (1990).

J.J. Charlesworth is a writer and curator who has contributed to art magazines such as *Art Monthly, Modern Painters* and *ArtReview*, where he is associate editor. He is tutor in painting at the Royal College of Art, London.

Barbara Clausen is a curator and art historian based in Vienna. Since 1997 she has written for numerous art publications and has curated exhibitions and screenings internationally. In 2002 she organized the film programme, artist archive and media coordination for Documenta 11.

Le Corbusier (Charles-Édouard Jeanneret, 1887–1965) was a Swiss-born architect, artist, urban designer and theorist who was a pioneer of modernist architecture and the International Style.

His books include *Towards a Modern Architecture* (*Vers une architecture*, 1923). The principal archive of his work is held by the Fondation Le Corbusier in Paris (http://www.fondationlecorbusier.fr)

Jonathan Crary is Meyer Schapiro Professor of Modern Art and Theory at Columbia University. A founding editor of Zone Books, he is the author of *Techniques of the Observer* (1990) and *Suspensions of Perception: Attention, Spectacle and Modern Culture* (2001).

Tacita Dean is a British artist based in Berlin. Solo exhibitions include Witte de With Center for Contemporary Art, Rotterdam (1997), Institute of Contemporary Art, Philadelphia (1998), ARC Musée d'art moderne de la Ville de Paris (2003), Solomon R. Guggenheim Museum, New York (2007) and Dia: Beacon, Riggio Galleries, Beacon, New York (2008).

Jacques Derrida (1930–2004), the French philosopher and literary theorist of deconstruction, also influenced the fragmentary and 'deconstructivist' tendencies in architecture with which architects such as Peter Eisenman, Frank Gehry, Zaha Hadid, Coop Himmelblau, Rem Koolhaas, Daniel Libeskind and Bernard Tschumi were associated during the 1980s.

Denis Diderot (1713–84) was a French writer, critic and philosopher, whose essays, novels, dialogues and collaborative project the *Encyclopédie* (1750–65) were key contributions to the emergent discourses of the Enlightenment and their dissemination.

Geoff Dyer is a British author and essayist based in London. His books include *The Colour of Memory* (1989), *The Missing of the Somme* (1994), *Paris Trance* (1998), *The Ongoing Moment* (2005) and *Otherwise Known as the Human Condition: Selected Essays and Reviews* (2011).

Richard Grayson is a British artist, writer and curator. He was a founder member of the Basement Group (1979–1984) at Newcastle. From 1992 to 1998 he was Director of the Experimental Art Foundation, Adelaide, Australia. He was Artistic Director of the 2002 Biennale of Sydney.

Jörg Heiser is an art critic and curator who lives and works in Berlin. He is Associate Editor of *frieze* and a regular contributor to *Süddeutsche Zeitung* and numerous catalogues and publications. He is the author of *All of a Sudden: Things That Matter in Contemporary Art* (2008).

Martin Herbert is a writer and critic based in Tunbridge Wells, Kent. He is a regular contributor to *Artforum*, *Art Monthly* and *frieze*, and is associate editor at *ArtReview*. He has been a visiting lecturer at the Royal College of Art and Goldsmiths, University of London.

Andreas Huyssen is Villard Professor of German and Comparative Literature at Columbia University, and a founding editor of *New German Critique*. His books include *Twilight Memories: Marking Time in a Culture of Amnesia* (1995) and *Present Pasts: Urban Palimpsests and the Politics of Memory* (2003).

Darian Leader is a psychoanalyst and writer on culture, art and psychology. His books include *Freud's Footnotes* (2000), *Stealing the Mona Lisa: What Art Stops Us from Seeing* (2002) and *The New Black: Mourning, Melancholia and Depression* (2008).

Mark Lewis is a Canadian-born artist based in London, and co-editorial director of the journal and publishing project *Afterall*. In 1996 he co-directed with Laura Mulvey the documentary *Disgraced Monuments*. In 2009 he represented Canada at the Venice Biennale.

James Lingwood is an independent curator and writer based in London who has organized numerous major survey and monographic exhibitions since the mid 1980s. Since 1992 he has been Co-Director, with Michael Morris, of the art commissioning and production organization Artangel.

Patrick Keiller is a British filmmaker and writer, and Research Fellow at the Royal College of Art, London. His films include *London* (1994), *Robinson in Space* (1997), *The Dilapidated Dwelling* (2000) and *Robinson in Ruins* (2010).

Rose Macaulay (1881–1958) was a British novelist, essayist and travel writer. Her books include *Life Among the English* (1942), *They Went to Portugal* (1946), *Fabled Shore: From the Pyrenees to Portugal by Road* (1949), *Pleasure of Ruins* (1953) and *Coming to London* (1957).

Tom McDonough is Associate Professor of Modern Architecture and Urbanism at Binghamton University, State University of New York, and an editor of *Grey Room*. His books include *'The Beautiful Language of My Century': Reinventing the Language of Contestation in Postwar France, 1945–1968* (2007)

Caomhín Mac Giolla Léith is a curator, critic and senior lecturer at the College of Arts and Celtic Studies, University College, Dublin. He has contributed essays to numerous exhibition catalogues on contemporary artists.

Jeremy Millar is a British artist, writer and curator based in Whitstable, England. He has curated numerous exhibitions for British and European galleries and has contributed to journals including *Afterall*, *Art Monthly*, *frieze*, *Modern Painters* and *Parkett*.

Celeste Olalquiaga is a Venezualan-born independent cultural historian. Her books include *Megalopolis: Contemporary Cultural Sensibilities* (1992) and *The Artificial Kingdom: A Treasury of the Kitsch Experience* (1998).

Nina Power is a Senior Lecturer in Philosophy at Roehampton University, London. She is the author of *One-Dimensional Woman* (2009) and co-editor of Alain Badiou, *Political Writings* (forthcoming). Journals to which she contributes include *New Humanist*, *Cabinet* and *Radical Philosophy*.

Ralph Rugoff is an American-born curator and critic, and Director of the Hayward Gallery, London. He was formerly Director of the CCA Wattis Institute for Contemporary Arts (2000–2006). He is the author of *Circus Americanus* (1995) and co-author of *Scene of the Crime* (1997) and *At the Threshold of the Visible* (1997).

Eric Schwab is a German-born scholar and lawyer based in Chicago, who as an assistant professor at Yale University (1998–2004) has taught and written extensively about Berlin's history and culture. He was the author, with Walead Beshty, of 'Willkommen in Irak!', *Cabinet*, no. 15 (Fall 2004).

Lytle Shaw is a poet and critic, and Associate Professor of English at New York University. His books include *Frank O'Hara: The Poetics of Coterie* (2006) and *Fieldworks: From Place to Site in Postwar Poetics* (forthcoming). He is a contributing editor of *Cabinet*.

Georg Simmel (1858–1918) was a German theorist of the emergent discipline of sociology and a cultural critic. His key books include *The Problems of the Philosophy of History* (1892), *The Philosophy of Money* (1907), *The Metropolis and Mental Life* (1903) and *Sociology* (1908).

Iain Sinclair is in his own words a British 'writer, documentarist, filmmaker, poet, flâneur, metropolitan prophet and urban shaman, keeper of lost cultures and futurologist'. His books include *London Orbital* (2002), *White Goods* (2002) and *Hackney: That Rose-Red Empire* (2009).

Robert Smithson (1938–73) was an American artist whose work intersected with conceptual art, Land art and Minimalism, and whose wide-ranging writings made a significant contribution to art discourse in the late 1960s and early 1970s. Retrospectives include Musée d'art moderne de la Ville de Paris (1982) and Centro Julio González, Valencia (1993).

Rebecca Solnit is an essayist, environmentalist, historian and art critic who contributes to numerous magazines, newspapers and journals. Her books include *Wanderlust: A History of Walking* (2000) and *River of Shadows: Eadweard Muybridge and the Technological Wild West* (2003).

Susan Stewart is a poet, literary critic and writer on contemporary art and aesthetics. Her books include *The Open Studio: Essays on Art and Aesthetics* (2005). She is the Annan Professor of English at Princeton University.

Adrian Stokes (1902–72) was a British art critic, painter and poet, much of whose writing focused on Renaissance art and architecture, and a Kleinian psychoanalytic investigation of aesthetic experience. His books include *The Quattro Cento* (1932), *Stones of Rimini* (1934), *Inside Out* (1947) and *Smooth and Rough* (1951).

Anthony Vidler is Dean and Professor of the Irwin S. Chanin School of Architecture at The Cooper Union, New York. He is the author of *The Architectural Uncanny: Essays in the Modern Unhomely* (1992) and *Warped Space: Art, Architecture and Anxiety in Modern Culture* (2000).

Paul Virilio is a French philosopher and cultural theorist of urban space, architecture and technology. His books include *Bunker Archaeology* (1975), *The Aesthetics of Disappearance* (1991), *Virilio Live: Selected Interviews* (2001) and with Sylvère Lotringer, *The Accident of Art* (2005).

Gilda Williams is an art and film critic and a lecturer at Sotheby's Institute of Art and at Goldsmiths, University of London. From 1997 to 2005 she was commissioning editor for contemporary art at Phaidon Press. A contributor to *Artforum* and a regular writer for journals such as *TATE Etc.*, *Sight & Sound* and *Parkett*, she edited *The Gothic* (2007) in the Documents of Contemporary Art series.

Bibliography

Arriola, Magali, 'A Victim and a Viewer: Some Thoughts on Anticipated Ruins', *Afterall* (Autumn/Winter 2005) 109–15

Ballard, J.G., 'A Handful of Dust', *The Guardian* (20 March 2006) 16

Bataille, Georges, 'Poussière' (Dust) entry in first instalment of 'Le Dictionnaire critique', *Documents*, no. 1 (Paris, 1929); trans. Ian White, in *Encyclopaedia Acephalica* (London: Atlas Press, 1995)

Baudrillard, Jean, 'The Anorexic Ruins', in *Looking Back on the End of the World*, ed. Dietmar Kamper and Christoph Wulf (New York: Semiotext(e), 1989)

Beasley, Mark, 'Walid Raad/The Atlas Group', *frieze*, no. 97 (March 2006) 152–3

Becher, Bernd and Hilla, *Industrial Landscapes* (Cambridge, Massachusetts: The MIT Press, 2002)

– 'Photographing Industrial Architecture: An Interview', *Parachute*, no. 22 (Spring 1981)

Benjamin, Walter, 'Über den Begriff der Geschichte' (1940); trans. Harry Zohn, 'Theses on the Philosophy of History', in *Walter Benjamin: Illuminations* (New York: Schocken Books, 1969)

– *Das Passagen-Werk* (manuscript, 1927–40); trans. Howard Eiland and Kevin McLaughlin, *The Arcades Project* (Cambridge, Massachusetts: Harvard University Press, 1999)

Boym, Svetlana, *The Future of Nostalgia* (New York: Basic Books, 2001)

– *Architecture of the Off-Modern* (New York: Princeton Architectural Press, 2008)

Brinckerhoff Jackson, John, *The Necessity For Ruins* (Amherst: University of Massachusetts Press, 1980)

Bruno, Giuliana, 'Modernist Ruins, Filmic Archaeologies', in *Jane and Louise Wilson: A Free and Anonymous Monument* (London: Film & Video Umbrella/Lisson Gallery/Newcastle upon Tyne: BALTIC, 2003)

Byles, Jeff, *Rubble: Unearthing the History of Demolition* (New York: Harmony, 2005)

Calvino, Italo, *Le Città invisibili* (Turin: Giulio Einaudi, 1972); trans. William Weaver, *Invisible Cities* (New York: Harcourt Brace, 1974)

Charlesworth, J.J., 'Signs of Life', in *Roger Hiorns: Seizure* (London: Artangel, 2008)

Clarke, Declan, 'The Weather Over Germany: Heinrich Böll's Literature of Ruins', *Cabinet*, no. 39 (Fall 2010) 40–44

Clausen, Barbara, 'Dorit Margreiter', *Artforum* (September 2008) 443–7

Colonna, Francesco, *Hypnerotomachia Poliphili* (1499)

Le Corbusier, *Vers une architecture* (Paris, 1923); trans. Frederick Etchells, *Towards a New Architecture* (Oxford: Architectural Press, 2000)

Crary, Jonathan, 'Vera Lutter: Specters of Negation', in *Vera Lutter: Battersea* (London: Gagosian Gallery, 2004)

Dean, Tacita, *Selected Writings* (Göttingen: Steidl/Paris: ARC/Musée d'art moderne de la Ville de Paris, 2003)

Dekkers, Midas, *The Way of All Flesh: A Celebration of Decay*, trans. Sherry Marx-Macdonald (London: Harvill, 2000)

Derrida, Jacques, *Mémoires d'aveugle: l'autoportrait et autres ruines* (Paris: Éditions de la Réunion des musées nationaux, 1990); trans. Pascale-Anne Brault and Michael Naas, *Memoirs of the Blind: The Self-Portrait and Other Ruins* (Chicago, University of Chicago Press, 1993)

Diderot, Denis, 'Le Salon de 1767' (Paris, 1767); trans. John Goodman, in *Diderot on Art. II: The Salon of 1767* (New Haven and London: Yale University Press, 1995)

Dillon, Brian, 'An Archaeology of the Air', in *Julie Mehretu: Grey Area* (Berlin: Deutsche Guggenheim, 2009)

– 'Modernologies: Contemporary Artists Researching Modernity and Modernism', *Artforum* (January 2010) 192–3

Dubin, Nina, 'Robert des Ruines', *Cabinet*, no. 20 (Winter 2005–6) 92–7

Dyer, Geoff, 'Leptis Magna', in *Yoga for People Who Can't be Bothered to Do It* (London: Abacus, 2004)

Gopnik, Adam, 'A Walk on the High Line/The Allure of a Derelict Railroad Track in Spring', in *Joel Sternfeld: Walking the High Line* (Göttingen: Steidl, 2001)

Grayson, Richard, '24A Orwell Street, Sydney, Australia 2002', in *Mike Nelson: Between a Formula and a Code* (Margate: Turner Contemporary/Cologne: Verlag der Buchhandlung Walther König, 2006)

Griffin, Jonathan 'New Romantic', interview with Cyprien Gaillard, *frieze*, no. 130 (April 2010) 85–7

Hatherley, Owen, *Militant Modernism* (Winchester: Zero Books, 2009)

Harbison, Robert, *The Built, the Unbuilt and the Unbuildable* (London: Thames & Hudson, 1991)

Heiser, Jörg, 'The J. Street Project', in Susan Hiller, *The J. Street Project* (2002–5) (Berlin: DAAD/Compton Verney, Warwickshire: Compton Verney Trust, 2005)

Herbert, Martin, 'Sifting Defunct Modernity in Search of Something Useful', *TATE Etc.*, no. 15 (Spring 2009) 62–8

Huyssen, Andreas, 'Authentic Ruins', in *Ruins of Modernity*, ed. Julia Hell (Durham, North Carolina: Duke University Press, 2009)

Irvine, Karen, 'Incident Control', in Sarah Pickering, *Explosions, Fires and Public Order* (New York: Aperture, 2010)

Jefferies, Richard, *After London, or Wild England* (London: Cassell & Company, 1885)

Keiller, Patrick, 'Imaging', in *Restless Cities*, ed. Matthew Beaumont and Gregory Dart (London and New York: Verso, 2010)

Leader, Darian, 'The Architecture of Life', in *Jane & Louise Wilson: Sealander* (Zürich: Haunch of Venison Zürich, 2006)

Lewis, Mark, 'Is Modernity Our Antiquity?', *Afterall* (Autumn/Winter 2006)

Lingwood, James, 'The Weight of Time', in *Field Trips: Bernd & Hilla Becher/Robert Smithson* (Porto: Museu de Arte Contemporanea de Serralves, 2002)

Mabey, Richard, *Weeds* (London: Profile, 2010)

Macaulay, Rose, *Pleasure of Ruins* (London: Thames & Hudson, 1953)

Macaulay, Thomas Babington, 'On Ranck's *History of the Popes*', *Edinburgh Review* (October 1840)

McDonough, Tom, 'The Archivist of Urban Waste: Zoe Leonard, Photographer as Rag-Picker', *Afterall*, no. 25 (Autumn/Winter 2010) 21–9

Mac Giola Léith, Caoimhín, 'The Light Gleams an Instant', in *Miroslaw Balka: Tristes Tropiques* (Dublin: Irish Museum of Modern Art, 2008)

Makarius, Michel, *Ruins* (Paris: Flammarion, 2004)

Marker, Chris, *La Jetée: ciné-roman* (New York: Zone Books, 1992)

Millar, Jeremy, 'Hinterland', in *Adam Chodzko: Plans and Spells* (London: Film and Video Umbrella, 2002)

– and Tacita Dean, *Place* (London: Thames and Hudson, 2005)

Olalquiaga, Celeste, *The Artificial Kingdom: A Treasury of the Kitsch Experience* (New York: Pantheon Books, 1998)

Orlando, Francesco, Obsolete Objects in the Literary Imagination (Yale University Press, 2006)

Paterson, Toby, and Ewan Imrie, 'In Conversation', in Toby Paterson, *Consensus and Collapse* (Edinburgh: Fruitmarket Gallery, 2010)

Pendle, George, 'The Ruined Man: The Melancholic Folly of William Beckford', *Cabinet*, no. 20 (Winter 2005–6) 61–3

Petrovsky, Helen, 'Lost in Time: Boris Mikhailov and His Study of the Soviet', in *Ruins of Modernity*, ed. Julia Hell (Durham, North Carolina: Duke University Press, 2009)

Power, Nina, 'Waiting for the Future', *frieze*, no. 129 (March 2010) 90–93

Purbrick, Louise, 'The Architecture of Containment', in *Donovan Wylie: Maze* (London: Granta, 2004)

Robbe-Grillet, Alain, *Topologie d'une cité fantôme* (Paris: Robert Laffont, 1976); trans. J.A. Underwood, *Topology of a Phantom City* (New York: Grove Press, 1977)

Rugoff, Ralph, 'Circling the Center', in *Overlook: Exploring the Internal Fringes of America with the Center for Land Use Interpretation*, ed. Matthew Coolidge and Sarah Simons (New York: Metropolis Books, 2006)

Ruskin, John, 'Of the Turnerian Picturesque', *Modern Painters*, vol. 4 (1856), in *Selected Writings* (Oxford: Oxford University Press, 2004)

Schwab, Eric, with images by Walead Beshty, 'Stumped: What Remains of the Thousand-Year Reich?', *Cabinet*, no. 20 (Winter 2005–6) 74–80

Sebald, W.G., *Die Ringe des Saturn* (1995); trans. Michael Hulse, *The Rings of Saturn* (London: Harvill, 1995)

– *Austerlitz* (London: Hamish Hamilton, 2001)

– *On the Natural History of Destruction* (London: Hamish Hamilton, 2003)

Self, Will, 'My Battersea Power Station ... All Mine', in *Vera Lutter: Battersea* (London: Gagosian Gallery, 2004)

Shaw, Lytle, 'The Utopian Past', in *The Present Tense Through the Ages: On the Recent Work of Gerard Byrne* (Cologne: Verlag der Buchhandlung Walther König, 2007)

Simmel, Georg, 'Die Ruine: Ein ästhetischer Versuch', *Der Tag*, no. 96 (Berlin, 1907) revised in Simmel, *Philosophisches Kultur* (Leipzig: Kröner, 1911); trans. David Kettler, in *Essays on Sociology, Philosophy and Aesthetics* (New York: Harper & Row, 1965)

Sinclair, Iain, *Lights Out for the Territory* (London: Granta, 1997)

Smithson, Robert, *The Collected Writings*, ed. Jack Flam (Berkeley and Los Angeles: University of California Press, 1996)

Solnit, Rebecca, *Storming the Gates of Paradise* (Berkeley and Los Angeles: University of California Press, 2007)

Stern, Ralph, 'The "Ruin" Film, 1945–50', *AA files*, no. 54 (Summer 2006) 48–60

Stewart, Susan, *On Longing* (Durham, North Carolina: Duke University Press, 1996)
Stokes, Adrian, *Stones of Rimini* (London: Faber & Faber, 1934); reprinted in *The Quattro Cento and Stones of Rimini* (Philadelphia: Pennsylvania State University Press, 2002)
Trigg, Dylan, *The Aesthetics of Decay* (New York: Peter Lang, 2006)
Vanderbildt, Tom, *Survival City: Adventures among the Ruins of Atomic America* (New York: Princeton Architectural Press, 2002)
Vidler, Anthony, *The Architectural Uncanny* (Cambridge, Massachusetts: The MIT Press, 1992)
Virilio, Paul, *Bunker Archéologie* (Paris: Centre Georges Pompidou and Centre de Création Industrielle, 1975); trans. George Collins, *Bunker Archaeology* (New York: Princeton Architectural Press, 1994)
de Volney, Constantin François, extract from *Les Ruines, ou méditations sur les révolutions des empires* (Paris, 1791); translated as *The Ruins* (London: Edwards Brown, n.d.)
Williams, Gilda, 'It Was What It Was: Modern Ruins', *Art Monthly*, no. 336 (May 2010) 1–4
Woodward, Christopher, *In Ruins: A Journey through History, Art and Literature* (London: Vintage, 2001)
Wylie, Donovan, *Maze* (London: Granta, 2004)

Index

ACKNOWLEDGEMENTS

Editor's acknowledgements
Thanks to Iwona Blazwick and to Ian Farr, Hannah Holloway, Sarah Auld and colleagues for bringing the book into being. It would not have been possible without the support of the Arts and Humanities Research Council. Much of the book's content was influenced by collaborations and public discussions with Bernd Behr, Svetlana Boym, Jeff Byles, Gerard Byrne, Tom Dale, Mark Fisher, Owen Hatherley, Susan Hiller, Jeremy Millar, Sina Najafi and Katherine Waugh. It is dedicated to Felicity Dunworth.

Publisher's acknowledgements
Whitechapel Gallery is grateful to all those who gave their generous permission to reproduce the listed material. Every effort has been made to secure all permissions and we apologize for any inadvertent errors or omissions. If notified, we will endeavour to correct these at the earliest opportunity. We would like to express our thanks to all who contributed to the making of this volume, especially: Magali Arriola, Mark Beasley, Walead Beshty, Svetlana Boym, Giuliana Bruno, J.J. Charlesworth, Barbara Clausen, Jonathan Crary, Tacita Dean, Geoff Dyer, Richard Grayson, Jörg Heiser, Martin Herbert, Susan Hiller, Andreas Huyssen, Patrick Keiller, Darian Leader, Mark Lewis, James Lingwood, Caoimhín Mac Giola Léith, Tom McDonough, Jeremy Millar, Chris Mooney, Celeste Olalquiaga, Nina Power, Ralph Rugoff, Fiona Russell, Eric Schwab, Lytle Shaw, Iain Sinclair, Rebecca Solnit, Susan Stewart, Anthony Vidler, Paul Virilio, Gilda Williams. We also gratefully acknowledge the cooperation of A.M. Heath, Afterall, Art Monthly, Artangel, Artforum, Atlas Press, Basic Books, Cabinet, University of California Press, The Estate of Italo Calvino, University of Chicago Press, Compton Verney, Dover Publications, Duke University Press, Faber & Faber, Film and Video Umbrella, The Paulo Freire Institute, frieze, Gagosian London, Granta, Guggenheim New York, Harper Collins, Harvard University Press, Haunch of Venison, Houghton Mifflin Harcourt, The Irish Museum of Modern Art, Little, Brown, The MIT Press, Penguin Group, Centre Georges Pompidou and Centre de Création Industrielle, Princeton Architectural Press, Random House, Semiotext(e), The Estate of Robert Smithson, Steidl, TATE Etc., Timothy Taylor Gallery, Thames and Hudson, Turner Contemporary, VAGA, Verso, The Wylie Agency, Yale University Press.